KEEPING

BUSES

MOVING

A GUIDE TO TRAFFIC MANAGEMENT TO ASSIST BUSES IN URBAN AREAS

Local Transport Note 1/97

London: The Stationery Office

ISBN 0 11 551914 9

CONTENTS

CHAPTERS

ANNEXES

FIGURES

CHAPTER 1

INTRODUCTION

1.1 The Government is committed to an integrated transport policy[1] which will address the important issues of traffic congestion and environmental pollution, both of which are serious and growing problems. A key part of such an integrated policy will be measures to encourage provision of more sustainable, environmentally friendly, forms of transport, including the development of more attractive public transport services. Buses already play an essential role in the transport systems of our urban areas and, in most cases, will remain the main means by which improved public transport services will be provided.

1.2 Transport policy needs to be integrated at national, regional and local level. The Government looks to local authorities to adopt an integrated approach to transport investment in their areas. They are best placed to identify what is needed to improve local conditions and the package approach to local transport spending reinforces the need to develop transport policy across modes while allowing local authorities to determine their own priorities.

1.3 Local transport strategies will include a range of measures. Although new road construction can sometimes be justified the Government believes that the role for new major roads in urban areas is limited. Other measures are required. Improvements to public transport services, coupled with measures to discourage unnecessary use of private vehicles, are likely to be an important part of a coherent and environmentally sustainable strategy for most urban areas. When it comes to improving public transport, although the Government has recently funded

Buses play an essential role in the transport systems of our urban areas

significant investment in the light rail systems in Manchester and Sheffield and construction of Midland Metro and Croydon Tramlink are underway, and in London the Docklands Light Railway has been extended, light rapid transit schemes will not be the right answer in most cases. Their capital cost is high, they are usually economic only in corridors where demand is high and they do not have the flexibility of buses to serve growing and changing suburban areas.

1.4 Bus services, on the other hand, can be more easily adapted to changing demands than fixed-track systems and, with their large carrying capacity, buses can make effective use of limited road space. Buses provide transport for people who for one reason or another are prevented from driving themselves - young, elderly and disabled people, those who are not able to drive a car, and those who do not wish to,either generally or for partcular journeys. Buses often provide these people with their only means of access to work, shops, education and social and leisure activities.

Buses are used by: the young, elderly and disabled people, and those without access to cars

1.5 However, if buses are to fulfill their potential in providing an alternative within a sustainable transport system, they must be made more attractive. To do that, it is important that buses are able to operate efficiently. Bus services are, however, particularly susceptible to traffic congestion. Buses are less manoeuvrable than private cars and their routes and schedules cannot be changed at very short notice

Buses are particularly susceptible to traffic congestion

because they are registered to run on fixed routes (and frequent re-routing would make it difficult for passengers to know when and where buses could be found). They must stop at regular intervals to pick-up and set down passengers. If land is available for segregated busways - such as those introduced in Ipswich and Leeds - buses may be able to bypass congested areas, but in most cases land is not available in intensely developed urban areas and buses are not able to avoid congestion in the way that is sometimes possible for cars and taxis. Delays to buses increase operating costs which may in turn lead to fare increases. Passengers are thus deterred because of the slower and less reliable services and higher fares; some take to their cars and so cause even more congestion.

1.6 For these reasons, it is frequently worthwhile to introduce traffic management measures to assist the movement of buses. These can take the form of measures designed to facilitate the movement of traffic generally along bus routes, and to protect access to bus stops. They may go further and permit buses to use lanes or dedicated tracks, or make movements which are denied to other traffic. Such measures can provide substantial benefits to bus passengers by allowing faster journey times and a more regular and reliable service; they can also help to attract additional passengers by eliminating unnecessary capital and operating costs by reducing the number of buses required to run the service.

1.7 Measures offering priority for buses are likely to be most successful where, singly or combined with other priority measures, their benefits spread to bus services over a wider area and where they are linked to other improvements such as passenger information systems, improved waiting facilities, more frequent services, and park and ride facilities. In combination, such measures can improve the image and public perception of the service in a way that encourages higher patronage and a transfer from other modes. When linked along a route, priority for buses can contribute towards an overall strategy for dealing with urban congestion, especially if supported by measures such as urban traffic control, new traffic management measures, parking control, and the provision of park and ride services. Giving priority to buses can cause other traffic some additional delay which should be assessed and taken into account in the overall appraisal. However, environmental considerations and overall transport policy objectives for the area in question may thus strengthen the case for providing priority for buses, even at the expense of delay to other vehicles. Bus priority measures can themselves be a component in a demand management strategy by reducing the road space available to cars.

1.8 The current document provides advice and guidance to local authorities wishing to implement measures to assist buses. It updates the advice first issued in Local Transport Note 1/91 issued by the Department of Transport, the Scottish Office and the Welsh Office. The revised guidance is published against the background of policy that seeks greater integration of transport with land use planning, as in Planning Policy Guidance (PPG) notes PPG6[2] and PPG13[3], and their Welsh and Scottish equivalents[4][5], as well as emphasising integration between and across modes. The guidance also builds upon the experience gained since the release of LTN 1/91. It includes new advice on innovative techniques such as bus advance areas, bus priority in SCOOT and other signal control systems, camera enforcement of bus lanes, and the importance of decriminalised parking control in assisting the movement of buses. It also updates previous advice, especially in relation to signing and road markings, road humps and traffic calming, the responsibilities of the PTEs, and developments in London; a revised emphasis is placed on the important subject of appraisal, reflecting the changed policy context.

1.9 The Government is clear that improved bus services will continue to have an important part to play in the development of transport strategies aimed at providing attractive alternatives to the use of private cars. It believes that there is considerable scope for providing more priority for buses as a main contributor to improving services. This guidance is being issued to encourage local authorities and bus operators to consider what more can be done in their own areas. As more experience is gained, further advice will be issued to disseminate knowledge of best practice as widely as possible.

Good advertising can help compliance.

CHAPTER 2

THE AGENCIES INVOLVED

2.1 Several different agencies are involved in providing bus services and the infrastructure on which they rely, including measures which provide priority for buses;

bus operators decide what bus services to run commercially and also provide services under contract to local authorities;

traffic commissioners are responsible for the licensing of operators, the registration of bus services and the enforcement of the appropriate standards, and have powers to impose Traffic Regulation Conditions at the request of the local authority;

traffic authorities are responsible for maintaining and managing the local road network, including making Traffic Regulation Orders under the Road Traffic Regulation Act 1984, and for providing traffic control systems, both of which can be used to the benefit of bus services. The Traffic Director for London is responsible for the Priority (Red) Route network in London which aims to provide special help for the efficient movement of buses;

local authorities outside London and the English metropolitan areas are responsible for the procurement and co-ordination of bus services, the operation of concessionary fares schemes, and the provision of infrastructure to assist the smooth running and increased attractiveness of bus services; they also have powers to promote the use of public transport services in their areas. London Boroughs, and those authorities outside London which have taken up the relevant powers, are also responsible for enforcing waiting and loading restrictions on local roads;

passenger transport executives, in the English metropolitan areas outside London, are responsible for the procurement and co-ordination of bus and rail services, the operation of concessionary fares schemes, and the provision of infrastructure to assist the smooth running and increased attractiveness of bus services. They also have powers to promote the use of public transport services in their areas;

the police are responsible for enforcing all traffic control measures that affect moving traffic, and for most waiting and loading restrictions outside London.

Users' groups are also important in advising these agencies about the improvements which are needed to make services more attractive to the travelling public.

The Department of the Environment, Transport and the Regions commissions research (sometimes jointly with the Scottish and Welsh Offices), produces guidance, and develops the legislative framework and regulations under which all these agencies operate.

Full details appear in Annex A

2.2 Bus priority involves managing the road system to make the best possible use of limited road space in terms of the overall transport objectives of the area. This requires these different agencies to carry out complex and inter-related tasks. Bus priority measures undertaken by a local authority must take account of the problems perceived by the bus operators, and are only likely to be effective if enforcement is taken into account at the planning stage. Local authorities should therefore discuss possible bus priority measures in their area at an early stage with bus operators and with others involved (including other local authorities and other interested departments and sections within the same authority), and should establish a proper framework for consultation and co-operation in their implementation. The benefits to the bus operator, and how these can be redistributed to the benefit of the travelling public (eg through improved reliability and/or service frequency) should also be established at an early stage. Such arrangements as may be agreed should be included in any TPP/Package Bid statements (see Chapter 9).

2.3 The duties, powers and responsibilities of the various agencies are discussed in more detail in Annex A. In particular the Road Traffic Regulation Act 1984 contains the provisions under which most bus priority measures may be introduced and the Road Traffic Act 1991 contains additional provisions that should assist the movement of buses in urban areas. More details appear in Chapter 3.

2.4 The London Boroughs, acting jointly and in discussion with London Transport Buses, the bus operators and other interested parties, have developed the London Bus Priority Network on those roads which carry large numbers of buses and are not part of London's Priority (Red) Route Network (see also paragraph 3.4). The new measures are seen as an important contribution to making bus services faster and more reliable as part of an overall strategy (which may also include other traffic regulation measures) to encourage more people to use bus services. Similar concepts are being pursued in some other areas.

2.5 The Government has been encouraged by the development of Quality Partnerships between bus operators and local authorities. Under such partnerships, operators provide vehicles to a specified quality, and the local authority provides assistance to the relevant bus services through traffic management schemes or other facilities. There are already a number of voluntary partnerships based on initiatives between local authorities and operators which include bus priority measures.

2.6 Good compliance, with the appropriate level of enforcement to achieve it, is essential to realising the full potential benefits from schemes providing priority for buses. If police/warden resources for enforcement are limited (see also Annex A, paragraph A9) then self-enforcing measures or automatic enforcement might be considered in order to maintain the same level of compliance. Automatic capture of details of vehicles illegally using bus lanes has recently been successfully trialled in London. Further details appear in Annex A, paragraph A11, and in "Bus Lane Enforcement Cameras"[6].

CHAPTER 3

PRIORITY THROUGH TRAFFIC MANAGEMENT

3.1 The movement of buses can often be assisted significantly by measures aimed at reducing congestion and improving the flow of traffic in general. For example, measures to remove through traffic from congested urban streets can greatly improve conditions for pedestrians, cyclists and local traffic, and offer the opportunity to improve bus access (see also Chapter 6). The potential impact of new traffic management measures on bus services should always be considered at an early stage in the planning of any scheme, whether its main intention is to improve bus services or not. Bus operators should always be consulted.

3.2 Indiscriminate parking can seriously reduce the capacity of the street network, and effective control of on-street parking and loading and unloading is essential to keep traffic, especially buses, moving. The Road Traffic Act 1991 provides powers under which local authorities are able to enforce on-street parking prohibitions and regulations. As required, all authorities in London had adopted the new powers by July 1994; the police and traffic wardens then ceased to be responsible for enforcement of waiting and loading restrictions except on Priority (Red) Routes (see paragraph 3.4), the Whitehall Zone and some other small areas, all of which has brought benefits to buses. Traffic authorities outside London may now apply to the Secretary of State to assume similar powers. To date (1997), few have done so, and the Department of The Environment, Transport and the Regions, would like more authorities to adopt these powers in the next few years as more experience is gained.

3.3 The number of on and off street parking places, as well as the type (eg. long or short stay, permits) and price of parking, need to be considered in the context of the overall transport strategy for an area. Adequate off-street parking, in conjunction with good on-street enforcement, can help to reduce parking on-street. Too much parking provision or inappropriate parking management polices may add to congestion on bus routes if too many cars are encouraged to use the highway or queue near to car park access roads. However, for parking spaces that do exist arrangements for directing drivers to car parks which have space free can help to reduce traffic circulating or queuing unnecessarily. Locating bus stops nearer to the main central area destinations than off-street car parking places can also help to improve the attractiveness of bus services.

3.4 The Road Traffic Act 1991 provides for the designation of a network of Priority "Red" Routes in London. These routes are subject to special parking controls and other traffic management measures designed to improve the movement of traffic so that people and goods can reach their destinations more easily, reliably and safely. On the pilot Priority "Red" Route in north and east London buses benefitted from this special attention because of the general reduction in congestion and more reliable journey times which have followed from new priority route controls. This improved reliability has made bus services more attractive to customers. Similar benefits should be evident throughout London as the network of Priority "Red" Routes expands. Local authorities outside London can use their existing powers to establish urban clearways, and to introduce stringent waiting and loading restrictions on what they regard as priority routes. These should be indicated with the conventional yellow signs and markings.

3.5 In the implementation of traffic management measures, some matters of detailed design such as turning radii at corners used by buses, and the siting of bus stops (see Chapter 8 for details) can have an important impact on bus services. Good access to major interchanges such as rail stations can also be important. Exemptions from prohibited turns can be useful; these are dealt with in Chapter 7.

3.6 In developing a traffic management strategy for an area, it may be desirable to introduce physical measures to ensure that vehicle speeds are not excessive in relation to the characteristics of a particular road. Unfortunately no ideal measure has yet been found which does not have some effect on buses and their passengers; the more "severe" physical measures can be especially difficult for disabled people. Horizontal deflections can be effective but the recommended spacing to materially reduce speeds (10 to 15 metres between the build outs forming the deflection) would be difficult for most buses to negotiate and a compromise may be needed. Road humps are the most effective speed controlling measure. Most bus operators have declared a strong dislike of road humps, but if there is no alternative then the following recommendations should be followed. Care is needed in choosing the most appropriate design for each site. The Highways (Road Humps) Regulations 1996[7] permit heights up to 100mm, but it is generally recommended that road humps should not be higher than 75mm in most cases. Conventional round top and flat top road humps built to the minimum height permitted by the regulations (25mm) are likely to have a minimal effect on speeds, and 50mm is normally regarded as a minimum. The maximum 100mm height might be desirable at raised junctions to assist pedestrians to cross more easily. Shallower exit ramps from road humps may be advantageous where humps can be separately related to a single direction of traffic. Whilst bus operators do not like any sort of road hump, most will reluctantly accept flat top humps with a plateau length equal to the bus wheel-base, or a minimum of 6m at restricted sites. Speed cushions can be straddled by buses with very little vertical movement, but even these do not always suit the wide variety of bus sizes (eg midibuses); the narrower they are the less effect they will have on buses, but a smaller reduction in the speed of other vehicles would have to be acceptable. Further guidance on road humps is available from the Department[7][8][9][10][11], the Scottish Office and the Welsh Office.

Busways and Tramways

3.7 Guidance for public transport systems running on segregated tracks is provided in two separate documents:

Advice about trams running on "line-of-sight" signalling, as they do when running on the highway, is given in "Railway Safety Principles and Guidance, Part 2, Section G, Tramways" [12]; and

for guided buses the Department's advice "Guided Buses"[13] is the most recent issued.

In the latter, guidance is given as to the most appropriate powers (in the Road Traffic Regulation Act or in the Transport & Works Act) under which guided busways are best introduced according to local circumstances.

3.8 Guided busways in the UK are new, and the experience from Germany and Australia where other guideways have been introduced is very limited. The Department is investigating the safety issues in the areas where guideways leave and rejoin the general purpose carriageway, and where guideways cross other roads and pedestrian ways; guidance on good practice will be issued as results from research become available.

Guided busways in the UK are new and experience from abroad is limited

CHAPTER 4

WITHFLOW BUS LANES

4.1 The "withflow" bus lane is the commonest form of bus priority measure. A traffic lane, usually on the nearside, is reserved for the use of buses and other vehicles which are to be accorded priority. Where road widths allow, double-width bus lanes can assist buses to pass slower or stopped buses, and cyclists. In some situations, for example in one-way streets or on the approach to a prohibited turn from which buses are exempt, an off-side withflow bus lane can provide considerable help for buses.

4.2 A Traffic Regulation Order under the Road Traffic Regulation Act 1984 must be made to identify the length of the bus lane and to limit its use to those types of bus and other vehicles (see paragraphs 4.10 to 4.18) which the authority wishes to allow. The restriction must be indicated using the prescribed signs and road markings which appear in the Traffic Signs Regulations and General Directions, 1994[14](TSRGD). Special drawings are being prepared by the Welsh Office for the bilingual signs which apply in Wales. An Order would normally specify the vehicles to which the bus symbol (with or without the word "local") on the mandatory bus lane signs to Diagrams 958 and 959 refers; these are:

(a) motor vehicles constructed or adapted to carry more than 8 passengers (exclusive of the driver) or

(b) local buses not so constructed or adapted.

Regulation 24 of TSRGD[14] gives more details.

An Order prohibiting vehicles other than buses from using a bus lane would normally also exempt emergency vehicles and cleaning or maintenance vehicles. There is normally no need to sign such exceptions. Pedal cyclists are normally permitted to use withflow bus lanes (see paragraph 4.11). Parking is not permitted in bus lanes during their operating times; where required, consideration should be given to the provision of parking nearby for orange badge holders. Loading and unloading is allowed unless a prohibition is specifically written into the Order and the appropriate signs and road markings displayed on street; it is recommended that loading in bus lanes should normally be prohibited unless there are special reasons why it should be allowed.

4.3 A withflow bus lane enables buses to bypass traffic queues, usually approaching traffic signals. This will often mean a substantial time saving to buses and their passengers, possibly offset by some additional delay to the vehicles which have been overtaken. So, although there may be other important considerations such as those mentioned in Annex B (paragraph B.7), an appraisal should be carried out to determine whether the overall benefits from the scheme are acceptable in terms of the scheme's overall costs; where appropriate the appraisal should include strategic transportation, environmental and other considerations. The appraisal may also give guidance as to whether the bus lane should operate in peak periods only, although it is recommended that withflow bus lanes which can be justified during peak periods should be provided all day unless other requirements, e.g.loading, preclude it; all-day bus lanes are easier for motorists to understand and so are less likely to be violated. The appraisal of bus priority measures is discussed in more detail in Chapter 9.

4.4 A plan of a typical layout of a single-width withflow bus lane is shown in Figure 1. Where roads are wide enough the bus lane should be 4.25 metres wide and the minimum preferred width is 4m; this allows buses to overtake cyclists safely and reduces the likelihood of interference from general traffic in the adjacent lane. The minimum recommended width is 3 metres. This will cater for up to 120 buses an hour without noticeable constraint, but there may be certain locations (e.g. at bus stops without lay-bys) where bus flow can be eased by providing a double-width lane.

The withflow bus lane is stopped short of the signal stop line to maintain saturation flow and accommodate left turns

4.5 If it is desired to minimise overall delay to all traffic, withflow bus lanes should normally be stopped short of the stop line at traffic signal controlled junctions. This "set back" ensures that the full width of the stop line at the junction is available to all traffic during the green period; it also facilitates, and makes safer, left turns at the junction. The aim should be to ensure that buses clear the stop line during the first available green period. As a general guide, a set back length (in metres) of twice the green time (in seconds) would normally achieve this, though it may be necessary to adjust this if there are special local site conditions or to take account of the variations in green time in active-response UTC systems. If a reduction in junction capacity is proposed as part of an area traffic management or demand management strategy, or if site conditions otherwise allow, then provided any left turning traffic can be safely accommodated and right-turning traffic does not restrict flow in the non-priority lane(s), a withflow bus lane may be continued up to the traffic signal stop line. An alternative method of allowing buses to reach the signal stop line ahead of general traffic is explained in paragraph 4.7.

4.6 At a roundabout, a set back should be provided to allow left turning traffic to take the nearside lane, and to ensure that the full width of the roundabout entry is available to all traffic at peak periods. Investigations by TRL suggest that the optimum set back distance should be at least 10metres but not more than 30m. These findings have not yet been tested in the field and the Department would like to hear from any local authority planning to introduce a bus lane on the approach to a roundabout with a view to confirming TRL's work. Where a roundabout is controlled by traffic signals, the set back distance should accord with the guidance in paragraph 4.5.

Bus Advance Areas

4.7 Buses can be given more priority, while still retaining full junction capacity, by stopping non priority traffic at a secondary stop line level with the end of the bus lane. This creates a Bus Advance Area and a possible layout is shown schematically in Figure 2A. During the red phase at the main signal, buses may proceed to the main stop line and take their preferred lane while non-priority traffic is held at the pre-signal. Shortly before the main signal turns green, non-priority traffic is released by the pre-signal to allow full use to be made of the green phase at the main signal. Such an arrangement has been trialled at sites inside and outside London. A schematic diagram of the layout at Shepherds Bush Green is shown in Figure 2B. An assessment of the trial undertaken for the Department of Transport by TRL[15] showed that buses and general traffic flowed more freely after the new measures had been introduced. Bus journey times being improved to the extent that the benefits produced by the total scheme (including other bus priority and traffic management measures) covered the cost of installation in just over a year.

4.8 The Bus Advance Area principle has also been trialled on an approach to a roundabout in Doncaster. A schematic diagram is shown in Figure 2C. It should be noted that the presignals are sited where a side road joins the main road carrying the bus lane. Because a certain amount of the presignal cycle had to be devoted to the traffic in the side road, the system was not as efficient as that in Shepherds Bush Green. Nonetheless the trial was useful in demonstrating that roads which contain obstacles (e.g. side roads, bus stops) which can cause delay to traffic between the presignals and the main traffic control - in this case a give way at a roundabout - are not good candidates for a Bus Advance Area.

4.9 Other than the trials mentioned in the above paragraphs, the Department has limited knowledge of Bus Advance Areas being trialled. The Department wishes to explore further the concept of using Bus Advance Areas to give priorities at junctions where suitable opportunities to introduce them might exist. However, such trials would need monitoring before the Department could advise on their general introduction. The Department is interested to hear from any highway authority having a suitable site, with a view to monitoring additional trials.

Use by vehicles other than buses

4.10 It may be appropriate to permit other classes of vehicle to use a bus lane. Issues which should be considered in this context include:-

* road safety;
* the operation of the bus lane, including potential delays to buses;
* delays to other traffic;
* the legality of the definition of the vehicle class;
* enforcement;
* any impact on modal split.

Vehicle classes which may be permitted to use bus lanes include pedal cycles, motor cycles, taxis, goods vehicles, and dial-a-ride services for disabled people, although it is not usual for all these classes to be included.

Cyclists are normally allowed to use withflow bus lanes…

…and where the carriageway is wide enough a 4m-wide lane should be provided for buses and cyclists

4.11 Pedal cyclists are allowed to use withflow bus lanes because they are more likely to be involved in an accident if required to ride in the main traffic lane with buses passing on their nearside. The Government are encouraging authorities to make special provision for cyclists and if there are no cycle lanes or tracks on a suitable alignment the presumption is that cyclists will be allowed in the bus lane unless there is a very good reason for excluding them, and the signing should accommodate this. Where bus lanes are only 3 metres wide, buses are unable to pass cyclists safely unless they pull out into the "non-priority" lane; in some cases it may not be possible to do this. With this in mind, bus lanes should be the preferred width of 4m or more wherever possible.

4.12 Motorcycles were officially allowed into bus lanes in Bristol starting in the summer of 1995. The safety record of these schemes is being monitored, but at the time of writing it was too early to say how the accident rate had changed, or whether bus journey times had been affected. Motorcycles have more power than pedal cycles and can maintain their position in the traffic stream, so they are not at risk from passing traffic in the same way as pedal cycles. Because there is, as yet, insufficient evidence from the Bristol experiment, and because there is likely to be a greater risk to pedestrians if motorcycles were able to use bus lanes, the Department recommends that motorcycles should not normally be permitted to use bus lanes.

4.13 Taxis are an important part of the public transport system. Where their average occupancy in any particular area is higher than other vehicles during the periods the bus lane is in force, it may be appropriate to allow them to use bus lanes. However, if this is to be done, it is necessary for enforcement purposes that the taxis be easily identifiable, as in the case of London's black cabs or where vehicles are required to carry prominent "Taxi" signs. Some assessment of the interaction between taxis and buses when using the bus lane should be carried out: where taxis would cause undue delay to buses they should not be permitted to use the bus lane. In some areas where taxis are permitted to use bus lanes there has been pressure from operators of **cars available for private hire**, most of which are indistinguishable from private cars, to be provided with the same priority; use of bus lanes by these vehicles is not recommended. The points about enforcement and interaction with buses mentioned above will be especially relevant to local authorities and police forces when deciding whether hire cars should be allowed to take advantage of bus priority measures.

4.14 Goods vehicles carrying high valued goods, or goods which are important to the national economy could, it is agreed, benefit from using bus lanes. However, the value of time of an average goods vehicle is no higher than that of other traffic, and the benefits to goods vehicles of using a bus lane are thus likely to be offset by delays to other traffic. There are, of course, some types of time sensitive traffic where a case for priority could be made, but these would be almost impossible to identify clearly for signing and enforcement purposes. In some situations where bus flows are too low to justify a lane exclusively for buses it may be that a combined bus and heavy goods vehicle lane would be worthwhile.

4.15 As part of a strategy to afford priority access to the central area for certain classes of vehicle, the City of Newcastle-upon-Tyne introduced a bus and goods vehicle lane in the autumn of 1992. The types of qualifying goods vehicle were agreed with the local police to minimise enforcement problems. The scheme was monitored for the Department of Transport by the TRL. The results showed that only a small proportion of goods vehicles used the priority lane which was probably due to a combination of lack of certainty among lorry drivers and local characteristics of the road carrying the priority lane. There is insufficient evidence from this trial to conclude whether or not, as a general principle, goods vehicles should be allowed in bus lanes; the appropriate regional Government Office for Environment and Transport, or the Transport Policy Division of the Welsh Office, or the Roads Directorate of the Scottish Office Industry Department, would be interested to hear from any other local authority in their respective area which wishes to install a trial bus and goods vehicle lane with a view to monitoring the result.

4.16 Dial-a-Ride Services for Disabled People are provided in some areas using mini-buses where seats have been removed (or not fitted) in order to accommodate wheelchair users. Some of these vehicles will not fall within the definition of a bus because they do not have enough seats, but they should normally be permitted to use withflow bus lanes if they can be defined adequately in the Order and recognised for enforcement purposes.

4.17 High occupancy vehicles (HOVs) carrying, say, three or more occupants have been provided with special lanes on freeways in the United States; in most locations there are grade separated junctions and no frontage access. The HOV lane has generally been most successful where it has been constructed as an additional traffic lane, rather than reallocating an existing lane. The main advantage obtained from HOV lanes in the USA has been that they have encouraged car sharing by people who previously travelled by car alone, thus reducing the total amount of traffic. In the UK an HOV lane could encourage the rather different result of a switch to car sharing by public transport passengers. A clear understanding of the definition of an HOV and easy recognition of such a vehicle would be essential for enforcement purposes.

4.18 During peak periods when most bus lanes operate, most car occupants are likely to be travelling in non-working time, so the value of time of a vehicle carrying three occupants would be little greater than the average for all traffic, and considerably less than the value of a well loaded bus. Enforcement of non-qualifying HOVs in a withflow bus lane would be extremely onerous. It is considered that while there can be no general case for allowing HOVs to use bus lanes, there may be special situations where an HOV lane would be justified. The appropriate

Department (see paragraph 4.15) would like to hear from any authority wishing to consider an experimental scheme.

Signing for withflow bus lanes

4.19 Clear signing of bus priorities is of utmost importance. Illustrations of the signs most relevant to bus priorities also appear in Figure 8, together with their Diagram numbers (from TSRGD[14]) which are referred to in the text below and the associated figures.

4.20 For lanes which are separated only by a white line from the remainder of the carriageway, Figure 1 shows the signing recommended for most situations arising from the introduction of a withflow bus lane. Only those signs applicable to the bus lane are shown; for example, signs relating to the one-way street in Figure 1 are not shown. Where a bus lane is in force, waiting restrictions are not required because parking is prohibited in a bus lane. However, if loading restrictions apply, the markings on the kerb (to Diagram 1019, or 1020.1) and No Loading Signs to Diagram 638 or 638.1 are necessary. The following signs should be provided:-

* Advance signing of a withflow bus lane should be provided by a sign to Diagram 958 sited as described in Chapter 3 of the Traffic Signs Manual[16]. The sign must indicate any other classes of vehicle which may be permitted to use the Bus Lane and should normally include the pedal cycle logo unless, in exceptional circumstances, pedal cyclists are prohibited from using a withflow bus lane. (In such a case, special authorisation must be sought from the appropriate Department (see paragraph 4.15) to omit the cycle symbol.) The appropriate permitted variant should be used. The sign should be upstream of the taper marking the start of the lane (Diagram 1010); the approximate recommended distances are:

85 percentile approach speed (private cars)	Distance of sign from start of taper	Minimum clear visibility distance of signs
up to 30 mph	30 metres	45 metres
over 30 mph	45 metres	60 metres

* Along the length of the withflow bus lane, signs to Diagram 959, with the appropriate time plates to Diagram 961, must be sited facing traffic at the commencement of the bus lane after the tapered road marking. Where other classes of vehicle are included, the appropriate permitted variant or specially authorised sign should be used, also with the appropriate time plates. The same signs should be erected at intervals of not more than 300 metres for the whole length of the bus lane. Generally these repeater signs should be sited on the downstream side of each side road, though local discretion may be used where side-road traffic is very light.

* Where there is a heavy left turning movement across the bus lane into a side road, two signs to Diagram 877 should be erected facing the oncoming traffic travelling in the same direction of flow as the bus lane. One such sign should be placed 30 metres in advance of the road junction between the sign and the

junction to which it refers. The second sign should be erected immediately on the upstream side of the junction (see also Figure 1).

* Every side road carrying traffic proceeding towards the bus lane should be provided with a sign to Diagram 962 using the appropriate variant indicating the direction of the bus lane. Where the road carries bus lanes in both directions the arrow should be omitted and "s" added to this word "lane". The sign should be erected facing traffic; where the road is one-way with two or more lanes a sign should be erected on each side of the road.

Bus lane signs should be repeated at intervals of not more than 300 metres along the whole length of the bus lane

* Where there are large numbers of crossing pedestrians, signs to Diagram 963 and its permitted variant should be erected to warn pedestrians to look in the direction of approaching buses.

* At the end of the bus lane a sign to Diagram 964 should be erected facing traffic proceeding in the same direction of flow as the bus lane. Where the bus lane forms part of a recommended cycle route, signs to Diagrams 2601 or 2602 should be erected to indicate the direction of the continuation of the cycle route.

Note that coaches operating excursions or tours are included in the new definition of vehicles to which the bus symbol applies. In some circumstances it may be desirable to exclude coaches from the priority lane. This may be achieved by the addition of the legend "local" to the bus symbol in the blue and white "bus only" sign to Diagrams 953, 958 and 959.

Where taxis are permitted to use a bus lane, this should be signed by the addition of the word "taxi" to the bus lane signs to Diagram 958 and 959.

Signs for withflow bus lanes which permit any other class of vehicle, or which exclude pedal cycles, and signs for bus lanes in the centre, or on the offside, of the road require special authorisation. Appropriate variants of the nearside withflow bus lane signs should be submitted to the appropriate Department (see paragraph 4.15).

Road Markings for withflow bus lanes

4.21 Road markings should be provided as follows. Figure 1 illustrates the text:

* Deflection arrows to Diagram 1014 should be placed 30 metres and 15 metres upstream of the start of the bus lane taper. Traffic should be deflected to the offside where the bus lane occupies the nearside lane, or to the nearside where the bus lane occupies the offside lane.

The carriageway approaching the bus lane should be marked with deflection arrows and a tapered broken line

The outer edge of the bus lane should be marked by a solid white line which terminates at the entrance to or exit from a side road

* A tapered broken straight white line to Diagram 1010 must be provided immediately in advance of the start of the bus lane. Its angle with the kerb (or the tangent to a curved kerb) from which it runs to connect with the solid line marking the outer edge of the bus lane (see below) should not normally exceed 1:10. Some adjustment may be required on sharp right hand bends, but it is recommended that the length of kerb over which the taper takes place should not be less than 30 metres. In any event the tapered line indicating the start of a bus lane (rather than its continuation after a junction) should not extend across a junction; the start of the bus lane in this situation should be moved sufficiently far down stream to allow the tapered line to run from the kerb to the solid edge marking within the angle specified.

* The outer edge of the bus lane should be marked by a solid white line 250 or 300mm wide to Diagram 1049. Wherever possible the wider line should be adopted to reduce the likelihood of wing-mirror conflict. The line should terminate at the entrance to or exit from a side road on the same side of the main road as the bus lane and recommence on the other side of the side road; a curved broken line to Diagram 1010 should be provided as a lead-in to the solid line on the downstream side of every side road entry point.

* The legend "BUS LANE", to Diagram 1048, should be marked on the bus lane at its commencement so that it is legible to drivers proceeding in the same direction of flow as the bus lane. The same legend should also appear in the lane after every side road on the same side of the road as the bus lane, and in every location where repeater signs appear.

* In advance of any junction with a major left turning flow across which the bus lane continues, it is recommended that the solid white line is replaced with a broken line to Diagram 1010 accompanied by advisory direction arrows to Diagram 1050 which should be positioned as near as possible to the first of the signs to Diagram 877 (see above).

4.22 The bus lane can be emphasised by the use of coloured surfacing (which is not a road marking and does not require authorisation), but care should be taken that the material used complies with normal skid-resistance criteria. Unlike prescribed road markings, coloured surfaces may be continued through the controlled area on the approaches to pedestrian crossings which are designated by zig-zag lines, and across junctions. Whilst there are no national standards for coloured surfaces, compliance appears to have improved in London and elsewhere where red has been used extensively. Compliance can also be encouraged by:

* designing the start of the bus lane so as to encourage the "natural" movement of traffic into the general traffic lane rather than into the bus lane; one way might be to build out the kerb using a suitable curved design; or

* where the road width permits, providing short islands along the length of the bus lane.

4.23 Cars straying onto the solid white dividing line between the bus lane and the remainder of the carriageway may obstruct buses. This is more likely where bus lanes are at or near the minimum recommended width of 3 metres. It has been suggested that better demarcation by longitudinal islands or such devices as raised rib marking could help to prevent this usually unintentional violation, and so reduce the need for police patrols. Research by the Transport Research Laboratory (TRL) in 1977[17] highlighted the danger to two-wheeled vehicles from the introduction of two styles of upstand then available (research on raised-rib markings in other locations on the highway is also reported in Traffic Advisory Leaflet 2/95). More modern methods such as raised rib marking similar to that used on the edge of motorway carriageways may be more successful, but no specification has yet been developed for its use as a bus lane demarcation and it cannot legally be used without authorisation from the appropriate Department (see paragraph 4.15). The safety of motorcyclists (who are not normally permitted to use bus lanes) and cyclists is of great importance, and there are implications for all traffic during the periods when the bus lane is not operating. In the few locations where raised rib demarcations have been installed they appear to have improved compliance. The Department would like to investigate this aspect further and would like to hear from any local authority wishing to promote a trial.

CHAPTER 5

CONTRAFLOW BUS LANES

5.1 By allowing buses to travel against the main direction of traffic flow in a one-way street, contraflow bus operation enables buses to avoid unnecessary diversions, to maintain route patterns when new one-way streets are introduced, and to gain better access to business and shopping areas. This can often be achieved on a two-way road by restricting the flow in one direction to buses and other permitted vehicles. In other situations a designated contraflow bus lane may be required; a typical plan is shown at Figure 3. Unlike withflow bus lanes, contraflow bus lanes normally operate 24 hours per day.

5.2 The introduction of a contraflow bus lane may cause delays to other traffic. As in the case of a withflow bus lane, the savings to buses and the delays to other traffic should be carefully assessed (see Chapter 9) to determine whether the benefits, including environmental and other considerations, are sufficient to justify the cost of the scheme. A contraflow bus lane will have particular road safety implications, and potential accident costs should be taken into account in the assessment; the servicing of premises fronting onto the contraflow lane may need special consideration.

5.3 Contraflow bus lanes should be at least 3 metres wide and separated from the rest of the carriageway either by a solid white line (see 5.14, or else physically separated by a continuous upstand or series of long islands. Although physical separation helps to keep the bus lane clear of other traffic, segregated lanes are costly to install, and by confining buses to a precise track can cause tracking of the road surface. Complete segregation also prevents buses from overtaking cyclists, a broken down vehicle or other obstruction, and may create a safety hazard by preventing the bus driver from steering to avoid a pedestrian. For these reasons, separation by white line supplemented by occasional traffic islands and/or solid white lines with hatching between them will usually be preferable to full physical separation. As for a withflow bus lane, the recommended width where cyclists are allowed to use the lane is 4.25 metres with a preferred minimum of 4m; the comments about coloured surfacing reinforcing the special nature of the lane (see paragraph 4.22) and about raised rib marking (see paragraph 4.23) are also relevant here.

Use by vehicles other than buses

5.4 As with a withflow bus lane it may be appropriate to permit other classes of vehicle to use a contraflow bus lane. Subject to consideration of the issues listed in paragraph 4.10, vehicle classes which may be permitted to use contraflow bus lanes include pedal cycles, taxis, and dial-a-ride services for disabled people, although it is not usual for all these classes to be included.

5.5 Research has shown that **pedal cyclists** using contraflow bus lanes can be at risk, mainly from conflicts with other traffic at the beginning and end of the lane[18]. However, over lengths of bus lane between junctions, accident risk tends to be low. If at all possible, safe junctions should be provided at the entry and exit points so that cyclists can use the contraflow lane. This is especially relevant where alternative routes are considered to be more dangerous for cyclists, or where they involve a substantial detour.

5.6 **Taxis**, and **dial-a-ride** services for disabled people, may be allowed to use contraflow lanes at the discretion of the local authority. It is recommended that motorcycles, goods vehicles and HOVs should not be permitted to use contraflow bus lanes.

Safety issues

5.7 A contraflow bus lane can create new road safety hazards. Based on investigations carried out by TRL in 1989[18] the following measures should be considered:-

* guardrailing to channel pedestrians to points where crossing facilities can be provided, and where clear signing indicates the direction of approaching buses.

* careful design of geometry, signing and road markings on the approach to the entry of a contraflow bus lane to control possible conflict between vehicles entering the lane and those turning across their path.

* reducing the number of uncontrolled junctions along the length of the lane, possibly by closing them off altogether or by banning turning movements in order to reduce the number of likely vehicle conflicts.

The use of contraflow bus lanes by unauthorised vehicles may create a particular hazard for pedestrians.

Road geometry, signing and markings on the approach to a contraflow bus lane

Signing for contraflow bus lanes

5.8 Signing and road markings should be in accordance with the Traffic Signs Regulations and General Directions 1994[14] . Particular note should be taken of the recommended signing at the entry to the contraflow lane which is designed to exclude all classes of vehicle except those permitted to use the lane. Illustrations of the most relevant signs and their Diagram numbers appear in Figure 8. Contraflow lanes are normally located so that buses travel along the lane with their nearside nearest the kerb. Contraflow lanes in other locations are extremely rare and are not recommended where stopping places are required or for anything other than a very short link in special circumstances. The following advice applies to the normal situation.

5.9 Vehicles approaching the beginning of a contraflow bus lane should be warned in advance by a map-type direction sign (e.g. to Diagram 2108) which shows "No Entry" into the road carrying the contraflow lane and the alternative route(s) for non priority traffic.

5.10 Figure 3 shows the signing recommended for a contraflow bus lane. At the beginning of the lane, No Entry Signs to Diagram 616 (see Figure 8) should be erected on either side of the main carriageway carrying the opposing flow; a traffic island should be provided between the contraflow lane and the opposing carriageway to accommodate this sign. The sign on the nearside kerb should be a blue and white sign (Diagram 953 or permitted variants) to show which vehicles may use the lane, and an "only" plate to Diagram 953.2. Where the lane is to be restricted to local buses, the word "local" must be added to the bus symbol in the sign to Diagram 953. Alternatively a No Entry sign to Diagram 616 may be used in conjunction with one of the following exemption plates:

* an "Except buses" plate to Diagram 954, or

* an "Except local buses" plate to Diagram 954.2.

Contraflow bus lanes must be signed with a blue and white sign (Diagram 953 or permitted variants) and an "only" plate (Diagram 953.2) or...

...a "No Entry" sign to Diagram 616 with an "Except buses" plate to Diagram 954 or "Except local buses" to Diagram 954.2

Where taxis are to be allowed to use the lane, the sign to Diagram 960 must be used and the word "taxi" must be added below the bus symbol. All traffic islands should carry, at both ends, "Keep Left" arrows to Diagram 610.

5.11 All side road approaches must carry signs to Diagram 612 or 613, and signs to Diagram 962 should be added to warn drivers of the bus lane. Signs to Diagrams 606 and 609 may be used to supplement the information.

5.12 Where provision is made to accommodate crossing pedestrians, refuges separating the bus lane from the other traffic lanes must be constructed. Signs to Diagram 963 must be erected on the refuge and on the kerb opposite the refuge on the other side of the bus lane.

5.13 At the end of the street where buses exit and general traffic enters, there will normally be no need to sign the end of the bus lane. Signs to Diagram 960 must replace the normal One Way Street Sign (Diagram 652), and be erected to face traffic entering the street. These signs should also be repeated, facing the direction of the main traffic flow, after every side-road junction, on whichever side the side-road is located.

Road markings for contraflow bus lanes

5.14 Figure 3 illustrates how road markings should be provided. The bus lane should be separated from the rest of the carriageway by a 250mm or 300mm solid white line to Diagram 1049 where there are no traffic islands or other physical separations. The line should be discontinued at nearside road junctions but, unlike withflow bus lanes, a broken line is not necessary on the approach to side roads since all non-priority traffic would be travelling in the opposing direction. "BUS LANE" road markings to Diagram 1048, together with appropriate direction arrows, should appear at both ends of the lane so as to be legible to drivers approaching the contraflow lane; these markings should be repeated each side of every side road junction. If cycles are to be allowed to use a contraflow bus lane, the road marking to Diagram 1048.1 must be used. "LOOK LEFT"/ "LOOK RIGHT" markings should accompany signs to Diagram 963 at pedestrian crossing places.

Road markings in a Contraflow bus lane

CHAPTER 6

BUS ONLY STREETS

6.1 A bus only street is a section of road for the use of buses only. It may be a section of road enabling the bus to take a more direct route, for example between a main access road and a residential estate, or it may be a "pedestrianised" street in a town centre where buses are exempt from a prohibition on all, or some types of, vehicles. Such streets enable buses to:-

* maintain route patterns in areas where traffic flow patterns have been changed; long detours which add to bus operating costs can be avoided whilst preventing unwanted short cuts by other traffic;

* gain close access to business and shopping areas at times when it is denied to other vehicles; such arrangements help to make bus services more attractive by providing convenient access for bus passengers, including elderly people and those with mobility handicaps.

6.2 The appraisal procedure recommended for bus lanes may be appropriate for bus only streets, but it is likely that in many situations, particularly in town centres, environmental considerations will predominate.

Pedestrianised streets

6.3 Allowing buses to use pedestrianised streets can help town centre businesses by encouraging bus use, especially where bus stops are nearer than major car parks are to the focal points in the town. A clear indication of which section of the carriageway is designated as a bus only street will encourage compliance and ease enforcement. Safety for pedestrians in a pedestrianised area into which buses are also allowed is paramount. Some successful schemes use a carriageway at a different level from the footway which is helpful to blind and partially sighted people. In others road surfaces flush with the footway are of different textures and/or colours from the footway. Excessive speeds are particularly dangerous in pedestrian streets. Bus operators should agree safe speeds with the local authority, and instruct their drivers accordingly. If extra measures are required to reduce bus speeds, road humps may be considered, although other measures which avoid the use of road humps are often preferable (see paragraph 3.6). In some bus only streets, it may be necessary to introduce defined pedestrian crossing places, especially when bus

Speed reducing hump with shallow approach gradients and flat tops extending along the length of the carriageways

service frequencies are high. Side roads having junctions with the bus only street should be closed off wherever possible to reduce the likelihood of accidents. The environment can be enhanced with features such as planting but good visibility between pedestrians and vehicles must be maintained.

6.4 Some authorities have used rising bollards to reduce or prevent entry violations of bus only streets. Such bollards have been activated by electronic devices fitted to the buses or by drivers using remote control panels. The rising bollards have been installed under Sections 92 to 94 of the Road Traffic Regulation Act 1984 to reinforce a Traffic Regulation Order. A traffic authority using rising bollards should be mindful of the duty of care which they owe to the public, and especially to ensure the safety of pedestrians, cyclists and other vulnerable road users. Signing would normally be used to show the times at which access can be gained to the restricted area. Advice should be sought from the appropriate Department (see paragraph 4.15) at an early stage as to whether site authorisation for signing or approval for equipment will be required[28].

Bus gates

6.5 Short lengths of bus only street are sometimes referred to as "bus gates". Short, standard width, sections of road protected only by signs are commonly used; violation rates are often high at such installations, especially away from central areas. Narrowing the road to the width of one vehicle in the bus gate itself (see Figure 4), using a different colour for the road surface in this section, and/or installing traffic calming features such as speed cushions or road-side furniture can often improve the compliance rate. Where more elaborate carriageway constructions designed to deter smaller vehicles from passing through the bus gate are proposed, the highway authority should ensure that suitable powers are available to introduce such measures. They should also be aware that such a construction may make it impossible for some emergency vehicles to pass. Local authorities should also be satisfied that adequate alternative routes are available before introducing such measures. Bus gates and entries to longer lengths of bus only street which are wide enough to accommodate only one vehicle at a time should not exceed 30 metres in length.

Bus only streets should be signed with a blue and white sign to Diagram 953, supplemented by an "Only" plate to Diagram 953.2...

...or a No Entry sign to Diagram 616 supplemented by "Except buses" to Diagram 954 or permitted variants

Signing for Bus Only Streets

6.6 Figure 4 shows a typical plan and the recommended signing for a bus only street. Figure 8 shows the most relevant signs and their Diagram numbers. The blue and white Buses Only Sign to Diagram 953 (see Figure 8) or permitted variants should be used (to show which vehicles may use the lane) with an "only" plate to Diagram 953.2. Where the street is to be restricted to local buses, the word "local" must be added to the bus symbol in the sign to Diagram 953. Alternatively a No Entry Sign to Diagram 616 may be used in conjunction with one of the following exemption plates:

* an "Except buses" plate to Diagram 954, or
* an "Except local buses" plate to Diagram 954.2.

Where taxis are to be allowed to use the lane, the sign to Diagram 953 must be used and the word "taxi" added below the bus symbol. These signs should be positioned on each side of the road, and on any central islands in the road, at each end of the length of restricted road. Adequate advance direction signs showing alternative routes for non-priority vehicles approaching the restricted street should be provided as for contraflow bus lanes (see paragraph 5.9).

6.7 Where other motor vehicles are also exempt from the restriction, the appropriate variant of the Pedestrian Zone sign to Diagram 618.2 or 618.3 should be used so as to exempt only those type(s) of buses which are permitted. Advice on signing where a variety of exemptions are in force is contained in Chapter 3 of the Traffic Signs Manual[16].

Different colour or texture of road surface can encourage compliance and ease enforcement

CHAPTER 7

BUS PRIORITY AT JUNCTIONS

7.1 Buses can be given priority at road junctions, either by permitting buses to make turning movements prohibited to other traffic, by giving preference to flows containing a high proportion of buses, or by adjusting signal controls when a bus is detected in the traffic stream.

Turning exemptions

7.2 Allowing buses to make a turn which is prohibited to other traffic is a measure which is usually cheap to install, and which can give buses a considerable advantage by allowing them to take a shorter route than other traffic. Exemptions can also be used to allow buses to enter a contraflow bus lane, or a bus only street. Research into the safety aspects of turning exemptions for buses[18] indicates that very few accidents involved buses making the exempted turn. Nearly four times as many accidents were caused by other vehicles making the turn illegally. This emphasises the importance of clear, well-located signs and road markings, and adequate enforcement.

7.3 To avoid long detours it may be appropriate to allow cycles to make turns prohibited to traffic other than buses. The safety aspects of any such proposal should be carefully considered. Pedal cyclists are much less visible than buses, and may be at serious risk when making a turn not made by other traffic.

7.4 Taxis may also exceptionally be exempted from turning prohibitions; again, safety aspects should be considered very carefully.

7.5 Where buses are exempted from turning prohibitions, No Left/Right Turn Signs to Diagram 612 or 613[14] (see also Figure 8) should be used immediately on the approach to the junction, supplemented with one of the following rectangular exemption plates below the sign:

* "Except buses" plate to Diagram 954, or
* "Except local buses" plate to Diagram 954.2.

Where the exemption is from a straight ahead prohibition, the Buses Only Sign or the No Entry Except Buses Sign should be used as described in paragraph 5.10. Where cyclists are also exempt, the Buses and Cycles Only sign to Diagram 953 must be used. At signalised junctions these signs should be fixed to an extended black backplate to which the signal lights are fixed, the extension being on the side away from the carriageway. Where other vehicle classes are included in the exemption, they must appear on the rectangular exemption plates. Advance warning should be given using a standard advance direction sign (see paragraph 5.9) with the appropriate roundel as described above but excluding the "Except buses" rectangular plate.

7.6 Exemption for pedal cycles should be signed by the addition of the exemption plate to Diagram 954.3 to the No Right/Left Turn Signs to Diagrams 612/613. Where it is intended that taxis should be permitted to make turns prohibited to other traffic except buses, special authorisation (see paragraph 4.15) will be required to include taxis in the exemption plate(s) to be used with the No Right/Left Turn Signs to Diagrams 612/613.

Turning exemption for buses at traffic signals

Selective detection of buses

7.7 Buses can be given priority at traffic signals more effectively if the signal can be made to respond to the arrival of the bus. This can be achieved by fitting buses with an electronic device which can be detected either by satellite using GPS techniques or by static equipment in the highway which is linked to the traffic signal controller. The most common form of this is a bus fitted with a transponder which is detected as it passes over an inductive loop slotted into the road surface. On receipt of the signal, a suitably equipped traffic signal controller can bring forward the start of the green phase, or hold the green phase to allow the bus time to pass the signal with minimum delay. Such systems have been found to provide significant benefits to buses[19] and have been widely installed at individual junctions (i.e. those not linked to others in a group) in London[20]. In some bus fleets, the traditional transponder is being replaced by a newer, cheaper, device called a "tag". Traffic authorities will need to ensure that these devices are sufficiently secure to prevent their use on non-authorised types of vehicle.

7.8 A traffic control system called MOVA (**M**icroprocessor **O**ptimised Vehicle **A**ctuation) has been developed by TRL for controlling individual junctions. MOVA aims to minimise both stops and delays to traffic, and uses microprocessor technology to apply logic beyond the capabilities of standard equipment. It has been found in trials to reduce delays by 13% compared to the vehicle activated system which is the present standard in the UK. The latest version of MOVA offers active bus priority via selective vehicle detection using loops in the road and transponders on the buses. Further guidance is available from the Department[21].

Urban traffic control (UTC)

7.9 In most large urban areas, traffic signals are controlled by some form of computer-based urban traffic control system. Approximately half of these are on "fixed time" plans based upon surveys of traffic flows and their variation by time of day and day of the week. Signal timings for these fixed time plans are usually calculated by the "TRANSYT" method developed by TRL[22]. A variation of this method, "BUS TRANSYT"[23], can be used where bus flows are significant. BUS

TRANSYT tends to favour signal approaches carrying significant bus flows, and thus takes more account of the high passenger carrying capacity of the bus.

7.10 UTC systems based on fixed time plans rely upon historical traffic patterns being repeated in a predictable way. Since traffic patterns tend to change over time, it is important that they are regularly monitored, and the timing plans recalculated. This is very labour intensive, and as a result many fixed time systems tend to operate inefficiently with out of date plans. Fixed time plans are also unable to deal with random variations in flows which cannot be predicted.

SCOOT

7.11 In order to deal with these problems TRL have developed an on-line UTC system called "SCOOT"(**S**plit **C**ycle **O**ffset **O**ptimisation **T**echnique). SCOOT responds continuously to actual traffic demands being detected on the network, and makes repeated small adjustments to signal timings to reduce traffic delays. The SCOOT system typically achieves 10-15% reductions in delays compared to fixed time systems, and has now been installed in over 130 cities in the UK and overseas. Facilities for active bus priority using selective detection by loops in the road or by automatic vehicle location (AVL) systems have been introduced as a result of recent research (see paragraph 7.13). These facilities are being further refined as part of on-going research commissioned by the Department of the Environment, Transport and the Regions.

7.12 The version of SCOOT used by many local authorities (version 2.3) offers a facility for weighting selected routes. This facility can be used to provide priority for buses by weighting routes with heavy bus flows; this is often called "passive priority" because the level of priority is programmed into the system rather than taking account of the real number of buses arriving at any particular time. A later version of SCOOT (version 2.4) offers additional facilities including a "gating" technique whereby the inflow of traffic to a sensitive area is controlled to ensure that any traffic queues build up outside that area. "Congestion offsets" can also be used to ensure that a specified main route is kept flowing and that any queues build up on the side roads. These "queue relocation" techniques can be used to give priority to buses by making sure that traffic queues do not affect buses, or else occur where they can be bypassed by bus lanes. Queue relocation techniques have been used to help buses successfully in the Bitterne Road scheme in Southampton, and more recently on London's Uxbridge Road on the westbound approach to a major junction in Southall. During Southampton's morning peak period when the bus priority scheme is in operation, a special fixed time plan is introduced which reduces the inflow of side road traffic in order to help traffic flow more freely on the main road which is a major route for buses approaching the city centre. This scheme has undergone a number of modifications since it was introduced in the early 70's, including the introduction of SCOOT control at certain periods of the day. It is a good example of a traffic management scheme which includes a number of bus priority features; a plan of the scheme is shown in Figure 5.

7.13 In 1995, TRL produced a version of SCOOT (3.1) in which the software kernel processes priority calls from buses identified by selective detection. The bus priority optimiser implements green-time extensions and priority recalls where the green phase is recalled earlier than it otherwise would be). The decision to make an extension or recall makes full use of SCOOT capabilities and account is taken of queues which may delay buses. This new version, developed as part of a European research programme, showed savings in bus passenger delay of between 20% and 30% in tests at TRL. Subsequent field trials in Camden Town, London, where traffic volumes are high and bus frequencies reach 150 per hour, produced average savings in bus delay of 22% per junction. Maximum saving to buses was achieved with local extensions and central recalls; other traffic suffered small delays with local extensions at all traffic levels but recalls caused the worst conditions for non-priority traffic at higher traffic levels. Nine junctions in Southampton have also been fitted with this new version of SCOOT. Further guidance is available from the Department[24], and more detailed information is given in the paper "Latest Developments in SCOOT"[25].

7.14 SCOOT is being further developed with a view to providing still more advantages to buses. Other methods with potential for offering new ways of giving priority to buses within traffic signal control systems are also being tried; for example a UTC system called SPOT was trialled in Leeds as part of the DRIVE Primavera project.

CHAPTER 8

BUS STOPS

8.1 The passenger's access to the bus network is normally at a bus stop. A formally agreed bus stopping place, normally designated by a bus stop pole and/or shelter, offers the opportunity to consider the road safety implications for stopping buses. There are therefore advantages to be gained for operators, the highway authority and the Police in agreeing sites for bus stops. Where agreement cannot be reached, the Traffic Commissioner is often asked to arbitrate.

The passenger's access to the bus system is normally at a bus stop

8.2 In town centres it is important that bus stops are located conveniently for the main shopping and business areas, and preferably nearer to those areas than major car parks. This makes services more convenient for passengers, particularly elderly and disabled people. The safety of passengers is most important, both while waiting at stops and whilst walking to and from them. For these reasons it is preferable that passengers do not have to cross major traffic flows to reach their destination. If this is unavoidable, bus stops should be located close to pedestrian crossing facilities. Where space is extremely limited a bus stop may be located in the controlled area of a pedestrian crossing (indicated by zig-zag lines) on the leaving side of the crossing, but not in the approach. Where one way traffic systems are involved, bus stops must be located on the nearside of the carriageway unless special provision is made for boarding and alighting. It is usually most convenient for pedestrians/passengers if bus stops are located close to junctions, especially where interchange between bus services is common, and the effect on vehicular capacity on the approaches to and exits from junctions may have to be balanced against the level of convenience offered to bus passengers. Where selective detection is in use (see Chapter 7) bus stops should not be located between the detector and the stop line. In any case, bus stops and shelters should be sited so that bus drivers can see waiting passengers and vice versa; any locations which are obstructed by large objects such as hoardings or trees also carry personal security risks and should therefore be avoided. Street clutter can be avoided by locating bus stops at existing lamp columns. Safety can be improved by the use of CCTV cameras. All these items should be considered during the consultations about the siting of bus stops which should take place between bus operators, traffic authorities, and the police, together with (where appropriate) frontagers and bus users groups.

8.3 When development takes place bus access should be considered. Bus stops should be located close to major generators of potential passengers, or to focal points in the footway network. Where new roads are involved, special arrangements may be required to give buses access to the development before the roads are adopted. In large developments it may help to construct special sections of road to provide buses with direct access to and through the development. Temporary stops and turning arrangements may be required as development proceeds. Some local authorities give guidance on these matters in design guides for developers, to ensure that appropriate provision is made for bus services from the outset. In some situations, developers may be prepared to contribute to the cost of passenger facilities at bus stops. Whatever arrangements are sought, early consultation between authorities, operators and interested private sector parties will be necessary to ensure the facilities are used.

When development takes place, bus access should be considered...

...and bus stops located close to focal points in the footway network

8.4 Bus stops should be well lit for road safety and personal security reasons, and should provide passengers with clear information about the services using the stop, either by static displays or by the use of real time information panels, or both. Shelters, seating, paved areas for waiting, and convenient access all help to make a bus service safe and more attractive to passengers. Guidelines for the design of public transport infrastructure, including bus stops, which address the needs of disabled and elderly people are contained in "Accessible Public Transport Infrastructure"[26]

8.5 One of the simplest ways of giving buses priority is to protect the road space by the bus stop so that it is kept clear for buses to use. This is vital in busy areas where there is often strong competition for access to the kerb from vehicles wishing to park or to load or unload. Keeping the bus stop clear allows the bus to pull in close to the kerb which is particularly important for low-floor buses if the benefits of step-free access are to be realised. It enables all passengers, especially those who are elderly or disabled, to board and alight without walking into the road; it also minimises the obstruction to the flow of other traffic. Special types of kerb such as the "Kassel" design can assist buses to approach as near as possible to the footway, but it should be noted that kerbs higher than 125mm may damage the underside of the bus if there is any overhang when the bus approaches at an angle; the potential conflict between street furniture and wing mirrors should also be taken into account. Sufficient road space should be kept free, by strong enforcement if necessary, to accommodate front and/or rear loading buses as appropriate. Where front loading buses are involved, kerbs should be located so as not to obstruct the swept path of buses with lowered front steps. Where more than one stop is required, sufficient road space should be kept clear for all the bus services involved.

8.6 Yellow lines (to Diagrams 1017, or 1018.1) to prevent parking, supplemented by No Loading markings (to Diagrams 1019, or 1020.1), are the commonest way of

Bus stops should provide passengers with clear information about the services using the stop

Bus stop boarder

keeping the road free for buses at bus stops. A bus stop clearway may also be used; the Traffic Signs Regulations and General Directions [14] allows total flexibility for the highway authority to choose the times of operation. All such measures will, of course, require a supporting Traffic Regulation Order.

8.7 Waiting restrictions and bus stop clearways both depend for their effectiveness upon adequate enforcement. In some locations where there is heavy parking a "bus stop boarder" may be more effective, and be largely self-enforcing because it deters kerbside parking. The "boarder" is constructed by projecting the footway into the carriageway by a distance which will vary according to the location. The optimal distance for bus passenger access will be the width of any adjacent bays designated for parking or loading, but shorter projections may be appropriate where general traffic flow may be unduly disrupted (eg. on the approach to signals or at heavily used bus stops. The projection of the footway into the carriageway provides passengers with easier access to the bus, and inhibits parking at the bus stop, while still allowing traffic to pass the stationary bus. The bus boarder may be provided with a raised area of footway and kerb to make access easier for elderly and disabled people. In some locations bus boarders can be used as traffic calming measures, but care should be taken if building out a considerable distance from the kerb to ensure that the gradient of the surface of the boarder is not so steep that it is awkward or dangerous (eg for wheelchair users) when approaching the bus.

8.8 Lay-bys can offer protection of road space at bus stops, but can create difficulties for buses seeking to rejoin a traffic queue on the main carriageway. Nonetheless, provision of a lay-by may help to improve traffic flow by removing the bus from the main traffic stream, so assisting buses further upstream in the traffic queue. Lay-bys should be provided where a stopped bus on the carriageway would present a safety hazard, or for any other safety reason, but they are not generally welcomed by bus operators. If lay-bys are provided they should preferably be constructed in material different from that used for the main carriageway so as to discourage other vehicles from parking and loading, and the crossfall should be arranged to avoid waiting passengers being splashed. Lay-bys should be clearly marked "BUS STOP" (see paragraph 8.10 for Diagram Numbers). Figure 7 shows both full-width and narrow bus lay-bys. Where a narrow bus bay is proposed to help buses rejoin the traffic stream, care should be taken that there is sufficient width for other vehicles to pass a stationary bus safely.

8.9 Lay-bys provided for other traffic to enable easier parking and loading away from the bus stop can help to discourage bus stops being blocked by cars and lorries. Traffic authorities may like to consult guidance on bus stops, boarders and lay-bys published by London Bus Priority Network Steering Group[27].

Signing for protection of bus stops

8.10 "BUS STOP" markings on the main part of the carriageway should be provided to Diagram 1025 (see Figure 8). In a lay-by at a bus stop, road markings to Diagram 1025.2 should be used. These are advisory, and can be supplemented with No Waiting and No Loading restrictions where necessary. A Bus Stop Clearway will, with full compliance, prevent all vehicles except buses stopping in the area of the bus stop. Road markings to Diagram 1025.1 (main carriageway) or to Diagram 1025.3 (lay-by), in conjunction with a sign to Diagram 974, must be provided.

8.11 Where waiting restrictions are in force, buses are allowed to stop only for the time needed to set down and pick up passengers. Where longer stops are required, buses should be specifically exempted from the restrictions in the Order. A bus layover place may be provided on the carriageway, signed with the "BUS STAND" permitted variant of the "BUS STOP" carriageway markings to Diagrams 1025, 1025.1, 1025.2, and 1025.3. Bus operators should ask the appropriate traffic authority to modify the necessary Traffic Regulation Order(s) so that such arrangements can be introduced.

Lay-bys improve traffic flow and access to bus stops. They are best constructed in materials different from the main carriageway...

... and narrow lay-bys help buses rejoin the traffic stream

CHAPTER 9

APPRAISAL AND FUNDING

Appraisal

9.1 The decision to implement a traffic management scheme on a local authority road, whether or not it includes any bus priority measures, rests with the local authority. Normally an authority would use its powers as highway authority under the Road Traffic Regulation Act 1984. On a trunk road outside London, decisions lie with the appropriate Department (see paragraph 4.15). On priority "red" routes, in London the Traffic Director for London's approval would have to be required, on designated roads he would also need to be notified.

9.2 A local authority considering whether to implement a scheme which provides priority for buses will require a sound basis for appraising the impact of the scheme. This should cover the operational, economic, environmental and planning aspects. Although it should not be the only criteria, and may not necessarily be the main one, an economic appraisal should always be carried out so that local authorities are able to satisfy themselves of the value for money of the priority measures before the decision is made to implement a bus priority scheme. Even where the estimated capital cost of the scheme is small, the impact on non-priority traffic (whether regarded as a benefit or disbenefit) may be significant or may affect a much wider area, and should be separately identified so that it can be properly considered as part of the appraisal.

9.3 The overall objectives of such an economic appraisal should be to evaluate the benefits of the scheme to buses and their passengers, including any additional patronage attracted to the services in question, and to compare these benefits with the effects on other road users. The net benefit should then be assessed in relation to the capital cost of the scheme. The final decision to implement bus priority measures should take into account wider considerations, particularly when it is judged that, with the development of the overall transport strategy for the area, there may be a transfer of passengers from car to bus. These wider considerations should include the benefits of bus priority as part of a package of measures to improve bus services, the overall transport objectives of the area (which may include traffic restraint), wider environmental issues such as air quality and noise, and planning concerns. Priority measures may therefore be justifiable even if, within the economic appraisal, net benefits would not cover the cost of the scheme for many years, or indeed if benefits to bus users fail to exceed costs to other road users.

9.4 Appraisals should not be confined to new schemes. Reappraisals should also be made of existing schemes when significant changes take place in either the bus service network or in the patterns of other traffic.

9.5 Annex B provides a detailed discussion of the principles, and presentation, of the appraisal of priority measures.

Funding

9.6 In England, under the package approach, spending on roads and public transport will be funded from the same allocation; this allows authorities to determine, within given resources, the optimal blend of transport measures for their areas. Capital expenditure by local authorities on bus priority measures will normally be eligible for support by way of annual capital guidelines or supplementary credit approvals. Except to the extent that a scheme whose cost is under £2m is expected to bring direct financial benefits to the local authority (e.g. rental for a trolleybus line or guided bus lane) such support will be reflected in the local authority's standard spending assessment for capital financing costs. Other sources of funding may sometimes be available; these may include funding from European funds and from private developer contributions.

9.7 Schemes estimated to cost under £2m will normally be funded by local authorities from the allocations of Supplementary Credit Approvals (SCAs) which they receive for transport minor works, including allocations made under the package approach. In exceptional circumstances, a specific allocation may be made for a particular scheme costing under £2m. Schemes costing £2m or more on roads of more than local importance may be eligible for Transport Supplementary Grant (TSG) towards 50% of the costs, with the balance funded through annual capital guidelines; other schemes costing £2m or more are eligible for support through SCAs. Major public transport infrastructure schemes such as busways are also eligible for support through SCAs; where the estimated cost of the scheme exceeds £5m and there are exceptional reasons for spreading the costs beyond users and local council tax payers, such schemes may also be eligible for partial support by grant under section 56 of the Transport Act 1968. Further details are provided in the annual TPP circulars.

9.8 In cases where users of a bus priority scheme - for instance a trolleybus scheme - are expected to pay through the fare box, a full cost-benefit appraisal must be submitted as well as an appraisal under the criteria appropriate to public transport schemes (such as those eligible for section 56 grant) in which the benefits to users are calculated by reference to the fare revenue.

9.9 In Scotland, the grant structure is different and Transport Supplementary Grant and credit approvals are not used. Local authorities must include all capital expenditure on bus priorities, whether it is grant aided (section 56) or not, in their TPP's for the Scottish Office to consider when determining capital allocations for individual authorities.

9.10 In Wales, local authorities are provided with basic credit approvals which are allocated annually by formula to cover a wide variety of services including transportation and highways. Projects are funded at local authorities' own discretion. In addition the Welsh Office administers funding for integrated transport packages through the arrangements for Transport Grant, including support for bus priority measures. Major public transport schemes may also be eligible for grant support under section 56 of the Transport Act 1968.

CHAPTER 10

IMPLEMENTATION, MAINTENANCE AND MONITORING

Implementation

10.1 This document gives guidance on various aspects of the layout and signing of bus priority schemes. Further information on the design of highways and traffic management schemes, including designing for buses, is included in "Transport in the Urban Environment"[29]. Measures to assist buses appear in Chapter 26.

10.2 All organisations, groups, and individuals likely to be affected by the scheme should be consulted about the proposals in good time. This "non-statutory" consultation at an early stage in the development of the scheme will allow time for the scheme to be properly understood by those who are not familiar with the techniques involved, and for them to comment. It also allows time for representations to be taken into account as the scheme is progressed. There is also a better chance of success where organisations are involved throughout the development of the scheme.

10.3 The Statutory consultation, required at the time the Traffic Orders are made, will be facilitated if the scheme has already been the subject of discussion. Standardised orders may also help to speed up this process. Adequate time should be allowed for processing orders, including preparing and publishing the Order, consulting police about enforcement, allowing time for objections and any public enquiry which may be either necessary or desirable, dealing with objections including amending the Order as necessary, and confirming the Order.

10.4 The Road Traffic Regulation Act 1984 permits an Order to be made on an experimental basis for a period of up to 18 months, during which the impact or extent of the Order may be reduced or suspended without the need to go through a fresh Order-making procedure. Authorities may like to consider using this approach where they are uncertain about the possible effects of introducing bus priority measures. When making an experimental Order, authorities must be able to explain what aspects of the proposed scheme are experimental , and what steps they will be taking to monitor the effects of the experiment.

Maintenance

10.5 Bus priority measures should be maintained to a high standard to ensure that all road users are aware of the priority arrangements. Broken, damaged, vandalised, faded or worn signs and carriageway markings do not encourage compliance; high levels of violation will mean that the benefits are reduced. Regular inspection is recommended so that any repairs required are carried out quickly. Full re-instatement of carriageway surfaces, coloured as appropriate, and of road markings is particularly important after road works of any kind have been carried out.

10.6 Work carried out anywhere on the highway will almost certainly cause a degree of disruption to traffic, and the effect on bus services is often disproportionate because of their fixed routes and greater vulnerability to delay. Chapter 8 of the Traffic Signs Manual[30] and the Code of Practice "Safety at Street Works and Road Works" published under the New Roads and Street Works Act 1991 advise how such works can be arranged safely and cause minimum disruption.

Where a road carries a bus route, minimum disruption to bus services should be the aim of the authority or agency undertaking the work. That might include giving priority to buses, for example by queue management and signal settings. As far as possible the removal or suspension of bus priority measures should be avoided in any traffic management associated with the road works. Where significant disruption from planned work is a possibility operators should be consulted in time to make and publicise amendments to their services. This may be more difficult for emergencies than for planned work, but the highway authority or street works undertaker can assist by complying with their respective duties to co-ordinate and co-operate on street works activities under the New Roads and Street Works Act 1991 and by:

* keeping as much of the plant and equipment as possible off the carriageway;

* phasing work to minimise carriageway obstruction, particularly at the busiest time of day;

* avoiding work in different places at the same time which affect the same bus route;

* giving bus routes priority in winter salting programmes.

Broken, damaged, vandalised, or worn signs and carriageway markings do not encourage compliance

Monitoring

10.7 Bus priority schemes should be monitored after implementation to ensure that the benefits to buses which were originally estimated, and upon which the decision to undertake the scheme was based actually accrue and that the scheme performs as intended.

10.8 Bus priority schemes often depend critically upon the number of buses and passengers. Changes in the bus network, or in traffic patterns as a result of changes in the road network elsewhere, can render a bus priority scheme obsolete. The scheme should be monitored and reviewed, and on occasion may need to be removed altogether.

10.9 Items which should be monitored periodically include:

(a) numbers of buses and bus passengers using the scheme;

(b) number and occupancies of vehicles on the roads affected by the schemes;
(c) any switch from car to bus;
(d) delays to buses and to other traffic;
(e) accidents on the roads affected;
(f) enforcement costs and levels of compliance.

Roadworks often disrupt bus services

CHAPTER 11

THE WAY AHEAD

11.1 The Government wishes to encourage greater use of buses in urban areas because they can cater efficiently for large numbers of people and it considers that the increased use of bus priority measures can make a significant contribution to making bus services more attractive. Co-operation between all those involved in the provision, maintenance, use and enforcement of priority measures is vital if their full potential is to be realised. New initiatives developed jointly by local authorities and bus companies are being encouraged, and new technology for enforcing bus lanes which reduces the need for human resources appears to have the potential for wide application. The Government is always keen to see new types of measure developed and tested, and good practice in bus priority disseminated as widely as possible.

11.2 The guidance in this document is based upon present knowledge and experience of bus priority measures. Research commissioned by the Department has been investigating the reasons that may be detering local authorities from implementing priority measures more extensively. Other projects are currently in hand. One is investigating how much relief from traffic congestion could be delivered by bus priority measures, and what effect such benefit may contribute to greater usage of buses compared with other ways of making bus services more attractive. Other projects are looking at innovative bus priority techniques, including automatic enforcement methods and the value of introducing long lengths of continuous bus priority. As results from these projects, and other being conducted elsewhere, become available, further advice will be issued.

11.3 From time to time, local authorities or operators may bring forward proposals for new types of bus priority measures. The appropriate Department (see paragraph 4.15) would like to be consulted about such measures with a view to setting up and monitoring trial schemes. It is important that innovations in the field of bus priority are properly monitored so that good practice can be established and disseminated widely.

1. Press Notice 206, Announcement of Integrated Transport Policy, Department of the Environment, Transport and the Regions, June 1997

2. Department of Environment: "Planning Policy Guidance No.6, "Town Centres and Retailing Development"", HMSO, Revised Edition, June 1996

3. Department of Environment and Department of Transport: "Planning Policy Guidance No.13, "Transport"", HMSO, 1993

4. Welsh Office: "Planning Guidance (Wales): Planning Policy", Welsh Office, Cardiff, 1996

5. Scottish Office: "National Planning Policy Guideline No. 8: Retailing", Scottish Office, Edinburgh, 1996

6. Traffic Director for London: "Bus Lane Enforcement Cameras", Traffic Director for London, London, 1996

7. "The Highways (Road Humps) Regulations 1996": SI 1996 No. 1483), HMSO, 1996

8. "The Road Humps (Scotland) Regulations 1990": SI 1990 No 2623 (s.218), HMSO, 1990

9. "Road Humps Regulations 1996", Traffic Advisory Leaflet 7/96, Department of Transport, June 1996, (for Scotland, Traffic Advisory Leaflet 3/91).

10. "75mm High Road Humps", Traffic Advisory Leaflet 2/96, Department of Transport, April 1996.

11. "Horizontal Deflections", Traffic Advisory Leaflet 9/94, Department of Transport, December 1994

12. "Railway Safety Principles and Guidance, Part 2, Section G, Guidance on Tramways", HM Railway Inspectorate, London, September 1995

13. "Guided Buses", A briefing note by Buses and Taxis Division, Department of Transport, July 1995.

14. "Traffic Signs Regulations and General Directions, 1994": SI 1994 No. 1519, HMSO 1994

15. A.J.Astrop and R.J.Balcombe: "Performance of bus priority measures in Shepherd's Bush", TRL Report 140, Transport and Road Research Laboratory, Crowthorne, 1995

16. Department of Transport: "Traffic Signs Manual, Chapter 3, Regulatory Signs", HMSO, 1986

17. G.R. Watts: "Assessment of vehicle handling when crossing two types of bus lane delineator", TRL Report SR 282, Transport and Road Research Laboratory, Crowthorne, 1977.

18. J. Brownfield and J Devenport: "Road Safety Issues for the Design of Bus Priority Schemes": TRL Report CR 180, Transport and Road Research Laboratory, Crowthorne, 1989.

19. N.B. Hounsell and M. MacDonald: "Bus Priority by Selective Detection": TRL Report CR 88, Transport and Road Research Laboratory, Crowthorne, 1988

20. N.B. Hounsell: "Bus Priority Using Selective Detection, Results and Recommendations of the Selkent Study": Traffic Control Systems Unit, London, 1988

21. "The MOVA Signal Control System", Traffic Advisory Leaflet 8/96, Department of Transport, 1996

22. R A Vincent, A I Mitchell and D I Robertson: "User Guide to TRANSYT Version 8". TRL Report LR 888, Transport and Road Research Laboratory, 1988

23. J R Pierce and K Wood: "BUS TRANSYT - a user's guide": TRL Report SR 266, Transport and Road Research Laboratory, 1977

24. "The SCOOT Urban Traffic Control System", Traffic Advisory Leaflet 4/95, Department Of Transport, April 1995

25. G.T.Bowen and R.D.Bretherton: "Latest Developments in SCOOT,Version 3.1", Institution of Electrical Engineers' 8th International Conference on Road Traffic Monitoring & Control, London, 1996.

26. P.Barham, P.Oxley and T Shaw: "Accessible Public Transport Infrastructure", Department of Transport, 1994

27. London Bus Priority Network Steering Group: "Guidelines for the Design of Bus Bays and Bus Stops to Accommodate the European Standard (12 metre) Length Bus", London Borough of Bromley, 1996

28. " Rising Bollards": Traffic Advisory Leaflet 4/97, Department of Transport 1997

29. Institution of Highways and Transportation: "Transport in the Urban Environment", Inst. of Highways & Transportation, 1997

30. Department of Transport: "Traffic Signs Manual, Chapter 8; Traffic Safety Measures and Signs for Road Works and Temporary Situations", HMSO, 1991

ANNEX A

DUTIES, POWERS, AND RESPONSIBILITIES

A.1 This annex reviews the duties, powers and responsibilities of the various agencies involved in providing and regulating bus services and associated infrastructure. It should be noted that it is intended only as a guide, not as an authoritative interpretation of the law. The agencies are bus operators, Local Authorities, Passenger Transport Executives (including London Transport Buses), the Traffic Commissioner, the Police and, in London, the Traffic Director, and their activities are controlled largely by:-

- the Road Traffic Regulation Act 1984;
- the Transport Act 1985;
- the Public Passenger Vehicles Act 1981.

Also relevant are the Local Government Act 1985 (in particular Section 51), the Road Traffic Regulation (Parking) Act 1986, the Parking Act 1989, the Town and Country Planning Act 1990 (Section 249), and the Road Traffic Act 1991. The main effect of these provisions on the agencies concerned are discussed below.

Operators

A.2 All bus and coach operators must have a valid Public Service Vehicle (PSV) Operator's Licence which is granted by the Traffic Commissioners. An operator may without further formality run a private hire service, long distance coach service or long distance excursion or tour. Outside London, if an operator wishes to run a local bus service under the Transport Act 1985 the service must be registered with the Traffic Commissioner 42 days in advance of the start date. If the operator wishes to vary or cancel the service 42 days notice must also be given to the Traffic Commissioner. This applies to all services whether run commercially or by the operator supported by a local authority. About 83% of the total bus network mileage is run commercially. No notice is required of fare changes.

A.3 When local services are introduced or changed, the bus operator must notify the relevant County Council, County Borough Council, Regional Council, or Passenger Transport Executive (PTE) in the Metropolitan areas outside London (London Transport Buses in London), by sending them a copy of the registration document so that they can consider appropriate changes to the supported network. Changes to services may also affect matters which are the responsibility of the highway authority*, such as traffic management measures to assist buses. Informal discussions about service changes between the operators, local authorities and, where appropriate, the police prior to the formal notification is important in establishing a way forward which is workable and acceptable to all. It is also important that formal notification of service changes is given promptly to the local authority so that their effect on bus priority measures can be assessed. Changes may also affect road maintenance and salting programmes, and arrangements where operators are notified directly by the highway authority about emergency diversions. Many local authorities and PTEs provide the public with comprehensive information about public transport services in their area. Prompt notification of service changes is essential to keep this up to date.

* *In Scotland "highway authority" responsibilities are discharged by the "roads authority"*

A.4 In London most bus services operate under contract to London Transport Buses [LTB], the main licensing authority, following competitive tender. Commercial services which provide a significant benefit to the network also operate under agreement with LTB. A system of local service licensing, from which London Transport Buses are exempt, also operates under the auspices of the Traffic Commissioner.

A.5 Operators are responsible for all aspects of vehicle operation, including vehicle safety, maintenance and cleanliness. All vehicles which are in service must display a disc issued by the Traffic Commissioner to the operator, and their drivers must have a Passenger Carrying Vehicle drivers licence. Operators are also responsible for their passengers' well-being, driver behaviour and courtesy, and information about their services and the fares to be charged. Staff and passengers are subject to the Public Service Vehicles (Conduct of Drivers, Conductors, Inspectors and Passengers) Regulations 1990 (S.I.1990 No.1020).

Traffic Commissioners

A.6 Traffic Commissioners are the licensing authority for public service vehicles (PSVs). They have powers to revoke or suspend a PSV Operator's Licence and may also revoke a Passenger Carrying Vehicle (PCV) driver's licence. They must take such action in respect of PSV Operator's licences if they consider that the requirements of good repute, financial standing or professional competence are no longer being met. Such action may also be taken if a condition attached to the licence has been broken or a vehicle examiner has prohibited the use of any vehicle because of its dangerous condition. They work closely with the Vehicle Inspectorate Executive Agency who are responsible for the annual testing of PSVs. All PSVs are subject to a statutory annual roadworthiness test which is to a higher standard than that for cars. In addition, vehicles and premises are subject to spot checks at any time.

A.7 Traffic Commissioners have powers to take disciplinary action against bus operators who fail to operate their local services in accordance with their registered particulars. If an operator does not run services reliably the Traffic Commissioner may place a condition on his PSV Operator's Licence; this could stop that particular service or any local service being operated. In addition, a traffic authority can ask the Traffic Commissioner to impose Traffic Regulation Conditions on the operating licences of bus operators to regulate the number and frequency of buses, their routes or stopping places (including banning bus operators from a particular street). The Traffic Commissioner can only do this is he is satisfied that such a condition is required to prevent danger to road users or reduce severe traffic congestion. In respect of services operated in London under a London Local Service Licence the Traffic Commissioner may attach conditions to an operator's licence regulating the routes to be used and the points at which passengers may be set down or picked up.

Police

A.8 The police are responsible for enforcing the Traffic Regulation Orders made by the highway authority to control moving and stationary vehicles. Traffic wardens may enforce parking and loading restrictions, but not the Orders which relate to moving vehicles. Keeping the highway free of unlawful obstructions is crucial to maintain sufficient road space for moving vehicles, particularly where traffic is congested. Police and traffic wardens are responsible for ensuring that priorities given to certain classes of vehicle (e.g. buses) are not abused by non-priority vehicles.

A.9 In some areas sufficient police and traffic warden resources may not be available to undertake all the traffic enforcement required. In such a situation the local authority sometimes makes a financial contribution to make additional resources available. It is therefore important that full consultation takes place between the police and highway authority at all stages during the development of traffic control measures requiring enforcement.

A.10 The decriminalisation of parking enforcement under the Road Traffic Act 1991 has in London led to police and traffic warden enforcement being concentrated on priority "red" routes (which also tend to be bus routes) whilst local authority parking attendants enforce permitted and prohibited parking on other roads. This appears to have resulted in better compliance with on-street restrictions and improved flow for all traffic, including buses. Local authorities outside London who adopt on-street parking enforcement powers are also likely to want to give a high priority to enforcement on arterial routes, and this can be expected to work to the advantage of buses.

A.11 A trial of bus lane enforcement by cameras in London has successfully demonstrated that video cameras are the most promising way forward using established technology. "Static" roadside cameras and "mobile" cameras carried on buses continuously recorded events in the bus lane, thus ensuring that there are no possible general defences which cannot be disproved. The mobile camera was found to be an effective way of dealing with stationary vehicles in the bus lane, and the tests also identified that "stopped" vehicles, whether parked illegally or moving offenders held up in the bus lane, are more critical to the effectiveness of bus lanes in improving the reliability of bus services if traffic conditions are congested. The trial also showed that to be cost effective a two-camera system (which includes a close-up camera to record a registration mark) is necessary. Testing is now being carried out over a wider area.

Local authorities

A.12 Local authorities are responsible for local transport policy, set in the context of policies on the environment and sustainability. They also have certain duties in the area of public transport procurement. They also have various powers and responsibilities enabling them as traffic authorities to control the use of highway and parking space by all classes of vehicle. Their responsibilities as local planning authorities have an important influence on transport generally and public transport services in particular.

A.13 The Transport Act 1985 has encouraged operators to provide bus services on a commercial basis. However, as it was expected that their services might not meet all the public transport requirements of an area, county councils, regional councils, and passenger transport executives were given a duty under the Act to secure, under contract after competitive tendering, the provision of other services to meet any requirements not being met by commercial services. Non-metropolitan district councils also have a power to secure the provision of additional bus services in their areas. Local authorities may thus provide bus services to areas not otherwise served, or increase the frequency of services beyond what would be provided commercially. Local authorities also have the power to promote public transport services in their area, including providing information on timetables and fares. Local authorities have a duty to monitor the bus services run by operators under contract to ensure that they are run correctly and reliably. Local authority contracts generally contain penalty clauses to ensure the authority can cancel the contract if the operator is in breach of its conditions.

A.14 Traffic authorities regulate moving and stationary traffic through their responsibilities mainly under the Road Traffic Regulation Act 1984, as amended by the Road Traffic Regulation (Parking) Act 1986 and the Parking Act 1989. Highway authorities have powers to make Traffic Regulation Orders on all roads except trunk roads (for which the Secretary of State's permission is required). The purposes for which these Orders may be made include:

- preventing dangerous conditions;
- preventing damage to the road;
- facilitating the passage of any class of traffic;
- preventing unsuitable vehicles using a road;
- preserving the amenities of the area in which the road runs;
- regulating parking on the highway.
- air quality management

Specific powers contained in the 1984 Act relate to:-

- the use of highways by public service vehicles [Section 19];
- the design, erection, and removal of traffic signs [Sections 64-80].

Section 122 requires, inter alia, that every local authority responsible for functions carried out under the 1984 Act should have regard to:-

"the importance of facilitating the passage of public service vehicles and of securing the safety and convenience of persons using or desiring to use such vehicles".

Where highway improvements or maintenance works affect local bus services, traffic authorities should discuss their work programme with the bus operators.

A.15 The Road Traffic Act 1991 provides for the designation of a network of priority "red" routes in London and for the Traffic Director for London to be responsible for that network. These routes are subject to a distinctive signing regime, special parking controls and other traffic management measures designed to improve the movement of traffic so that people and goods can reach their destinations more easily, reliably and safely. One of their specific aims is to improve the efficient movement of buses. Buses benefit from this special attention and from the general reduction in congestion which has followed from the priority "red" route controls and from more reliable journey times. This improved reliability should make the bus services more attractive to customers. Outside London it will be for the local authorities to apply to the Secretary of State to establish priority routes using their existing statutory powers.

A.16 Provisions concerning the regulation of parking, both on and off the highway, and of loading on the highway, are contained in the Parking Act 1989, the Road Traffic Regulation (Parking) Act 1986, and those sections of the 1984 Act not superseded by either of these Acts. Provision of parking, both on and off street, and policies related to parking charges can affect bus ridership. Sections 95-111 of the 1984 Act deal with the powers available to control and enforce Traffic Regulation Orders. Provisions in the Road Traffic Act 1991 enable the local authorities to exercise greater control over enforcing parking restrictions (see paragraph 2.10). Other provisions in these Acts allow, amongst other things, restrictions to be placed on parking in the highway in order to keep all traffic, including buses, moving more freely. Bus priority measures are normally introduced under the powers conferred by Section 2(2)(a) and (b) of the 1984 Act and, in London, Section 6 of, and Schedule 1 to, the 1984 Act. Where buses are to be permitted to travel on pedestrianised streets, the authority may use its powers as local planning authority under the Town and Country Planning Act 1990. Local authorities require the permission of the Secretary of State to carry out any of these functions on a trunk road.

Co-operation between agencies

A.17 The provision, operation and enforcement of traffic management measures which assist buses involve a number of agencies, each responsible for a variety of complex tasks. Close co-operation between these agencies is essential if such measures are to operate satisfactorily.

ANNEX B

APPRAISAL OF BUS PRIORITY MEASURES:

RECOMMENDED METHODS

Good practice when appraising schemes

B.1 Appraisal methods should be:

a) practicable
b) affordable
c) consistent
d) informative
e) capable of demonstrating value for money

B.2 The following advice is intended to be practicable from the point of those who carry out appraisals, affordable to those who commission them (and to be in proportion to the cost of the project and their potential impacts), and to encourage consistency across projects and locations and with appraisals of other transport projects. It is intended to encourage the provision of full and accurate information about schemes and their effects to policy and funding authorities. Underlying all is the need to incorporate all significant costs and benefits within sound analytical techniques.

Presentation

B.3 Many bus priority appraisals will be components of a wider presentation of a package submission within the local transport capital expenditure round. The Department issues advice on appraisal, presentation, and other aspects of packages each year in "Supplementary Guidance Notes on the Package Approach". (Contact Local Transport Policy Division, Great Minster House London SW1P 4DR.)

B.4 Other appraisals are made for individual priority measures or strategies for other sources of funding, from DOT or elsewhere. The broad Framework Tables described in the package approach guidance will generally be inappropriate for these schemes, but the same broad principles will in many cases still apply.

B.5 This Annex is intended to provide additional advice to those completing appraisals of priority measures, be they stand-alone measures, related to other schemes or projects, or part of a package bid.

Priority measures within packages

a) Objectives

B.6 All transport investments should be appraised within the context of policies, objectives and problem solving. (As background and illustration, brief descriptions of general traffic, environmental, and business conditions are valuable.) The overall strategy for achieving objectives needs to be explained, highlighting the role of priority measures. It is therefore important that these factors are presented clearly and in full at the beginning of an appraisal, and the effects assessed against them at the end. It is difficult or impossible to assess projects against very general objectives such as "To regenerate the local economy"; more quantifiable objectives, which can be shown to contribute to the wider aims, should be adopted. The nature of bus priorities should make them one of the elements of a package most suitable for this purpose.

B.7 Packages of measures (whether within a package approach bid or any other systematic grouping of projects) will generally have been designed with local policies and objectives to the fore, but relevant national ones, such as on emissions or safety targets, should also be included in appraisals. Any additional significant effects, beyond clearly defined objectives, also need to be presented.

B.8 Appraisals should also describe current conditions. Delays to buses, and effects on reliability of services and waiting times at stops, should be presented, for the route as a whole and at specific black spots. A brief description of service frequency, type of service, and patronage levels is important.

b) Methods

B.9 A brief but informative description of modelling techniques and data sources should be presented. Consistency with other local modelling exercises should be demonstrated, or the reasons for any differences justified.

B.10 All other relevant significant factors should also be included, such as details of consultation exercises. Bus operators may respond to priority measures by running extra services, or by maintaining current services with fewer buses. Details of consultations with operators should be presented, along with details of how the likely responses have been modelled.

B.11 Many priority schemes consist of a series of measures (e.g. along a corridor) introduced over a period of time. The effectiveness of such measures, and the interaction with other transport initiatives, can depend significantly upon the sequence in which they are implemented. Appraisals should demonstrate the rationale for the planned programme, in terms of incremental effectiveness through achievement of objectives and value for money.

c) Project costs and benefits

B.12 The Supplementary Guidance Notes on the Package Approach provides tabular frameworks for scheme appraisal; one for transport, environmental, and economic development impacts, and one for economic and financial consequences. Comparable frameworks have also been constructed for specific major bus priority investments. Such tables are intended to act as a checklist for local authorities to ensure that all relevant impacts are considered, and to satisfy them (and demonstrate to the Government if necessary) that all measures are consistent with local authority policies and play a part in achieving objectives.

B.13 The framework is a minimum requirement for package bids; the results of any additional analysis should also be presented. However the Department no longer requires that authorities automatically submit tables with submissions, but may call for them later for clarification.

B.14 The Department does not require full economic analysis for individual measures of less than £2m within TPP submissions. Qualitative assessments of physical/traffic and environmental consequences are required.

B.15 B.13 and B.14 should not be taken to imply a relaxed attitude to economic appraisal. Local authorities should satisfy themselves of the value for money of bus priority and other measures even though they may not be required to present them to the Department.

B.16 Table I is a suggested framework for the presentation of bus priority appraisals. Like the package approach tables it is meant as a guide. Alternative approaches may more clearly present the effects and economics of individual measures while retaining the same basic content.

Stand-alone priority measures

B.17 There will continue to be a place for bus priority measures which are not part of a recognised package of measures. Nevertheless the basic principles of identifying overall strategies and objectives will apply, and in many cases their contributions may be significant. Even where there is no significant impact on wider objectives a "nil response" is a useful piece of information.

Table 1

Appraisal Framework

CONTEXT
Brief description of local traffic, environmental and economic conditions, traffic growth.
Relevant local policies/strategies;
How priority measures contribute

SCHEME
Discussion of do-minimum.
Description of scheme. (Map)
Expected reactions of operators
Description of modelling techniques and data sources
Discussion of its reliability

TRANSPORT IMPACTS;

A [Table]	Opening year Do-min	Opening year Option
Traffic levels, vehicles[1][2][3]		
Car		
Other private		
Bus		
Cycle		
Pedestrians[4]		
Bus load factors		
And mode shift		

Highway speeds / Time savings in minutes
Car/other private vehicles (On route, parallel)
Bus (Distinguish routes where available)
Pedestrians

Accidents
(Quantitative estimates if available, otherwise qualitative in discussion section)

B [DISCUSSION/SUMMARY]
Additional information to that provided in the Table

ECONOMIC APPRAISAL
A Discussion of occupancies, trip purposes, values of time etc

B [TABLE] Opening year (Year, £000 in 19XX prices, discounted to19XX)
COSTS
Capital costs (in year 19XX)
Operating costs
Delays during construction
BENEFITS
TIME;
Car occupants
Bus occupants etc
FUEL COSTS;
Ditto
[RELIABILITY]
Buses
TOTAL

Benefit/cost ratio, payback period etc
Sensitivity tests
C DISCUSSION/SUMMARY

ENVIRONMENTAL APPRAISAL
Land take, noise, air quality, etc. Reference to local policies, scheme objectives.

ECONOMIC DEVELOPMENT IMPACTS
Discussion/quantification

Notes
(1) Specify units
(2) For appropriate point(s) on main corridor and any parallel routes which change significantly as a result of reassignment.
(3) Separately for different time periods if necessary
(4) Effect on total pedestrian flows and diversions

Appraisal methods

a) Depth of assessment

B.18 This requires a balance between the need for detail - to provide sufficient information for decision makers and funders - and cost and practicability. This applies to the operational assessment of priorities as well as an economic and environmental appraisal. Two useful underlying principles are;

a) models and other analytical devices should be used as an aid to decision making; they do not remove the need for qualitative or political judgement.

b) do not attempt to obtain direct measures where they are inherently unsuitable; there will be cases where indirect indicators or qualitative and objectives related approaches, are more appropriate.

B.19 One consideration will be the ease with which schemes with effects of modest proportions can be modified after opening. For example if initial modelling/simulation produces uncertainty as to which of two designs will be most effective it may be more sensible to try one, with the recognition that change may subsequently be necessary, rather than attempt a series of expensive, and perhaps uncertain, more complex simulations.

B.20 In general however, expensive schemes and schemes with larger impacts should receive more rigorous appraisals. Such schemes may require some assessment of reassignment effects of other traffic (and possibly modal split) away from the route of the priority, while this would be unnecessary where capacity and journey times for such vehicles are effectively maintained.

B.21 Congested assignment models can be expensive and time consuming to set up from scratch, and without careful handling (such as close attention to convergence) can give misleading results where small network changes are applied. More ad hoc methods of assessing reassignment effects may be attractive, especially where the local network is uncomplicated, and with realistic sensitivity analysis. In other circumstances, especially where detailed models have been built for analysing package proposals, reassignment effects of priority measures may be more practical.

B.22 Models for package bids may include mode shift and other demand effects, which may be appropriate to consider where priority measures provide major time savings for buses. Alternatively, conventional congested assignment models, or even a series of junction models, may provide a realistic estimate of major bus journey time savings which could be used to make some assessment of potential mode shift. However mode shift estimates will always be uncertain and are obvious candidates for sensitivity analysis, (and, perhaps, more detailed modelling) especially where initial estimates suggest the scheme is marginal. Priorities may also encourage existing bus users to make additional trips.

B.23 Other factors relating to the depth or complexity of appraisal methodology include;

* variability of traffic flows through the day or week. Even modest differences in levels and tidal flows, and even such factors as differences in origins and destinations, can affect the operational consequences of bus priorities. Thus in

heavily congested networks it may be necessary to consider each peak, inter-peak, and Saturdays separately. For less congested or complex networks a sensible (e.g. adopting sensitivities) use of factors applied to journey times or monetised effects may be possible to compare different periods outside the peak, or even to relate them to estimated effects of the peak itself.

* variations in the regulations throughout the day or week will also affect the degree to which appraisals need to be fragmented. Some priorities along a corridor may operate at times of the day after others have ceased to apply. This may also affect the interrelationship of different sections or junctions.

b) Principles of economic appraisal

B.24 Project appraisal of transport investments should be a composite exercise which takes account of all significant consequences. Within that, economic appraisal should aim to compare the discounted costs and benefits of those factors for which money values can acceptably be derived. For larger road investments some environmental consequences are being examined as to the appropriateness of their valuation and incorporation within economic appraisal, although this is unlikely to be of major significance for most bus priority measures. But investment decisions can never become mechanistic operations and will continue to depend upon an overall judgement of economic and other factors, with particular reference to relevant policies and objectives.

B.25 The essential components of an economic appraisal of a bus priority measure are;

- capital costs and (possibly) operating costs including enforcement
- journey time savings to occupants of buses on the bus route
- benefits to new bus users, totally new trips or shifts from other modes
- changes to journey times of occupants of other vehicles on the route and on other links of the network (including other buses) and pedestrians.
- the value of changes in journey time reliability
- effects on fuel and other vehicle operating costs
- any consequences for accident levels
- any encouragement towards a transfer from car to bus

B.26 Some projects may involve significant capital expenditure, on land take, junction redesign, highway redesign to enable contra-flow bus lanes etc. though generally very much smaller than urban highway investments (e.g. inner relief roads, road dualling,). In some schemes it might therefore be thought necessary to carry out appraisals over a project's economic life, comparable to a COBA or URECA appraisal for highway investments. Long term traffic forecasting in congested, capacity constrained, networks is fraught with difficulties, introducing additional uncertainty on those priority measures which appear to require many years to achieve pay-back (or, which amounts to the same thing, have marginal npvs after even 20 to 30 years). Detailed attention to these calculations can also distract from the important question of whether priority measures do actually provide benefits to bus users and how they compare to costs imposed on other road users. In general therefore even priority measures costing in the region of £1 - 2M (greater expense would be very rare) should be expected to achieve payback within a couple of years and should not require complex forecasting exercises. If schemes do appear marginal when assessed over such periods (where an 8% real discount rate should be used) it is likely that annual net benefits are low because there are costs to other vehicles to set against the benefits of buses, rather than low benefit levels to buses. In such circumstances it is better to assess the worth of the scheme by examining such costs and benefits in terms of local policies and objectives rather than mechanistically extending the appraisal period.

B.27 An original intention was that bus priorities would permit buses to get to the front of a queue of traffic, obtaining significant time savings with minimal effect upon other vehicles. In practice many schemes inevitably take some road or junction capacity and other vehicles will suffer delays. In terms of economic efficiency the gain to bus users should be sufficient to outweigh such costs to other users, capital costs, and any other net costs (e.g. vehicle operating costs). However, the final decision on whether to implement schemes which fail to achieve a net benefit depends, as noted earlier on other factors also. These wider considerations apply only where the measures contribute to the overall transport objectives of the area, and wider environmental and planning considerations.

B.28 However it would generally not be appropriate to use priorities as a deliberate measure to restrain car use. That would be a particularly inefficient method, unable to discriminate between vehicle types or trip purposes, and tending to hit hardest those with highest values of time. The justification for npv negative schemes needs to be well argued, cogent, and consistent.

B.29 Improved public transport services can contribute to net economic regeneration, for example by improving employment supply. However, within local policies for economic regeneration or growth there are frequently specific objectives of gaining or regaining economic activity from surrounding towns. These may apply particularly to Park and Ride schemes associated with bus priority measures. While these are clearly proper local concerns it must be recognised that they do not count as national resource benefits. The exception would be where there is an accepted national policy for the regeneration of a specific area or inner city.

c) The "do minimum"

B.30 The correct appraisal of a project is not, normally, with respect to current network design and operations (the "do nothing") but against the network as it will be at the time of implementation (ie incorporating other schemes and measures which are committed and have funding agreement). Such schemes need to be explained. In addition the "do minimum" should take account of other minor changes that could, and indeed in the absence of the priority measures, should be implemented. Particular examples are to examine whether existing traffic light settings could be optimised, which might improve journey times for buses and other vehicles. Enforcement of existing parking and other restrictions should be examined. A common failing of priority measure appraisals is to assume proper enforcement of the new measures while ignoring the potentially valuable contribution which enforcement of current restrictions could bring. For both do-minimum and do-something cases the modelled effectiveness of enforcement policies should be realistic rather than idealistic.

B.31 The "do nothing" retains an important role in being the only scenario in which models can be calibrated and validated.

d) Model inputs

B.32 The Department's current advice on values of time and vehicle resource operating costs for use in economic appraisals is set out in Highways Economic Note 2 (HEN2). This is updated from time to time and is published as Appendix II of the COBA Manual. Resource values of time per person are listed in Table 1 of HEN2 for each vehicle type, and for working and non-working time. It is important that working time values apply only to journeys made in the course of work. Non-working time values apply to all non-work journeys, including travel to work, by all modes.

B.33 Table 2 of HEN 2 gives average vehicle occupancies, and average proportions of cars in working and non-working time. While these values may be used in the absence of other local data, it is strongly recommended that where bus priority measures are involved, local surveys should be carried out to establish local values for these factors for the times when the bus priority scheme is to be operational. Bus priority measures are often used at times and places where the traffic mix and vehicle occupancies are quite atypical, and for this reason local survey data should always be used in favour of national averages. Since the essence of a bus priority measure involves trading off time savings to one type of road user against delays to others, every effort should be made to establish accurately the numbers of each type of road user affected. The proportions of car occupants in working and non-working time are important. It may be appropriate to carry out roadside interview surveys to obtain local information on this if none is already available. It may be found that in some situations, significant numbers of light goods vehicle occupants are in non-working time. Where the bus priority scheme is to operate at both peak and off-peak times, a separate appraisal should be carried out for each time period.

B.34 Local policies and strategies may aim to favour/discourage particular categories of trip purpose by mode of travel, e.g. to discourage commuting by car. It is recommended that the impact upon different categories are distinguished in the presentation of the appraisal, but applying additional weights to the basic HEN2 values of time is not acceptable.

B.35 HEN 2 also gives a formula for calculating resource vehicle operating costs and a table (Table 5) of parameters for each vehicle type. Because vehicle operating costs depend on speed and delays, the introduction of a bus priority scheme will affect vehicle operating costs, and these should, wherever possible, be taken into account in the assessment. The vehicle operating costs in HEN2 are based upon national averages. Although they will be sufficient in many situations, there are circumstances where a more detailed estimate of the effect on bus operating costs would be appropriate. For example, if the introduction of a series of bus priority measures meant that the number of buses required to run a particular service could be reduced, the bus operating cost savings could well be greater than the formula would indicate.

B.36 Priority measures may have consequences for safety, for vehicle occupants, cyclists or pedestrians. Highways Economics Note No 1 gives the Department's estimates of the values for the prevention of road casualties and accidents for use in cost-benefit analysis.

e) Reliability and regularity

B.37 Improved reliability is often seen as a major benefit of bus priority measures, and an invaluable factor in the attempt to persuade more people to switch from their cars. The Department has therefore commissioned research towards the preparation of a methodology for estimating and presenting reliability benefits from priority measures. This will report in 1997. In the meantime, if reliability benefits are thought to be significant any estimate of their value should be presented in a way in which their impact upon the total value of the scheme can be readily identified. All methods and assumptions should be clearly expressed. The following advice is offered.

B.38 Reliability and regularity benefits can be defined as follows:

Reliability benefits result from a reduced spread of on-bus journey times.

Regularity benefits arise from a reduction in waiting times at stops due to a more even headway between buses.

In assessing the overall reliability of a service people will normally consider the two aspects together.

B.39 Passengers with a need to reach their destination at a specific time are likely to value reliability and regularity more highly than those who do not, and in many cases will allow for risk by leaving home earlier than in most cases would be necessary. For each priority measure the overall value of improved reliability will depend upon trip purpose as well as the predicted change in the distribution of journey times, and these should be examined and findings presented.

B.40 Although priority measures may significantly reduce differences in headways along their course, it cannot be guaranteed that improvements will be maintained downstream, and are less likely to be so in congested areas. Appraisals should therefore not assume regularity benefits for all passengers along a route.

B.41 Improved regularity of headways reduces average waiting times at bus stops. If it is possible to predict the distribution of arrivals after the scheme is implemented, and this is compared with estimates of the do-minimum distribution, then one element of the reliability benefit can be estimated, assuming, which is the standard assumption in transport appraisals, that waiting times are valued at twice the ordinary value of time. (This will not give the full value of regularity benefits; it does not, for example, reflect that some people may be able to spend an additional X minutes at home each morning with reasonable confidence of getting to work on time.) Average waiting times can be calculated using:

$$W = H/2 + V/(2H) = H/2 + E$$

where: W = mean waiting time H = mean headway between buses
V = variance of bus headway E = excess waiting time owing to service irregularity

B.42 Detailed advice on estimating reliability benefits will be prepared on completion of the current research project.

B.43 Estimates of current unreliability and irregularity should be based upon properly compiled evidence (e.g. an appropriate number of headway counts and journey time measurements).

B.44 Although detailed modelling of the effects on journey time reliability for other road users will generally not be practical, some qualitative assessment should be made.

f) Mode shift and other demand responses

B.45 The two principal effects of priority measures on travel patterns are on bus users (direct time savings) and other road users (time savings or costs). However there are a number of other, more complex, responses. A shift from private cars to bus travel will be an expressed objective of many schemes, but other effects, such as retiming of trips and change of destination are also possible, but will almost always be too trivial to attempt to incorporate within the appraisal. One other effect which may need to be considered is an increase in bus travel which is not a shift from other modes.

B.46 Any predicted shift from car to bus should be incorporated into the economic appraisal according to the "rule of half". This should be with reference to the change in consumers' surplus across the relevant particular trips, but in most cases the changes in journey times would be a reasonable proxy. However it should be recognised that where the measures make car travel slower, the rule of half calculation needs to take that factor into account also. If a bus trip improves by 5 minutes and the equivalent car trip deteriorates by 5 minutes, those car travellers who change mode will on average be no better or worse off than before the scheme opened. (Their "gain" is in avoiding the 5 minute penalty to car travellers.)

B.47 A further complexity is the assessment of additional bus trips which are not a result of mode shift. It can be argued that these people impose a trivial cost on other bus users (if they significantly slow down services through longer dwell times at stops this should be incorporated directly in journey time calculations) or other resources. However their expenditure on bus tickets represents a freeing of equivalent resources (though netting off any relevant tax on such expenditures) elsewhere, which should enter the appraisal as a benefit. However, in a competitive bus market it can be argued that such additional revenue to the bus industry would be competed away by increased supply. This does involve additional resource costs, though also benefits other users since higher supply means lower waiting times or improved departure opportunities. It is impossible to make hard and fast rules on this question. If it is thought reasonable to include an additional benefit to reflect increased bus use it should be clearly explained in the presentation, and a check made to see whether the value for money calculation is sensitive to it.

WITHFLOW BUS LANE TYPICAL LAYOUT

FIGURE 1

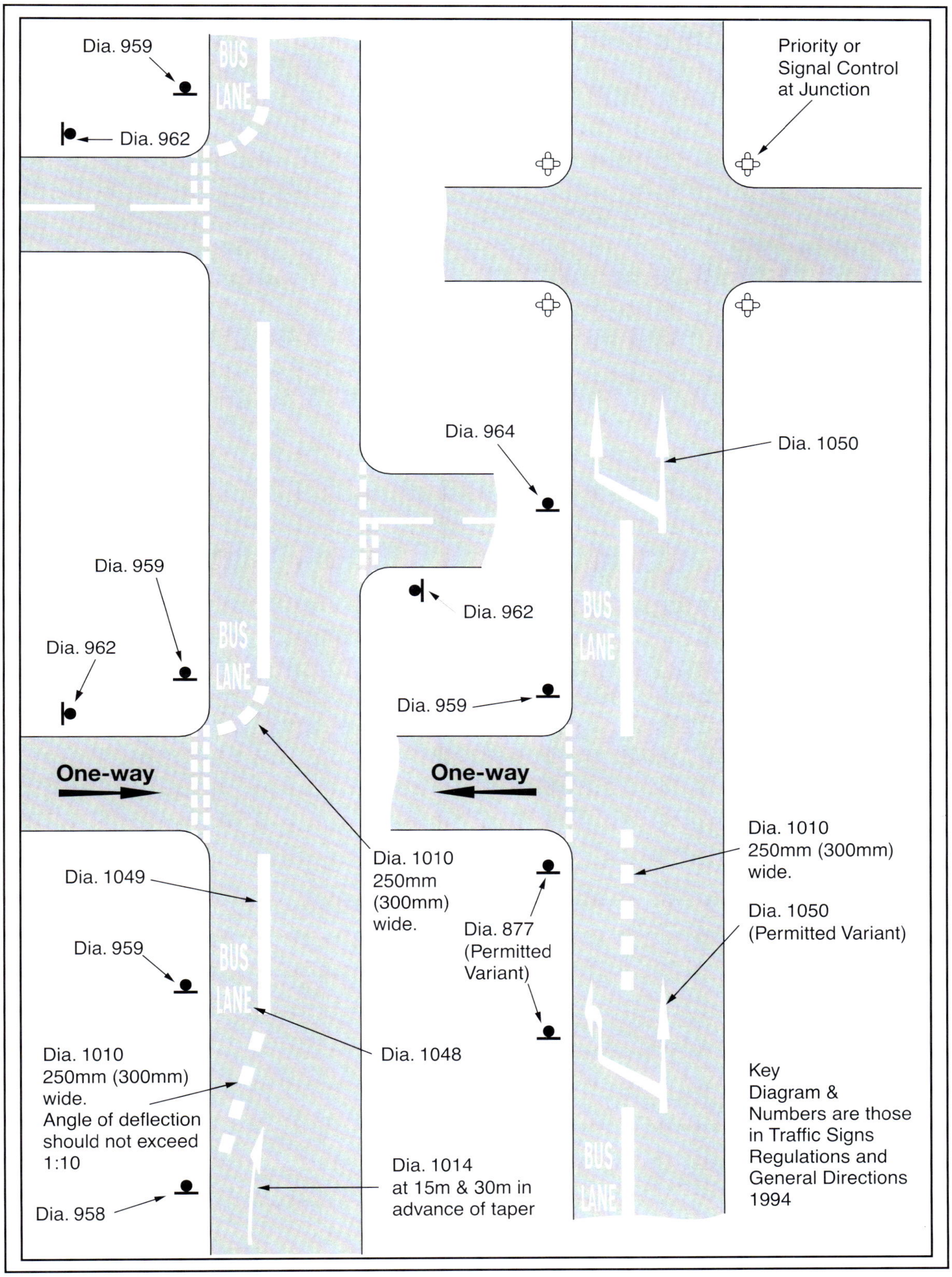

BUS ADVANCE AREA

FIGURE 2

Bus advance area

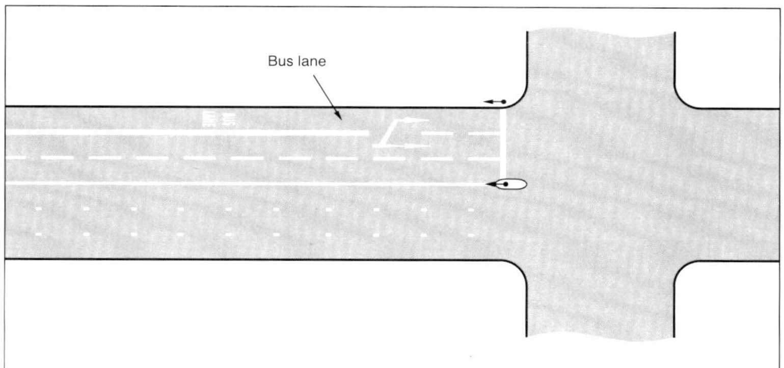

Bus lane with "traditional" set back

Fig. 2A

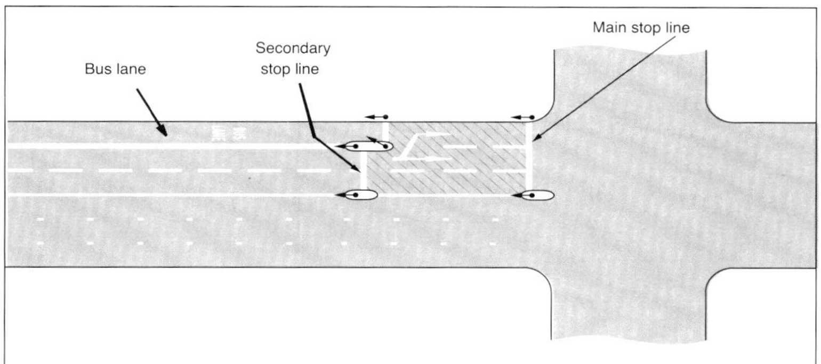

Bus lane leading to bus advance area (detailed signal arrangements will depend on site circumstances)

Fig. 2B

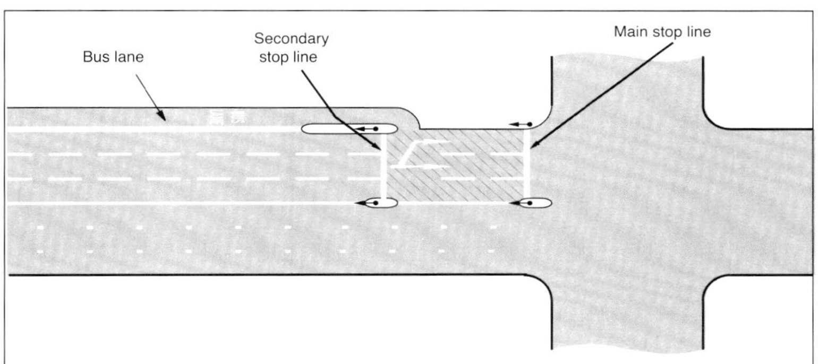

Bus lane on wider section leading to bus advance area on narrower section

Fig. 2C

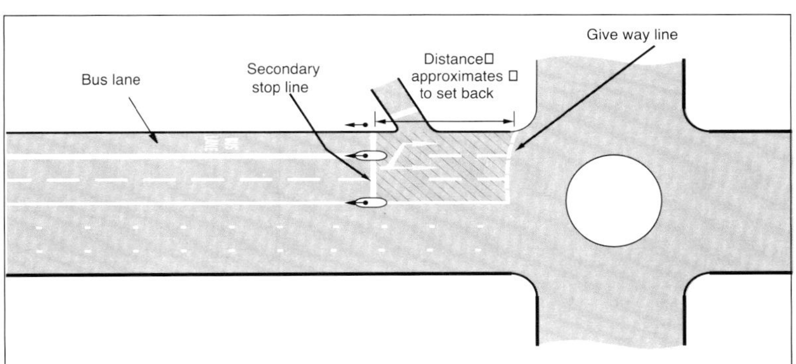

Bus advance area on approach to roundabout

CONTRAFLOW BUS LANE TYPICAL LAYOUT

FIGURE 3

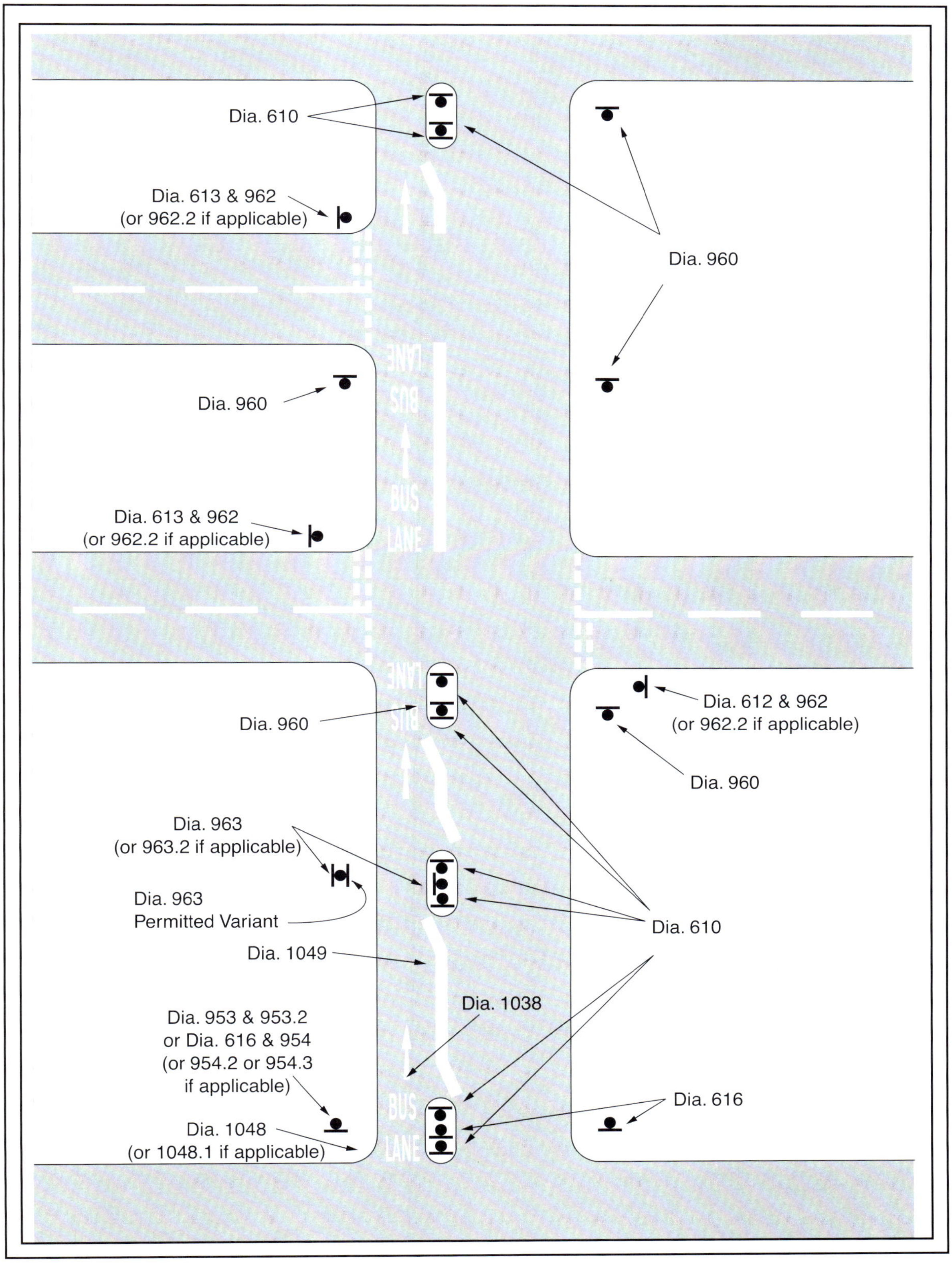

BUS ONLY STREET TYPICAL LAYOUT

FIGURE 4

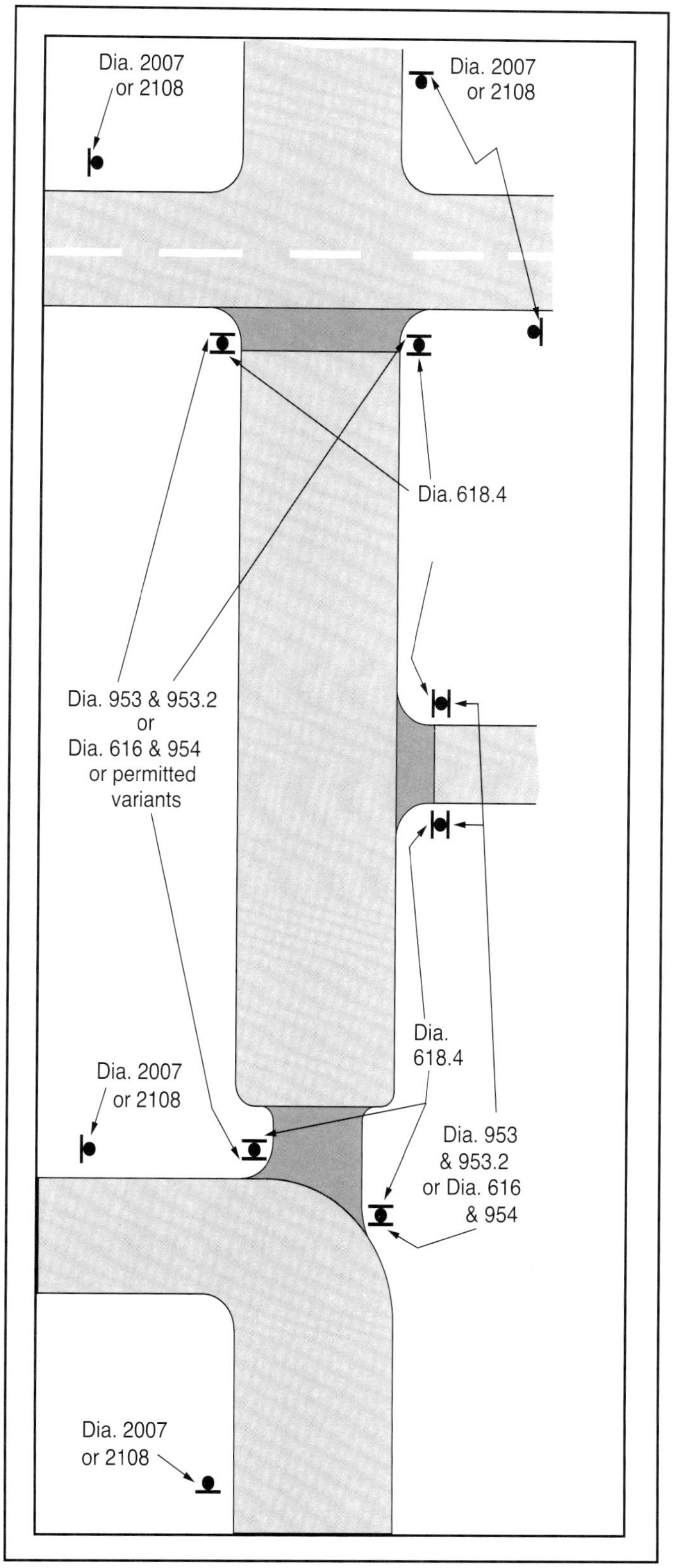

Notes:

1. "BUS ONLY" Carriageway markings may be authorised.
2. Signs to dia. 2007 or 2108 should be varied to include either
   a) dia 616 (with no plate) or
   b) dia 953 plus 953.2 plate according to entry signs used at commencement of Bus gate.

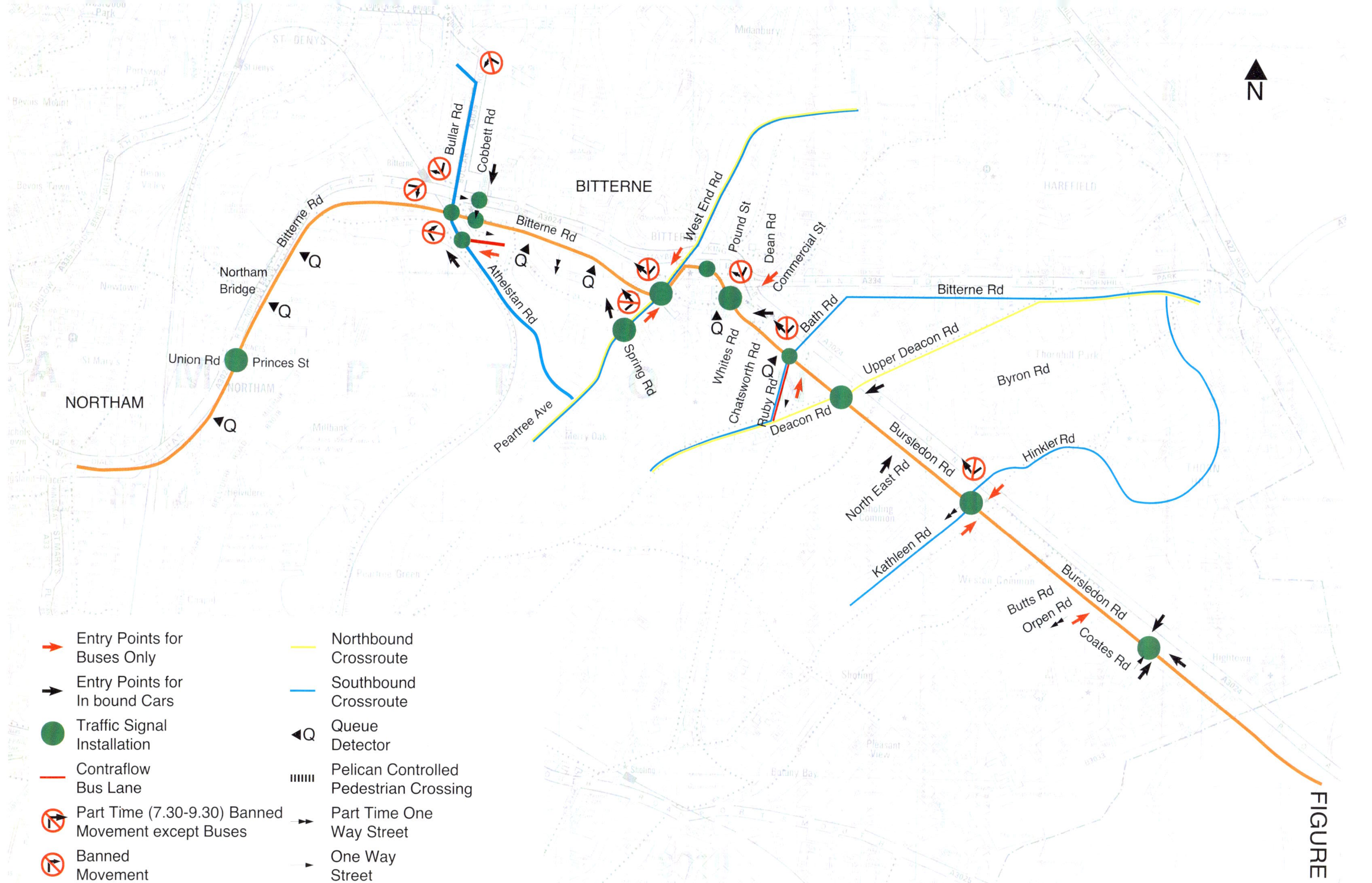

The Scheme as Implemented Bitterne, Southampton

BUS STOP BOARDER TYPICAL LAYOUT AND DIMENSIONS

FIGURE 6

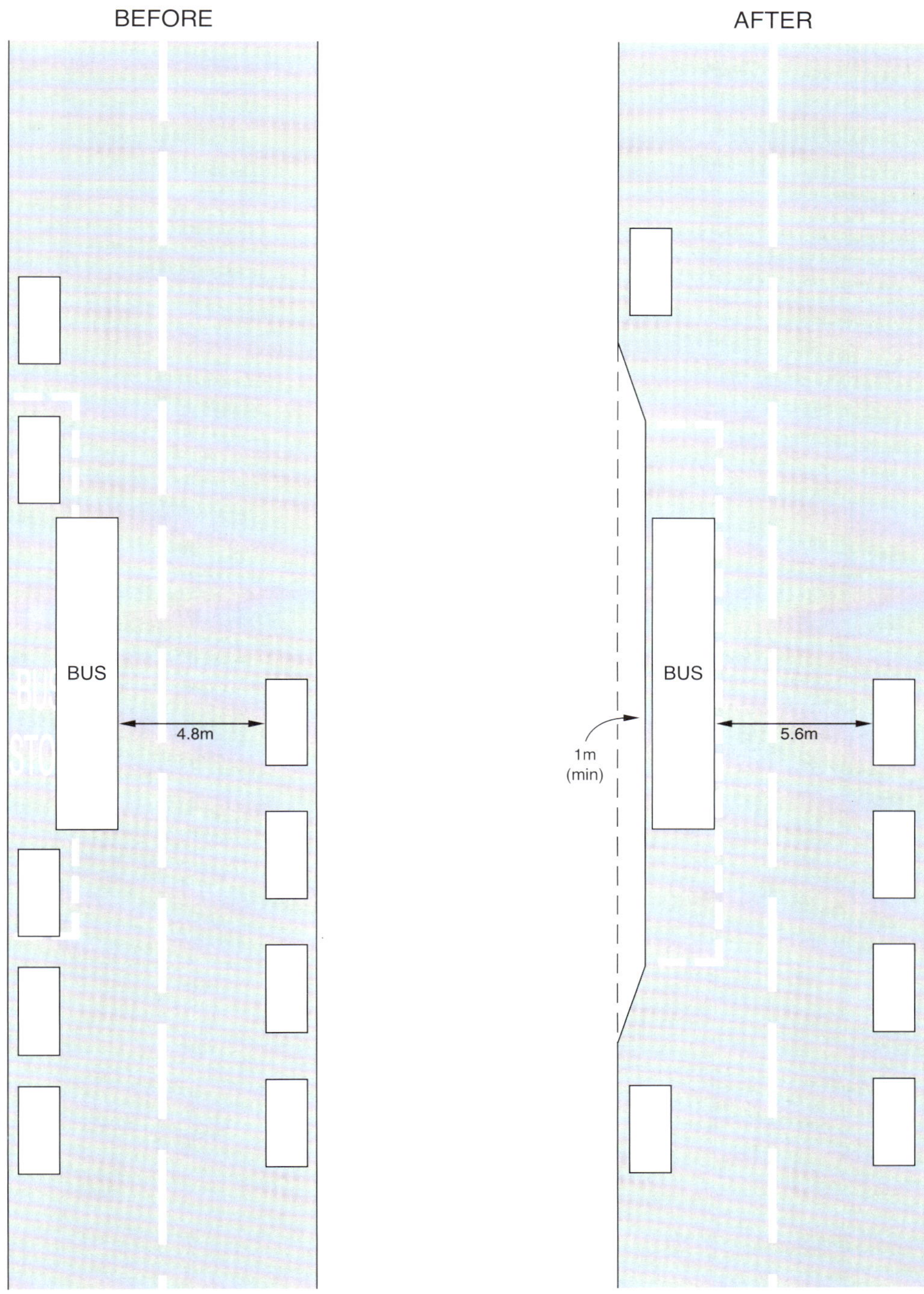

Bus stop on typical 11m two-way road showing cars parked illegally at bus stop

Bus stop boarder on typical 11m two-way road

Source: London Borough of Barnet

LAY-BYS AT BUS STOPS

(See also Reference 27)

FIGURE 7

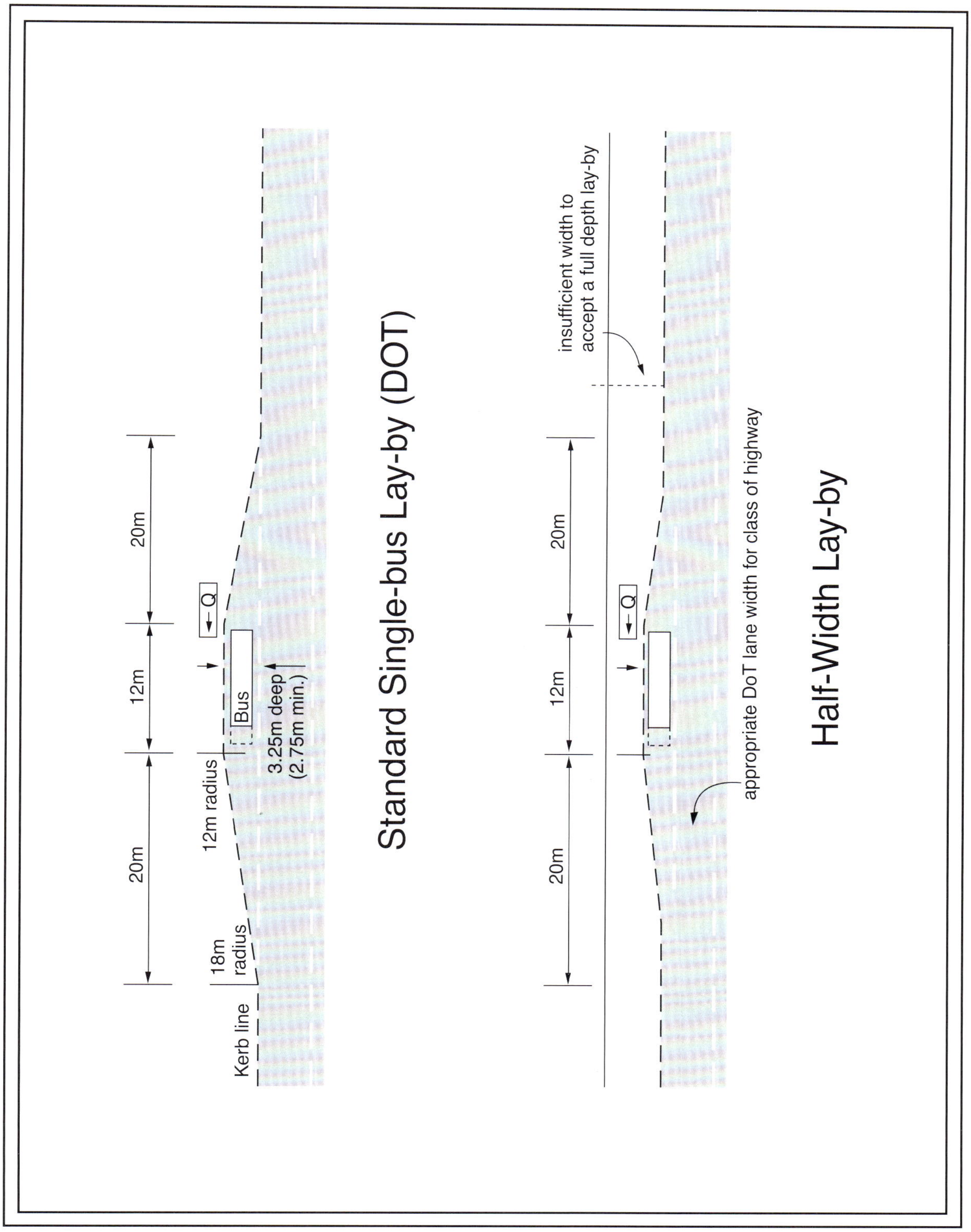

SIGNS FOR USE WITH BUS LANES

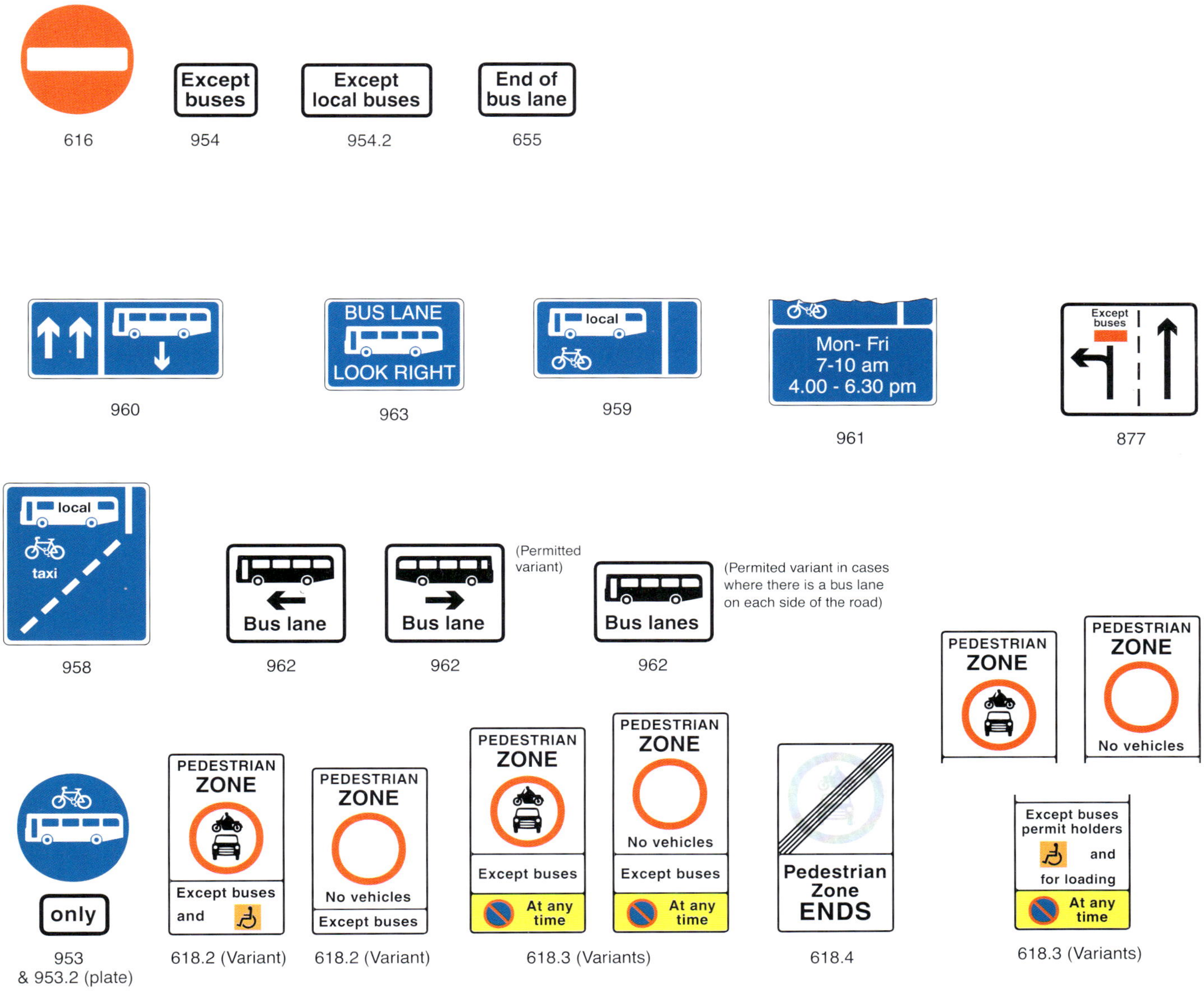

SIGNS FOR USE AT BUS STOPS

CARRIAGEWAY MARKINGS FOR USE WITH BUS LANES

Printed in the United Kingdom for The Stationery Office.
Dd.J8041, 10/97, C10, 5673, N10420.

100
GREATEST MONEY-MAKING CRIMES OF THE WORLD

100

GREATEST MONEY-MAKING CRIMES OF THE WORLD

igloo

igloo

Published in 2011
by Igloo Books Ltd
Cottage Farm
Sywell
NN6 0BJ

www.igloo-books.com

10 9 8 7 6 5 4 3 2 1

ISBN: 978-0-85734-651-3

Printed and manufactured in China

CONTENTS

INTRODUCTION

The fight against financial fraud is with us every day.

The world has always been fascinated by the faker and the forger, usually with a mixture of disapproval and admiration. The dictionary definition of a fake is "something that is made to appear more valuable or real by fraud or pretence" – such as a painting in another artist's style to which someone has added the original artist's signature, or a composite from parts of other authentic pieces of the same period. It is easy to see, therefore, how restoration can come close to fakery if it is not properly acknowledged.

Forgeries usually refer to documents and signatures, and include copies and facsimiles. A hoax is usually an innocent object with a tall story attached. However, there is certainly an overlap between all these terms, and they are used virtually interchangeably in this book.

A Brief History of Fakes and Forgeries

Art forgery has been occurring since ancient times. The Ancient Egyptians, Phoenicians, and Babylonians were all prolific fakers of jewelry and other objects.

In the 14th century, a piece of colored foil was placed between a gemstone and its setting to give extra shine. Or, alternate layers of clear and colored glass were used to give the appearance of a gemstone. The 17th century saw a huge number of fake gems and pearls.

Often, whether something is a fake or not is down not to the intention of its creator but to the spirit in which it is sold. Manufacturers in the 19th century sold reproductions as "Historical Revival" pieces but they were sold on as originals.

Goldsmiths of the 19th and 20th centuries were responsible for most fake jewelry; before that time hallmark protection was enough.

The 21st-century phenomenon in terms of fakes is in collectables. Such items make huge sums at auction, so naturally there are people prepared to create fake versions.

How to Spot a Fake

Early 20th-century fakebuster Bernard Berenson infuriated Italy with his inability to articulate what it was that told him something was a fake. He was particularly frustrating in court, where he would say only that a fake gave him a ringing in his ears and a depression.

But, presumably, behind the showmanship was an individual who knew his trade. He had learned about fake works through experience, for which, unfortunately, there is no substitute where fake-spotting is concerned. If you visit galleries, museums, and auction houses – where you will be able to handle items – you will begin to be properly equipped.

You will start to know that the so-called "Ming" vase is not quite rounded enough, and that its mouth is not quite as flat as it should be. And if you really look hard in these places, you will have something against which to compare pieces. You will start to know that 18th-century silver salvers and trays were plain and 19th-century ones more ornate, so you will be able to spot a suspect date.

With even a little knowledge, you will be able to spot other anachronisms, too. You will look at faces in paintings or on porcelain and say to yourself, "he looks too kind to be an 18th-century depiction of a huntsman – he must have been made in the Victorian era." If you are buying old, typed letters, you will look at the typeface. Using a font that was too contemporary for the document's alleged date gave the "Pre-First Editions forgers" away (see page 24).

You'll know if a piece has been converted from something else – not a problem with silverware unless the converter has omitted to re-hallmark it, in which case we are in forgery territory. You'll look at a design and know not just whether it is good but whether there is too much or not enough detail in it for its supposed date. Most fun of all, like a flamboyant Italian art connoisseur, you'll be able to listen to your gut instinct.

But, in the meantime, here are some general pointers.

Learn how to tell whether a Ming Vase is genuine.

TOP TEN TIPS TO AVOID GETTING DUPED

1 **Smell it!** Especially if it is a painting. It should smell old and not just of chemicals, paint, and varnish. The smell of succinic acid gives a false amber varnish away.

2 Beware the **halfway price**. If a seller knows their work is fake, they will often price it at around halfway between what it's worth – approximately nothing – and what they wish it was worth.

3 Be on your guard at auction houses. Check that the **catalog description** and label description are the same as the description on the receipt. Make sure the receipt also carries any important information that the seller gave you verbally. Watch the wording in the catalog, too – and don't buy anything less than a piece with the name of the artist, its date (and its factory, if it is a ceramic). Terms such as "after" or "in the style of" won't do. And don't be fooled by oak paneling and expensively suited experts. Smart auction houses can contain the crooks – and dodgy merchandise.

4 Study the **pattern of wear** on the piece. Is it consistent with everyday use or is it a bit random? If it is a chair you are considering, look at the bottom of its feet. The wear should not be too even. It should look like it has withstood years of being dragged about.

5 Study the **signs of ageing** hard. Some "antiqued" furniture comes complete with woodworm, but it isn't real. Looked at with a magnifying glass, stress cracks coming from the hole will show that it was made by a man with a spike rather than an expert craftsman. Look for clumsy attempts at ageing, such as hidden nooks and crannies that don't look old. If it is a painting, does the back of the canvas look really old or has it been aged? If it is really old, it should be worn down, and not rough. If it is a piece of furniture and you can do so, turn it upside down. Often, it is here that signs of pieces not being so old can be seen.

6 Sometimes a forger will overcome the problem of ageing by **overpainting** another plate or canvas. If a very bright light is available, you may be able to use it to establish if this is the case. Often, shapes from the old work can be seen underneath.

7 Look at any **labels** that are on the piece – particularly if it is a violin! Are they frayed at the edges? This suggests that they may have come from somewhere else. Or they may themselves be fake and aged with tea.

8 Ceramics are made in factories, so they invite the mass reproduction of imitations. Look out for guidelines – or any lines – on your porcelain, made from **transfers**. Sometimes, these can be seen with the naked eye; sometimes you'll need a magnifying glass. Sometimes, printed designs are used, too. Not only are these flat in tone, but your magnifying glass will reveal that colors are made up of lots of little dots.

9 Look at the fixings – at hooks, nails, and screws on paintings and mirrors. Are they old? Are you sure they haven't been aged? And, of course, even if they are old, this is no guarantee that the painting is old, too; but if the fixings aren't, the artwork probably isn't, either.

10 Letters and documents. There are specific guidelines on this in the book but, overall, beware **generalized letters**. These are less likely to be genuine than specific, personal letters and, if they are genuine, they are less likely to be valuable.

Don’t get carried away at the auction.

ARTS & LITERATURE

The art forger or literary impostor is more than just a criminal. In the pages that follow, there is much to admire – some real talent and ingenuity. Many forgers of words and pictures are subversive scholars, who spend hours researching and honing their craft. So it attracts loners and outsiders, and those who wish to impress their fathers (Shaun Greenhalgh, William Ireland) or their readership/editor (Jack the Ripper letters, Lincoln love letters, Hitler diaries).

Conversely, there are those who fake out of sheer mischief, or for adventure. Clifford Irving, the "biographer" of Howard Hughes, for instance, who left the tedious business of research to his accomplice, while saving the adrenaline-inducing bits for himself: the misleading of the publishers, the dreaming up of the scams, the serving of the mistresses while he toured the world pretending to interview his subject.

Irving was already an accomplished author at the time of his hoax, and William Boyd and David Bowie were already huge names in their respective fields when they created Nat Tate. What they all needed was a new challenge – to find a new and bigger way of spinning a yarn and being believed.

But they are in the minority. The vast majority of art forgers were first rejected as artists. Most are painted as bitter and vengeful as a result, but perhaps this is not fair. Had they succeeded as artists, they would not have had the need to be forgers; as it was, they settled for the next best thing.

And perhaps, ultimately, it is the forgers who have the last laugh, since what all successful forgers become, eventually, is collectable.

THE FAKE PICASSO

A very talented art forger and something of a fantasist, de Hory was also a bad judge of character as he found out to his cost – literally.

Elmyr de Hory was born in Hungary in 1906. Immediately truth and fiction become blurred because, although he told his biographer Clifford Irving that his father was an Austro-Hungarian ambassador and his mother came from a family of bankers, a little investigation showed the family to be staunchly middle class and unremarkable.

When he was 18, Elmyr went to study classical painting in Munich. Paris followed, where he was taught by the famous artist Fernand Léger. Here, it is said, he got a taste for high living.

De Hory also found himself irresistibly drawn to people that spelt trouble. He returned to Hungary where he struck up an intimate friendship with a journalist who was also a suspected spy. The upshot was a spell in a Transylvanian prison in the Carpathian Mountains. The crafty De Hory got the prison officer on his side by painting his portrait and was released.

Pablo Picasso in his studio.

But he was released into a war, and another prison beckoned – this time in Germany, and this time for the twin crimes of being Jewish and homosexual. As it turned out, he was probably not Jewish but Calvinist. He was beaten so badly in prison that he was transferred to a prison hospital in Berlin. He escaped and found his way back to Hungary. Having established that both parents had been killed and their estate taken into Nazi hands, he decided to be an artist back in Paris.

It was not easy for de Hory to make a living from his art. But he did have a great talent for copying the work of other artists. He started selling Picasso reproductions to art galleries at \$100–\$400/£50–200 a time.

In 1946, de Hory made another unfortunate alliance, this time with a certain Jacques Chamberlain. Although Chamberlain secured a nice split-profit deal with de Hory, it emerged that, while they had been touring Europe and South America together selling forgeries, Chamberlain had been keeping the majority of the money for himself.

The following year, de Hory visited the US and liked it. He stayed. The intention was still to make his name as an artist in his own right. It remained so all his life, but the world did not appear to be listening. So he expanded his repertoire, forging the work of other masters like Renoir and Matisse. In order to avoid flooding the same art galleries, he began to deal by mail order, under a number of assumed names.

A Chicago dealer recognized his works as fakes and so he fled to Mexico, where he was imprisoned for the murder of someone he said he'd never met. Both his lawyer and the Mexican police tried to relieve him of much of his money. He returned to the US, where he attempted to overdose on sleeping pills.

Then dealer Fernand Legros came into his life. Like Chamberlain before him, Legros was keeping much of the profit, despite having an already more than reasonable 50-50 deal with de Hory. Still, he continued to work with, and be fleeced by, Legros and his partner Lessard.

Eventually Legros and Lessard were caught and imprisoned for check fraud. A few years later de Hory was convicted by a Spanish court of homosexuality and

Elmyr de Hory photographed in 1969 with one of his fake Matisse sketches.

consorting with criminals. It could not be proven that he had created forgeries in Spain. But Spain turned him over to the French authorities. Not long after, he tried the sleeping pill trick again. This time it worked.

De Hory always maintained that he did not sign his works – so technically he could not be classified as a forger. If he had been believed then Legros or another of his unsavory business partners might have taken the rap for adding the signatures of the greats on to De Hory's creations.

De Hory's biographer Clifford Irving went on to create his own forgery in the form of the famous Howard Hughes biography.

THE GIACOMETTI FORGER

An unlikely 20th-century coupling that resulted in 200 fake masterpieces being circulated on the world's art market. The majority have not been recovered.

John Drewe made fraudulent use of the archives of the V&A, London.

In 1999, John Drewe, the man who orchestrated one of the 20th-century's biggest art frauds, was sentenced to six years in prison. But the creative talent behind the forgery was the extraordinary John Myatt who, "deeply ashamed", was sentenced to 12 months – although in the end he only served four.

It all began when Drewe spotted a classified advertisement that Myatt had placed in the UK satirical magazine, **Private Eye**. In it, he offered "genuine fakes" from the 19th and 20th centuries. The ad had run four times when he received the call from John Drewe that was to change his life.

Myatt had no reason to suspect Drewe. Here was a well-heeled, plausible man who claimed to be a professor of physics. Soon Myatt was painting a "Matisse" for him and then several portraits in the Dutch style. He became a regular visitor to Drewe's house, where he saw his creations hanging on the stairwell.

Next came a portrait by French cubist Albert Gleizes that Myatt had seen in a book and which, once completed, joined the others on the stairs. What Myatt did not know was that Drewe had then taken it into Christie's auction house for valuation and been offered $50,000/£25,000.

That is, he did not know until he got a call from Drewe asking him, the hard-up, recently separated teacher with two kids to raise: "How do you fancy $25,000/£12,500 in a brown envelope?" "It did not take me any time at all to make the wrong decision," he told the UK's **Guardian** newspaper. "It was as much money as I earned as a teacher in a year."

It had begun.

Starting with copies of Giacometti, Myatt produced around 200 works between 1986 and 1994. Some were aged using mud or the dust from a hoover. Gradually he learned the correct materials and how to water down his emulsion with KY jelly to give it the right glazed look. He began to enjoy himself.

Meanwhile, using deception, Drewe obtained access to the archives of the Victoria and Albert Museum and the Tate in order to slip new references to art works into card indexes there. He also collected old gallery receipts and used these to claim his works as genuine. In court, Judge Geoffrey Rivlin, QC, was astonished by the level of creativity applied to these "provenances".

Not only is Drewe believed to have amassed a fortune of up to $3.6 million/£1.8

The authenticity of some of the works was just luck. Myatt happened to use the same cotton duck canvas that had been favored by Giacometti.

million, his nerve was such that he donated $40,000/£20,000 to the Tate. Unlike Myatt, he went down fighting. When first accused, he insisted that "a cesspit of festering corruption" in the art market sought to make him a scapegoat, to conceal international arms deals. It was high drama, and at one time Drewe is believed to have threatened Myatt with a gun when their relationship was at its worst.

Police have since recovered 60 of the forgeries but believe that around 140 remain undetected.

In common with many successful forgers throughout history, Myatt began his career as an optimistic legitimate artist hoping to make a living by making his own name in the art world. His approach has always been scholarly and respectful. He surrounds himself with books on the artist, he says. He wants to know everything about them.

Myatt's genuine fakes were exhibited in the prestigious Air Street Gallery in London's Mayfair in 2005 – it was a sell-out – and he is now a committed Christian, living a happy, settled life. A film on the story of his life, **Genuine Fakes**, is in the making.

Alberto Giacometti – the starting point for Myatt's career as an art forger.

TOM KEATING

The talented artist, turned forger, turned TV star, who created 2,000 fakes in the style of more than 130 different artists, from Rembrandt to Modigliani.

Tom Keating made no attempt to hide the fact that his works were copies.

It had all looked so promising. Born into a poor family in Lewisham, south London, in 1917, Tom Keating had been a house painter but, via evening art classes at Croydon and Camberwell schools of art, he won a scholarship to the prestigious Goldsmith's College. However, he failed his diploma twice, which meant that he could not become a teacher, so he turned his hand to restoration.

Like other forgers before him, a whole heap of disappointment and bitterness helped speed him on his way in his chosen career, although he portrayed it as a kind of crusade for impoverished artists against, in particular, American "avant garde fashion" led by critics and dealers. From his days at art school, Keating was already well versed in copying the styles of other painters. It was only a short hop from this to becoming a real-life forger. Like many copyists today, he would put "time bombs" into his paintings, to protect himself against accusations of fraud. He might use modern materials or introduce flaws or anachronisms into the subject matter. More blatantly, he would write "FAKE" on the canvas in lead white before he made the painting. If the owner of the painting took the precaution of having it x-rayed, the writing would be there for all to see. Keating's particular method of ageing paper was to employ brown juice from boiled apples and sometimes a teaspoonful of instant coffee.

His favourite artist was Rembrandt, whose work complemented Keating's preferred oil painting technique perfectly. This was a variation on Titian's technique, which took time to achieve but resulted in wonderfully rich colors and subtle textures.

Whatever else he was to be charged with, no one could accuse Keating of a lack of care. To make a Rembrandt, he would boil nuts for ten hours, before filtering the resulting pigment, to ensure that with time the painting would fade, revealing itself as a fake. He learned the chemistry of his craft too: a layer of glycerine under the paint ensured that when the painting was cleaned, the whole thing would dissolve.

He enjoyed several years of success, with his paintings often making it onto the art scene by way of more obscure, rural salesrooms.

In an oddly old-fashioned, British manner, Keating was finally uncovered and confessed within the pages of the UK's **The Times** newspaper. An art critic wrote in,

Over the years, Tom Keating faked all the big names, including Constable, Cézanne Degas, Renoir, Turner, Gainsborough, and Modigliani.

questioning the authenticity of a work by Samuel Palmer, which had recently sold for $18,800/£9,400. There had been a crop of new Palmers over the preceding years, and up until then they had all been accepted as genuine.

Sensing the net tightening, Keating wrote to the newspaper confessing all and protesting that he had done it all for impoverished artists. His trial, scheduled for 1979, was dropped in the end due to his ill health. In the final analysis, he had achieved a phenomenal amount more than he would have done had he passed that diploma and become a teacher. By the time he died in 1984, he had been the subject of a 1977 biography, **The Fake's Progress: The Tom Keating Story**, by Tom Keating, Geraldine Norman, and Frank Norman; had presented a television program about the techniques of old masters and – irony of ironies – had seen Christie's stage a sale solely of his pictures.

Things had come full circle for Tom Keating. In the old days, when he had been a restorer as well as a forger, he would sometimes be in touch with the auction house in a less legitimate capacity. Whenever he came across a frame with a Christie's catalog number on it, he would ring them up to establish what the frame had contained – and then paint a fake for it accordingly.

ERIC HEBBORN

The artist with an uncanny ability to reproduce the work of Rembrandt, Rubens, and other Old Masters amassed a fortune – but came to a sorry end.

Eric Hebborn was born into an impoverished single-parent family in the East End of London in 1934, to a gypsy mother. He had difficulties settling in at school, later claiming that he was charged with arson at one stage, but one thing he was always extremely good at was painting. His art teachers were encouraging and one in particular took the young Eric under his wing. Through this assistance, Hebborn had his first exhibition at the Maldon Art Club at the tender age of fifteen and it was a huge success.

Against the odds, Eric was soon accepted at the Royal Academy of Arts. Even amongst these students, he was considered gifted, and after graduating, he gained a scholarship to the British Art School in Rome where he came out as homosexual and led an extremely high life during which he made many exceptionally well-connected friends including Sir Anthony Blunt – who was later to become the Queen's art historian and, even later, to have his title removed for betraying his country. Blunt happened to mention that one of Hebborn's drawings reminded him of a work by Poussin.

This comment seems to have fired something up in Hebborn and, on his return to London, he found himself a job with an art restoration expert called George Aczel. Spotting his talent at imitation, Aczel was soon advising Eric on how to make money by "copying" onto a blank canvas and then selling the product. A row inevitably developed over commissions and payments and the pair soon fell out.

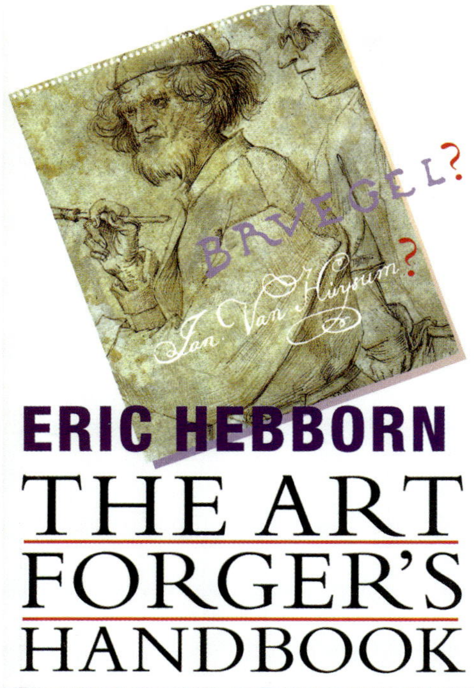

The fakers' "how-to" manual.

Eric found a new boyfriend, Graham Smith, who had a drug habit and needed cash. The pair began hanging out at an antique shop in London where they became friendly with the owner. Eric offered to catalog her antique prints and had the neat idea of using the genuine antique paper as the canvas for his only too contemporary drawings.

His first out-and-out forgeries were of pencil drawings by Augustus John, most of which he sold through Bond Street galleries and even Christie's auction house. Eventually, Hebborn and Smith went to live in Italy where they set up their own gallery which sold a mixture of paintings called "Hebborns" as well as thousands of other paintings by Hebborn which were labeled "Corots", "Mantegnas", and "works by Rubens". Gushing art critics came to the gallery's shows and declared the paintings to be genuine and brilliant and worth tens of thousands of pounds.

In 1978, a curator from the National Gallery of Art in Washington, D.C., called Konrad Oberhuber was examining a pair of drawings he had bought from a dealer of Old Masters in London called Colnaghi. He noticed that they were both painted on similar paper. The likelihood of this being a coincidence was negligible. Oberhuber got in touch with colleagues. They, too, had paintings from

The Massacre of the Innocents by Rubens, being hung by Sotheby's staff, London.

Colnaghi executed on the very same paper. Oberhuber discussed this with the London dealer who said that he had purchased every one of these contentious works from a man called Hebborn in Italy.

Colnaghi, though convinced that Hebborn had forged the paintings himself, was reluctant to say so for fear of a libel suit and he therefore took no action, leaving the artist free to paint at least another 500 more forgeries between 1978 and 1988.

As the evidence against him grew, Hebborn eventually confessed. Yet the canny forger managed to use his new status to make still more money by writing the best-selling autobiography **Drawn to Trouble**. His book was vitriolic and personal and, in 1996, shortly after the publication of the Italian edition **The Art Forger's Handbook**, another work that was bitingly critical of the art world, Eric Hebborn was found dead in a street in Rome with his skull crushed. He had made one enemy too many.

THE FAKE VERMEER

The artist who had to prove himself a forger by creating a fake Vermeer for the court – in front of six witnesses and under police guard.

Hans van Meegeren, shown painting his perfect copy of Vermeer's Young Christ in the Temple.

For nearly twenty years, Hans Van Meegeren was a successful part of the Dutch art world. Born in Holland in 1889, he spent six years studying architecture at Delft University before deciding to concentrate his efforts on painting and drawing.

He then became an establishment figure, joining societies, contributing to art magazines, and – most importantly you would think – holding exhibitions. But he was restless. It was not enough. In 1932 he moved to France.

Once there, his career path changed in radical style. Opinions differ as to why it changed in the way it did. Some say he was another disgruntled artist who had not made it as big as he had hoped while others insist that he just wanted cash, and lots of it. Whatever the truth of the matter, he tried his hand at painting in the style of Frans Hals. None of his first four efforts sold. It was time to try another tack.

He would fake a Vermeer.

It took Van Meegeren four years of trial and error to achieve his aim. Four years to research the master, his methods, and his materials. He worked on a huge old canvas – buying the work of a contemporary of Vermeer's and stripping it.

Instead of creating a pastiche of existing Vermeers as he had with Hals, and as had a thousand forgers before him, he decided to take the more courageous option – he would invent. The subject was to be the same as one of Caravaggio's: **The Supper at Emmaus**.

He mixed the paint himself and used badger brushes. He learned to age the painting. In order to ensure that it would pass the alcohol test, which experts employed to test for very old paint, he alternated between using paint and a mixture of phenol-formaldehyde (Bakelite) and lilac oil. He then made a special oven and baked it at 105 degrees centigrade.

He was ready. The unfortunate man who was to help him with his scam was a respected lawyer and ex-Dutch MP called G. A. Boon. Much previous experience of fakers should have set off alarm bells for Boon as soon as he heard Van Meegeren's story about smuggling what he thought was a Vermeer out of Italy to protect the name of his mistress's family who owned it. But Boon was an innocent in this respect.

For art expert Thomas Hoving *Christ and the Adultress* was "one of Van Meegeren's "truly putrid fakes, a sloppy and saccharine daub".

The lawyer duly took it to the great Dutch art connoisseur Abraham Bredius, now an eighty-year-old-man with failing sight – who still keen to make discoveries. Bredius's famous gut instinct led him to proclaim: "It is a wonderful moment in the life of a lover of art when he finds himself suddenly confronted with a hitherto unknown painting by a great master, untouched, on the original canvas, and without any restoration, just as it left the painter's studio!"

The French art market was not convinced, but in 1938, the painting was bought by the Rembrandt Society for a sum of 520,000 gilders – about $300,000/£150,000 – and presented to Rotterdam's Museum Boijmans Van Beuningen. Van Meegeren returned to Holland where he continued to make himself rich, creating and selling Vermeers. The hitch was that Holland was now under Nazi occupation. He was going to have to collaborate with the Germans. He did so.

Then, in 1945, the Allies drove the Germans out of Holland. Captain Harry Anderson discovered Van Meegeren's work **Christ and the Adultress** in Hermann Göring's own collection. It was traced back to its creator. So had he been colluding with the enemy? To save his own skin, Van Meegeren confessed to forging it and the other "Vermeers".

Over two months, he was made to prove it by painting another "Vermeer", **Young Christ in the Temple**, in a guarded room with six witnesses. Eventually he was convicted of forgery and fraud and sentenced to a year in prison. He fell ill and died the following month.

FRANÇOIS FOURNIER – FAKER OF STAMPS

Accurate copies of stamp collections by the master Swiss forger appealed to the masses but appalled genuine stamp dealers.

The first postage stamp was issued in Great Britain in 1840 and was followed, just twenty years later, by the first stamp forgery. François Fournier, a well-known early stamp forger, was born in Switzerland in 1846, and became a soldier in the Franco-Prussian War in 1870. After the War ended, he returned to Geneva where, in 1904, he bought the company of a man called Louis-Henri Mercier who had been awarded several gold medals for his ability to produce stamps.

Fournier used Mercier's remarkably well-equipped studio to make more reproductions, selling them at a large profit as "extremely accurate copies of the real thing". He made so much money that he could afford to employ engravers to make even more stamps. For this reason, the quality of the Fournier stamps have come to vary quite considerably, ranging from the excellent (Fournier's own work) to the amateurish (those produced by his sub-contractors). Between 1910 and 1914, Fournier was so successful that he produced his own mail order catalog "Le Fac-Simile" with over 20,000 registered customers.

Some experts looked at Fournier as someone who had enabled the masses to put together satisfying stamp collections at a fraction of the cost of a "real" collection while others objected strenuously, maintaining that he was a criminal, profiting from deliberate forgeries. Authentic dealers were furious as they lost out on a potential fortune as collectors bought Fournier's stamps, in the full knowledge that they were cheap copies, but enjoying the thrill of collecting.

It was not technically illegal to produce copies of stamps, merely to claim that they were genuine, so Fournier was never charged with an offense. However, the First World War meant that the public had more important issues to deal with than their amateur stamp collections and Fournier's business went into decline. He eventually got into financial difficulty and died in 1917 but his stamps still live on in thousands of cheap but cheerful stamp collections.

NAT TATE – THE FAKE NEW YORK ARTIST

How rock singer David Bowie and novelist William Boyd fooled Manhattan art lovers into believing in a tragic artist.

It was 1998, and New York's literati was enjoying a lavish party to celebrate the launch of a biography of a little-known but influential abstract expressionist artist called Nat Tate, written by the surprisingly well-known novelist, William Boyd. He must have been good, this Nat Tate, because not only was it being published by David Bowie's company, 21 Publishing, but the rock star had agreed to do some readings at the event. Bowie also put extracts from the biography on his website.

Tate's was a tragic story. He had befriended Pablo Picasso and Georges Braque, and having visited Braque's studio and witnessed real talent first hand, he was thrown into such despair that he committed suicide at the age of 31. Gore Vidal, who endorsed the book on the dust jacket, described Tate as, "an artist too well understood by his time". In the book he remembered Tate as being "essentially dignified, drunk with nothing to say".

Except that he wasn't, because he didn't exist. 21 Publishing insisted there was nothing malicious in the hoax. Apparently they had done it simply to amuse

David Bowie and artist Jeff Koons at the launch of Nat Tate's biography.

themselves. The photographs in the book had mostly been collected from sales and antique shops by Boyd. "Part of it was, we were very amused that people kept saying 'Yes I've heard of him'," said co-director Karen Wright. "There is a willingness not to appear foolish. Critics are too proud for that." Several British newspapers, including the **Sunday Telegraph**, had run extracts from the book, believing it to be genuine.

The editors, and another co-cirector at 21 Publishing, said they thought of the exercise as conceptual art in itself. It was not designed, they insisted, to expose the shallowness of the art world, as hoaxes so often are. Boyd, who also procuced a couple of "Nat Tate" drawings for the book, said that this was a "literary exercise" for him. "I wanted to see what illusions I could spin," he said, "what tricks I could turn." A savvy journalist might have spotted, however, that the name Nat Tate was a mischievous amalgamation of Britain's two leading art galleries – the National Gallery and the Tate Gallery.

FIRST EDITIONS FORGERY

Literary shenanigans at the end of the 19th century caused confusion and conflict among bookish types of the 20th.

This deception was particularly scandalous in its day because of the several then-famous names attached to it. It was the 1930s and two London booksellers, John Carter and Graham Pollard, decided to get together to solve a particularly puzzling literary problem.

Written evidence, including a biography of the great thinker John Ruskin, suggested that there existed rare, valuable pamphlets by certain Victorian writers. However, Carter and Pollard's knowledge of pamphlets and of the authors themselves suggested to them that something was afoot.

In the case of the Ruskin pamphlets, the problem was that these were said to be first editions – but contained within them was text from a later date. A "first edition" pamphlet of Elizabeth Barrett Browning's **Sonnets from the Portuguese** was printed in Reading, but the Brownings were living in Italy in 1847, when it was published. Why had they not used an Italian printer?

According to the literary critic Edmund Gosse, a friend of his had informed him that Barrett Browning's friend Mary Russell Mitford had arranged for the printing. It was also said that Mitford had cleverly held on to some of those pamphlets and that they had since been sold to collectors for $1,250/£625 each.

Bibliographer Thomas J. Wise explained that while researching the Barrett Browning pamphlets, he had established that the documents had been passed on from Mitford to another friend of hers who sold them on to Browning collectors.

Two types of analysis showed that this story did not add up. Analysis of the paper revealed that the pamphlets were made from wood pulp, which had only been used from the 1840s; analysis of the lettering showed that the font used was one that had not emerged until the 1880s.

Now that Carter and Pollard were satisfied that several pamphlets were "wrong", all that remained was to establish who the forger was. The printers of the pamphlets were Clay and Son, who told detectives that a fire in 1911 had destroyed their records. So the person who had the Elizabeth Barrett Browning pamphlets printed could not be established.

The booksellers found a lot of other forged pamphlets, by authors including George Eliot, Tennyson, and Matthew Arnold. In each case the title page of the document contained a "rider", explaining its early publication.

So was Wise the friend of Gosse's with the Barrett Browning information? Certainly they knew each other. He had a great reputation, but then the best forgers often have. And Wise had sold hundreds of forged pamphlets to innocent antiquarian bookseller Herbert Gorfin.

Wise was intimately connected with the Browning Societies, so he was perfectly placed for such a scam.

When questioned years before about a couple of forged first editions, Wise had accused two other literary figures, both of them dead. By the time Carter and Pollard got to Wise he was 73 and acting the part admirably. He was vague and said he had a bad memory, but that he would try and find records of the Gorfin sales. The records never materialized.

Soon after Carter and Pollard visited him, Wise offered Gorfin $800/£400 for any pamphlets he still had and asked him to say he had bought them from Buxton Forman, another esteemed bibliographer. Forman was also dead but he had known Wise and might well have been involved in the forgeries in some way. Gorfin took the money but would not lie about Forman. Wise maintained in letters to the **Times Literary Supplement** that Forman was behind the pamphlets. He died in 1937, still protesting his innocence.

As in so many spheres, literary collectors since Wise's time have become interested in the forgeries and forgers themselves. Frank W. Tober was one of those. His Wise forgeries formed the most prized elements of his library. When he died in 1995, he left his collection to the University of Delaware.

Elizabeth Barrett Browning.

FRITZ KREISLER

The great Austrian violinist Fritz Kreisler was a man of many talents. Not only a violinist, but also an author, a doctor, a war hero, and a talented forger.

Kreisler: more famous for his forgeries than his undoubted musical talents.

These days Kreisler's undoubted talents as a musician tend to dominate accounts of his life, but in his day it was the exposure of his forgeries that caused perhaps the greatest sensation.

Kreisler was born in Vienna in 1875 and at the age of just seven he went to study at the Vienna Conservatoire. Within five years the boy's talents were obvious, nurtured as they were by teachers such as Léo Delibes and Joseph Massart. His Jewish father decided that the boy should be baptized into the Catholic faith of his mother at this point to overcome the latent anti-semitism of late 19th-century German society. Equipped with his new faith, the young Kreisler embarked on a concert tour that took him to the USA to make his American debut at the Steinway Hall in New York.

On his return to the Austro-Hungarian Empire, Kreisler applied for a position at the Vienna Philharmonic, but was turned down. Apparently his style of playing did not fit in with that of the orchestra. Dispirited and needing to earn a living, Kreisler began to study medicine, then joined the army. But in 1899 he obtained a position with the Berlin Philharmonic and returned to full-time music. By 1910 he was one of the foremost violinists of his day, and Edward Elgar dedicated his Violin Concerto to Kreisler.

When the First World War broke out, Kreisler returned once more to the Austro-Hungarian army and served with distinction on the Eastern Front. His fighting career was cut short by a Cossack saber, which sliced into his shoulder during a confused night action. Kreisler then moved to the USA, taking up his violin playing again, and did not return to Europe until 1924.

It was at this point in his career that he began to undertake historical music research. Working in Berlin and other European capitals, Kreisler apparently developed a knack for turning up lost works by assorted 17th- and 18th-century composers. Among the men he studied, and whose lost works he claimed to unearth, was Gaetano Pugnani, an Italian violinist and composer who died in 1798. Kreisler claimed to have found three works by this obscure figure, **Praeludium**, **Allegro** and **Tempo di Minuetto**, which he then premiered to great acclaim from both historians and audiences.

Inspired by this success, Kreisler began to research another Italian violinist-composer, Giuseppe Tartini, and again found previously unpublished works by the composer, who had died in 1770. Works by Antonio Lucio Vivaldi followed. But Kreisler's greatest success came when he began discovering unknown works by the obscure French court composer Jacques Marnier Companie, who had been most active in the 15 years or so before the French Revolution. Kreisler's research turned up a huge amount of music by this previously unregarded figure, including

When Kreisler's "discoveries" were revealed to be fakes the music world was aghast. But Kreisler felt he had done nothing wrong.

marches, suite de dances, and festive music. Suddenly Companie's reputation soared – and the man everyone wanted to hear play his works was Kreisler.

Unfortunately, it was this very success that led to Kreisler's unmasking. Study of the watermarks on the newly discovered works by Companie indicated that he had been working in places that he was known not to have visited, and to have been using paper made after he died. Finally, Kreisler was forced to admit that the entire body of works was an outright forgery. He had written them all himself.

Kreisler decided to brazen out the controversy declaring boldly that, "The name changes, the value remains". For the most part, he got away with it. Audiences still loved his playing and even though the works were now known to be forgeries, they were remarketed as "pastiches" and several remained concert favorites.

Kreisler left Europe in 1939 to escape Nazi persecution and settled in the USA. He gave his last public concert in 1947 and died in 1962.

THE TURIN SHROUD

An ingenious 14th-century forgery? A genuine relic? Or an object whose true origins have yet to emerge? The Turin Shroud has always been defended and attacked in equal measure.

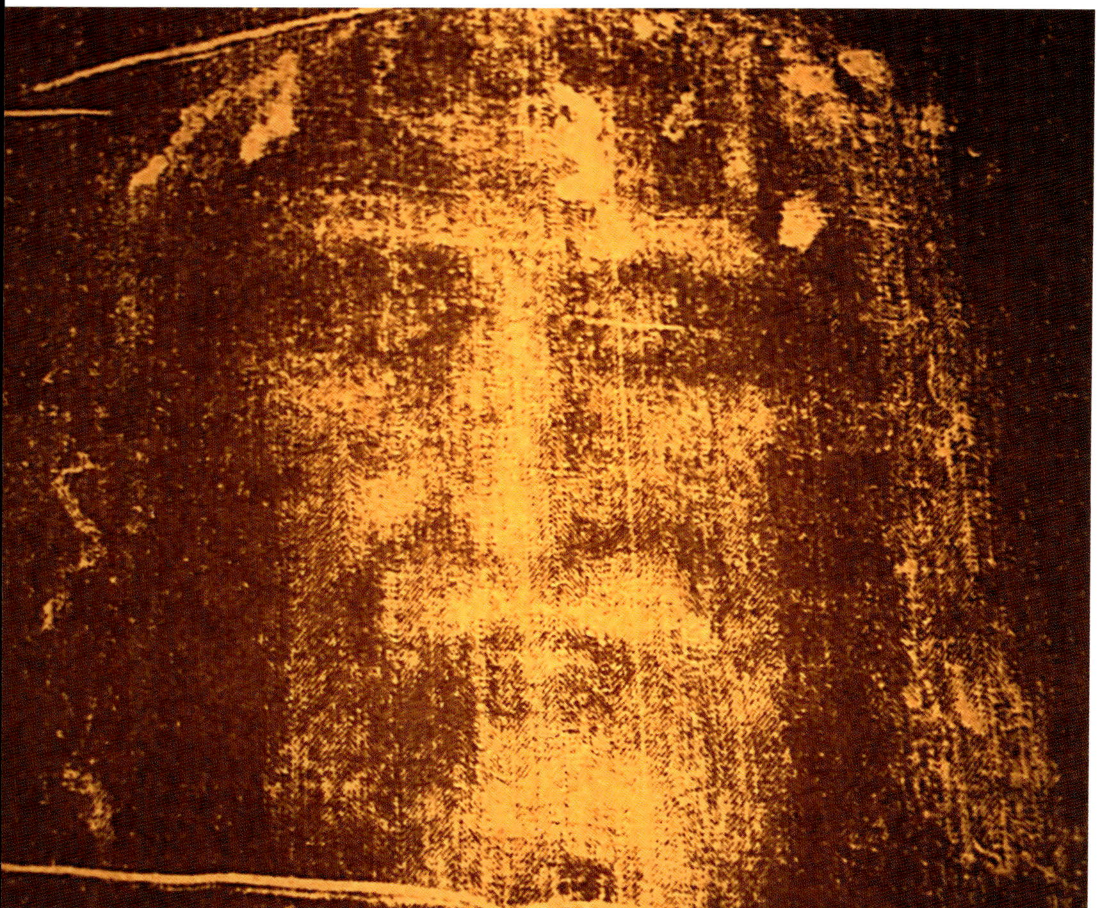

Detail of the face depicted on the Turin Shroud, believed to be that of Jesus.

The Turin Shroud is a riddle. It is a large piece of linen which carries the faint image of a long-haired man with a beard. He appears to have wounds consistent with crucifixion and laceration, as well as a wound on the right side of his chest where Jesus is supposed to have been lanced on the cross. There are also marks along his forehead consistent with the wearing of a crown of thorns.

Ever since its authenticity was first challenged by Bishop Pierre d'Arcis in 1389, the origins of the shroud have been hotly debated. The Bishop was unconvinced of its authenticity as Jesus's shroud. However, because it concerns faith itself, there have always been those who will defend it to the death as being such, maintaining that somehow his image was transferred onto the material.

In the past few decades, the shroud has been subject to much scientific scrutiny. In 1988, three independent teams of researchers used carbon-14 dating techniques in an attempt to establish the age of the fabric. They concluded that the shroud was created between 1260 and 1390.

In other words, it was probably a medieval fake – yet so sophisticated that it was an accomplishment in itself.

Ten years earlier, another scientific experiment, also using carbon dating, concluded that the image on the shroud was a painting. Undeterred, scientists, convinced that the shroud was that of Jesus, claimed that the carbon dating process had been corrupted by the use of a bioplastic coating which threw off the results by a neat 1,300 years, i.e. the shroud could actually be dated back to around the time of Jesus's birth.

And the idea of it being a painting? No problem for the pro-shrouders: paint flecks from other paintings had clearly been transferred on to the shroud when the owners of the works had pressed them against it to sanctify them.

If it dates from further back than 1389, say those who believe the shroud to be a fake, where are the references to it? Journalist Ian Wilson says they are there. It is the Edessan icon, he claims, a piece of cloth imprinted with the image of Jesus's head that is referred to from the 4th century onwards.

The Turin Shroud seems to invite conspiracy theories. In the 1960s, one UK researcher pointed to the similarity between this type of burial and the burial rituals of the small sect of ancient Israelites responsible, many claim, for creating the Dead Sea Scrolls. Without much in the way of clear scientific proof, others claim that it was in the possession of the Knights Templar for 150 years from 1204. Some speculate that it is the Holy Grail.

There is a degree of silly theorizing on the parts of shroud defenders certainly, but there is also enough science for it to remain a knotty problem. For every pro-shrouder asking why, if it is a fake, more relics were not made and profited from, there is a chemist who has done some real research. Alan Adler claimed in **Time** magazine that the blood was not only real but that long before such processes were understood, it was clotted.

Even if the shroud was forged in the mid-14th century, it is still intriguing, because it continues to confound us. How was the extraordinary detail achieved? And why is the style not more typical of the medieval era? Why and how is the image in negative? If it isn't a painting, what is it? Although science is able to provide persuasive evidence that the shroud is a mere seven centuries old, no clues about motivation, method or identity were left by its creator.

References to the Edessan icon only mention the head on the cloth. Ian Wilson claims it was folded, so that only the head was visible.

A member of the Knights Templar.

HEINRICH SCHLIEMANN

The archeologist who believed he had discovered the treasures of the great ancient city of Troy.

Heinrich Schliemann was born in Germany in 1822, the son of a Protestant minister. His mother died when he was nine and Heinrich was sent to the local grammar school where he learned to love the classics. Just a few years later his father was caught embezzling church funds and Heinrich had to leave school. At 14, Schliemann was forced to become a grocer's apprentice; he always felt his lack of education keenly.

After five years, he ran away to become a cabin boy but was soon shipwrecked and ended up in the Netherlands where he began working for an import/export company. By 1846, he had become so successful that he was sent to St. Petersburg to represent the company. Heinrich's brother, meanwhile, had been digging for gold in California and, after his death in 1850, Heinrich followed in his tracks. He set himself up as a middleman between the gold-panners and the banks and, within two years, he later claimed, he had become extremely wealthy, acquired American citizenship, and had dined with the President. In fact, he had cheated his business partner, acquired citizenship by lying, and had never had dinner with the President.

In 1852, he returned to Russia in a hurry and married a woman called Ekaterina. The couple had three children and Heinrich made a new fortune from the indigo dye trade. He also cornered the saltpeter market and, on the outbreak of the Crimean War, made yet another fortune from ammunitions. By 1862, Schliemann could afford to retire and dedicate himself to his one true interest – the ancient city of Troy.

A British archeologist called Frank Calvert had located a site near Hissarlik in Turkey and, based on his work, Schliemann was convinced that the ruins of Troy must be nearby. With Schliemann's wealth and enthusiasm, he and Calvert dominated the field for the next few decades. Schliemann, meanwhile, divorced Ekaterina and advertised in an Athens newspaper for a new, Greek wife. The Archbishop of Athens suggested a 17-year-old relative called Sophia and the couple had two children, Andromache and Agamemnon.

Schliemann sketching Troy.

By 1871 Schliemann had dug straight through to the lowest level of the site. He and Calvert fell out over these drastic methods and Calvert stormed off, claiming Schliemann had destroyed vital records. Within a year, Schliemann had located a treasure trove exactly where he had earlier predicted and he immediately labeled this "Priam's Treasure". He claimed that he and Sophia had been the sole witnesses of the discovery as they had sent all the workmen away at the crucial moment in order to relish the "discovery" on their own. Sophia was soon to be seen modeling "Helen's Jewels".

The Turkish government soon revoked Heinrich's digging license and demanded a share of the treasure, particularly after it emerged that it was not the first time that

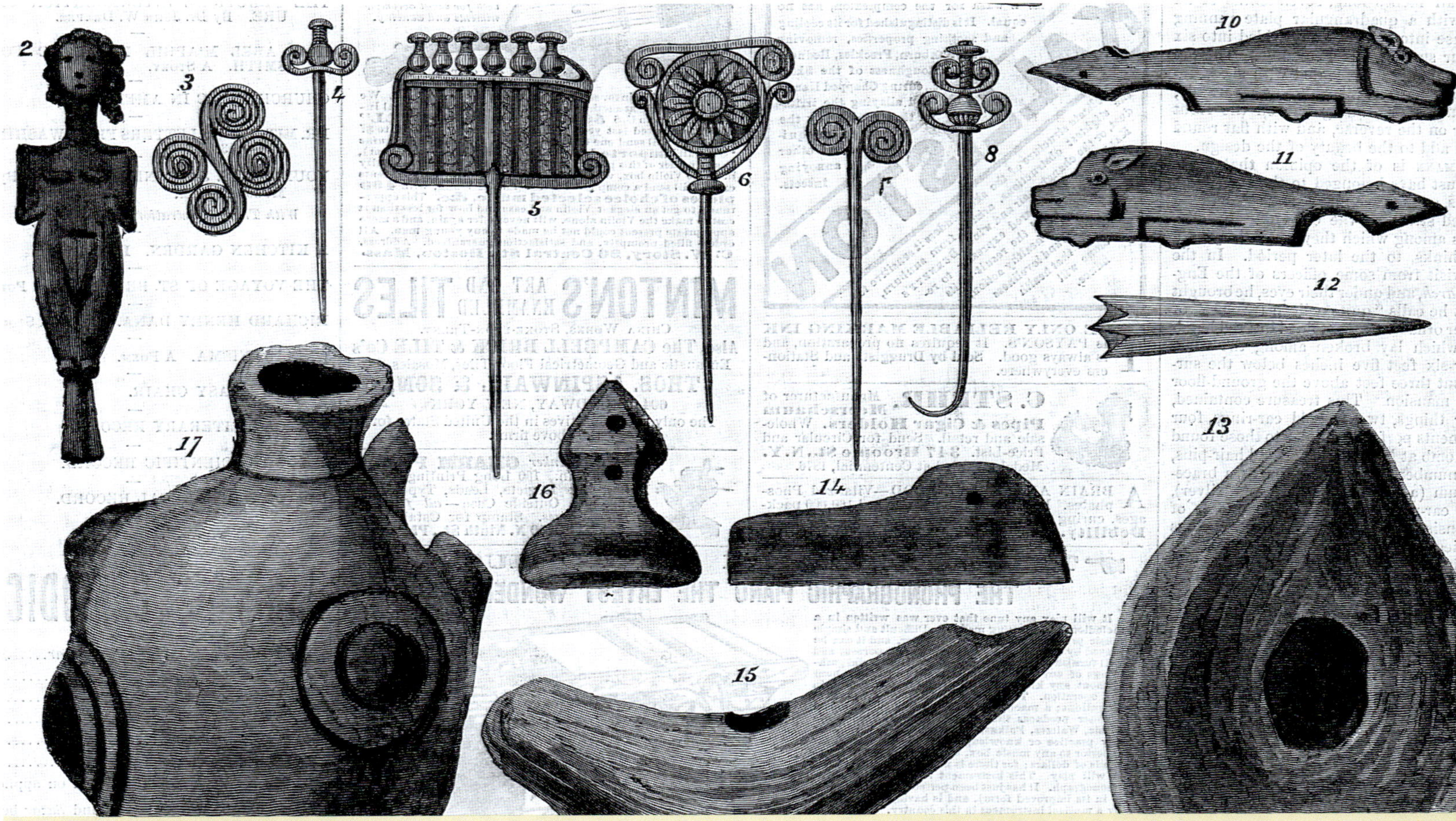

Some of the artifacts discovered by Schliemann at Troy.

Schliemann had been caught "smuggling". By 1878, however, the government had realized they were missing out on a profitable enterprise and allowed Schliemann to return. He participated in three more major digs until his ears became infected and he died in Naples on Christmas Day, 1890. He was buried in a neo-Classical mausoleum in Athens.

Subsequent research showed that the level he had named "Troy" could not have been that of Homer's **Iliad**. His digging had been so coarse that he had destroyed parts of the real Troy and his servant testified that "King Priam's Treasure" had actually been found in a tomb some distance away, was not of the correct period, and contained no gold. Schliemann had, apparently, hired a goldsmith to plant gold nearby in order to "authenticate" his finds.

In spite of the lies to further his own ends, Heinrich Schliemann's finds were nonetheless genuine antiques, and can be seen today by visitors to the Athens Archeological Museum.

THE GREENHALGH FAMILY

The art forgers from the north of England who fooled the world with their Egyptian artifacts, knocked up in a garden shed.

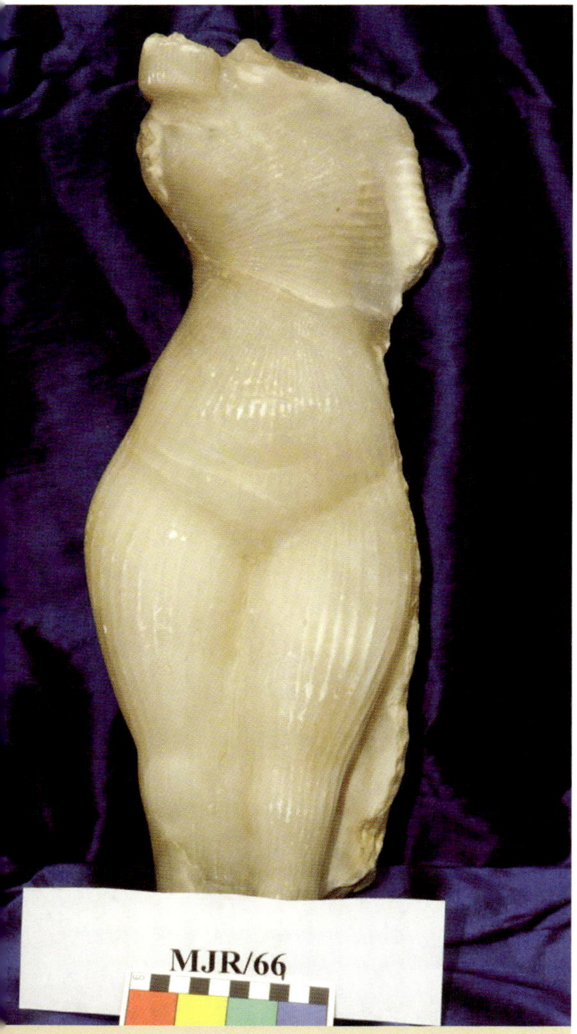

The Amarna Princess.

The world, and in particular the UK, is divided in its response to the Greenhalghs: the working-class family from Bolton, UK, who conned the art world on many occasions between 1989 and 2006 with a huge array of forgeries.

The creative force behind the counterfeits was the son, Shaun; the father, George, did all the negotiating. According to Bolton locals he had always been something of a storyteller. Although he was forever showing off about how he had been decorated during the war, the truth was that he spent most of it in prison for desertion.

The story really began when George found out that his son was a talented artist. Having left school at 16, Shaun, something of a loner with curiosity, a creative urge, and a desire to please his father, began visiting libraries and teaching himself art history.

He then began to turn his attention to more obscure books and to investigating lost artworks. It began with a silver Roman plate, which he recreated. George took it to the experts. The verdict was that it was not the original, but an 18th-century cast. A British Museum donor bought it for $186,000/ £93,000. They were on their way.

A few prolific years followed, with Shaun turning his hand to everything from metalwork to sculpture to painting in oils. He produced a fake Anglo-Saxon helmet, L. S. Lowry paintings, a sculpture by Barbara Hepworth, a lost Gauguin sculpture. Gauguin expert Waldemar Januscek referred to the very beautiful little statue of a faun on a TV program in 2003. And all that George had to do was keep inventing new members of the family and contacts from whom he had obtained the pieces.

The Greenhalgh's greatest and most audacious coup took place close to home – at the Bolton Museum. Shaun created a statue of Tutankhamun's sister, which became known as "The Amarna Princess". The British Museum thought it dated from 1350 BC and valued it at $1,000,000/£500,000. Bolton Museum was hugely excited by the find, but raising that kind of cash was a problem.

So George threatened to sell the statue to the highest bidder. His threat paid off. $740,000/£370,000 of public money was found and used in addition to existing funds to purchase the statue for Bolton for $880,000/£440,000. It was the pride of the museum. Overnight the statue became a huge visitor attraction. The little museum was full to bursting. Even the Queen visited.

Shaun's mother Olive created provenances for the works. Her other son got a six-month suspended sentence for taking $20,000 from the sale.

Shaun decided to turn his hand to making Assyrian reliefs, from "stone" purchased from a local DIY store. A feature of the Greenhalghs forgeries had been that they were not made of quite the right materials, but the experts so wanted them to be genuine that it blinded them to it.

When he had finished the reliefs, for once Shaun had to take them to London himself. The British Museum was excited, but Bonham's auction house was not quite so sure. There were a couple of problems with the reliefs. A detail on a horse's bridle was wrong for the period. There was a spelling mistake in the inscription.

Scotland Yard were contacted and an 18-month investigation into the Greenhalghs culminated in a visit to their house. Seasoned detectives could not believe what they found. Everywhere was evidence of forgery: "old" paper was being pressed under beds, apparently ancient statues thrown into wardrobes with shoes, drawings in pastels, paintings in oils. When Shaun confessed to the forgeries he was not believed at first, because of the vast array of work.

Shaun Greenhalgh – an unassuming exterior hid a talented artist.

Shaun was eventually jailed for four years and eight months. His father appears to have escaped conviction because no prison would take him with his wheelchair.

A neighbor observed that he had never been in a wheelchair before his court case.

THOMAS CHATTERTON

The child prodigy with a little too much imagination who invented his own fictional author and whose life was cut short in dramatic fashion.

The Death of Chatterton by Henry Wallis.

Thomas Chatterton was born in Bristol on 20 November 1752. His father died four months before he was born and his uncle, Richard Phillips, was the local sexton in one of the most beautiful churches in the west of England. Thomas's mother supported her young son and daughter by establishing a local girls' school and their life was educated but abstemious.

At the age of eight, Chatterton was enrolled at the local charity school, though he was always more fascinated by his Uncle Richard's duties in the church. He spent hours in dark corners staring at statues of knights and tombstones and, in particular, in the "Muniment Room" which contained an abandoned, antique oak chest. Inside this, he discovered old parchment deeds that fired up his imagination.

Although his family considered him a little over-studious, no one doubted his ambition when he took the chest's contents home. Here he spent weeks studying the 15th-century documents and writing his own commentaries. His teacher encouraged his efforts and, by the age of eleven, he had begun sending contributions to local newspaper **Felix Farley's Bristol Journal**, including a poem commemorating his own communion.

By 1764, he had begun sending anonymous, satirical poems to the local paper and, just before his twelfth birthday, he composed a poem called "Elinoure and Juga", which was published but which, perhaps through fear of rejection or to make it more attractive to a publisher, he claimed was the work of a 15th-century poet that he had somehow "found" in the oak chest.

Everyone believed him and, encouraged, Chatterton spent all his money on books – one of which was John Kersey's **Dictionarium Anglo-Britannicum**. He used this as the main historical source for his most important literary creation – a 15th-century monk called Thomas Rowley who was a "great, undiscovered poet". Chatterton had soon given Rowley an entire life history, regularly "discovering" more of his writings.

Local scholars were convinced of the poetry's authenticity and "Thomas Rowley" became the great, undiscovered Bristol poet – regularly appearing in local history books and poetry collections. Two local businessmen, George Catcott and Henry Burgum, were hugely influential in this, particularly after Chatterton "discovered" in Rowley's poetry that they were both descended from noble blood. The men rewarded Chatterton for this fortuitous discovery with five shillings.

In July 1767, Chatterton became an articled clerk while continuing to write "antique" poems for local papers using the pseudonym "Dunelmus Bristoliensis". One of these appeared in the **History and Antiquities of the City of Bristol**, which lent the writer even more credibility. Threatening to commit suicide unless he could further pursue his literary career, Chatterton persuaded his family to give him enough money to move to London where he continued to contribute to prestigious periodicals but got paid very little and was often rejected. In desperation, Chatterton revived his Thomas Rowley character and "transcribed" a poem called the "Excelente Balade of Charitie". This, too, was rejected. He had been in London for less than two months, had run out of money and, worse, had to face public failure. On 24 August, 1770, still only 17, he locked himself into his room, tore up his work, and drank arsenic.

The Chatterton myth endures partly because his literary output by the age of 17 was so extraordinary.

A sketch of Chatterton at his desk, discarded poems strewn across the floor.

Chatterton's death attracted little attention at the time, since he was still recognized merely as the "transcriber" of the literary masterpieces of Thomas Rowley. It was only after his death that the legend, and the controversy, began to grow. By 1789, a collection of poetry had been published under his own name. But it was the pre-Raphaelite painting of the **Death of Chatterton** by Henry Wallis in 1856 that brought him near-legendary status. The British Museum now holds the main collection of "Chattertoniana" and the writings are still an endless source of fascination for many since one so young, with such prodigious talent, managed to pull off such an astonishing literary feat.

THE FAKE BESTSELLING AUTHOR

When a young man rises above a life of drugs and prostitution to become a gifted novelist, the scene is set for a literary sensation – if only it were true.

Savannah Knoop disguised as J. T. Leroy.

Few tales of suffering tug at the heart strings quite like that of a young man's abused childhood at the hands of an addict mother and his own descent into drugs, prostitution, and HIV infection. Jeremiah "Terminator" LeRoy captivated readers by pouring out his pain on the printed page. Unfortunately, both name and life history were entirely bogus.

In public, LeRoy appeared as a 5ft 5in/165cm cross-dressing blond in a wig and huge sunglasses. She was finally unmasked in court in 2007.

Brooklyn-born Laura Albert, a 42-year-old writer of fantasy and mystery tales, based in San Francisco, was found guilty of defrauding Antidote International Films. The movie company had paid for the rights to film one of LeRoy's most successful novels, **Sarah**, which told the sorry saga of truck-stop hookers. Albert was assisted in the deception by Savannah Knoop, who played the cross-dressing blond, and who was a half-sister of one of Albert's former partners. Between them, Albert and Knoop spun a web of deceit that entangled the literary establishment.

LeRoy burst onto the book scene with the acclaimed **The Heart is Deceitful Above All Things** (1999), allegedly based on

J. T. LeRoy fan Courtney Love.

his own tragic childhood in West Virginia. When **Sarah** appeared in the same year, LeRoy became a publishing phenomenon, described by the trendy British magazine **The Face** as "a literary wunderkind".

The novella **Harold's End** (2005) came next – the heart-rending tale of a rent boy with a snail for a pet. By the – alleged – age of 24, LeRoy's works were being translated into twenty languages. Celebrity poets and authors including Dennis Cooper, Dave Eggers, Mary Gaitskill, Sharon Olds, Mary Karr, Tobias Wolff, and Michael Chabon all gave praise and support. LeRoy was invited to contribute to well-respected publications.

Soon LeRoy had added the worlds of film and music to his conquests. His screenplay for the Gus Van Sant film **Elephant** won the 2003 Palme d'Or award at Cannes Film Festival and **The Heart is Deceitful Above All Things** was turned into an acclaimed art-house movie in 2004. LeRoy even had his life turned into song courtesy of "Cherry Lips (Go Baby Go!)" by Shirley Manson.

At first LeRoy shunned publicity, leaving others to read his works at public recitals. A New York book editor laden with groceries for the malnourished maestro tracked "him" down to his San Francisco squat, but LeRoy refused to see her. Then a svelte figure in wig and shades appeared on the scene wearing a raccoon bone necklace. Even hard-nosed newsmen were hooked.

A 2004 **New York Times** article entitled "A Literary Life Born of Brutality" describes LeRoy's descent into sado-mashochistic sex and self-mutilation. LeRoy poured out his heart to the interviewer: "For a long time I tried to get people to hit me, because for my mom, it was better if she hit me than ignored me." Not once did the reporter suspect that the reason the author spoke in a "quiet, girlish voice" was because "he" was a girl!

The charade was revealed a year later when the **New York Times' Sunday Magazine** outed Albert. She had written an article about Disneyland Paris under the "LeRoy" by-line. They were suspicious because her expenses receipts were for three people, not the four mentioned in the article. Paris hotel staff later identified Albert from a photo.

A year later, the **Times** named Albert's accomplice, Knoop. Film company Antidote immediately sued. Albert's defense in court was that LeRoy was her alter ego – a created character who just "took over". The Manhattan jury were not convinced, however, and Albert was ordered to pay the company $116,500/£58,125, including $6,500/£3,250 punitive damages. This was a story with a sting in the tale.

Troubled stars such as Winona Ryder and Courtney Love were all caught out by the fake "LeRoy," calling press conferences to "relate to his suffering."

THE "SUN KING" DIARIES

The apparent discovery of the diaries of Louis XIV, with their unveiling of his secret wife, caused much excitement in a publishing world eager for headline-grabbing memoirs.

Following a doctorate at the University of Oxford, a historian called Veronica Buckley wrote a biography of Christina, a former Queen of Sweden. Born in New Zealand, Buckley now lives in Vienna with her husband. **Christina, Queen of Sweden** appeared in 2004 to excellent reviews. It was swiftly acknowledged as a first-rate piece of historical research and Buckley looked set to have a stellar career as a professional historical biographer.

Just a few years later, she thought that she was onto another winner. An unnamed acquaintance had drawn her attention to "a packet of yellowed papers, wrapped in string, and sealed with faded red wax" which had been located "inside a heavy old chest in a Loire valley manor house". The chest apparently contained the secret diaries of Louis XIV, the legendary Sun King of France. Nothing like this had ever appeared in the public domain before and, despite her years of research, Buckley took these papers in good faith. Perhaps thrilled by the potential importance of her new discovery, she began work on a new book about Louis XIV's mistress, which was to be largely based on writings from these diaries

The Sun King, Louis XIV of France.

and entitled **Madame de Maintenon: The Secret Wife of Louis XIV**.

Sadly for Buckley, she was apparently unaware that the "diary" had actually been written by French historian François Bluche. Bluche had put the material together as a work of fiction by using a variety of original sources as well as his own imagination. Amid much excitement, Buckley quoted at length from the "diaries" and even copied a large chunk that purported to be Louis' own version of a day in his life. Louis, of course, had never written a diary.

The manuscript was snapped up by her publishers, Bloomsbury, who were as excited as she was, and was due to appear in May 2008. On April 19, however, literary editors, who had received early copies of the book in order that they could have it reviewed, also received a note out of the blue which was headed "Erratum" and contained the slightly startling news that **Le Journal Secret de Louis XIV** was not in fact written by Louis himself, but had instead been reconstructed from historical sources by historian François Bluche, a specialist in the reign of Louis XIV. Buckley was only too happy to confess to her error and apologized "unreservedly" for any confusion to which it might have given rise.

Reviewers condemned both Buckley and her publishers for relying on "anachronistic, novelistic speculation" over genuine historical detail and evidence.

Every single copy of the original Sun King diaries ended up on the scrapheap.

Editors were quick to point out that the main confusion seemed to be that of the publishers, who had been only too eager to believe Buckley's story, in order to turn a quick profit. They were soon to reap the consequences, however, as every single copy of the book had to be pulped and a new one produced without the offending quotations, and with new uncontroversial material in its place. This would take some months.

A variety of academics rushed into the debate to claim that Buckley was not qualified to carry out primary archival research and, indeed, it should never have been presumed that she could. The publishing industry had woken up to the fact that "dry" history books were not big sellers and was keen to produce as many "racy" versions of history as possible. Editors had become less than zealous about checking the historical veracity of a version that would sell more copies.

Bloomsbury, the publishers of JK Rowling, put a brave face on the incident, and were quoted as saying that "errors are an occupational hazard" and "mistakes happen". They stood by the volume as "an absorbing account" while Buckley herself remained unavailable for comment.

MUSSOLINI'S DIARIES

The writings of Italy's fascist wartime leader, Benito Mussolini, have been the target of numerous attempted forgeries. In 2007, one such forgery caused worldwide excitement.

Benito Mussolini, Italy's proud dictator, stands next to a bust of himself.

In 1957, an Italian mother and daughter produced thirty volumes of what they claimed were the diaries of their leader. They were so convincing that even the dictator's son was persuaded of their authenticity. At the time, no one could believe anyone would bother to forge thirty volumes of writing – they had to be the real thing. However, handwriting experts and historians soon realized that the details did not add up and dismissed the diaries as fakes.

Perhaps it was the success of this earlier attempt that led Italian senator Marcello Dell'Utri to claim, in February 2007, that he knew of the location of the "real" Mussolini diaries. According to Dell'Utri they were in a suitcase that the Italian leader must have been carrying when he was caught by Italian partisans near Lake Como as he attempted to flee Italy towards Switzerland at the end of World War II. Dell'Utri said that the diaries had been in the hands of an (anonymous) ex-partisan for some time, and on that person's death they had passed to his son, who subsequently offered them to Dell'Utri.

The fact that Mr. Dell'Utri was simultaneously appealing against a nine-year sentence for Mafia dealings seemingly didn't make him think anyone would doubt his version of events.

In an interview with the respected Italian newspaper **Corriere della Sera**, he revealed that the writing covered the years 1935 to 1939 and stated that he had read the diaries very carefully and that "the handwriting is clear and recognizably Mussolini's". He added that he had left

Alessandra Mussolini.

them in the custody of a reputable lawyer in an Italian-speaking part of Switzerland. Dell'Utri also relied on the evidence of an unnamed handwriting expert to support his claim.

The diaries tell of how Mussolini had only entered the War reluctantly and that he was a peace-loving person who had tried his best to stop the war from spreading to Italy. The writings were greeted with great enthusiasm by his supporters, including his politician granddaughter, Alessandra. She was quick to claim that she had seen the diaries; she was sure that they were real and they would allow her grandfather's life to be "interpreted with greater objectivity". Clearly, plenty of people had vested interests and much to gain by proving that the work was real.

Those who were of an age to remember the 1957 forgery were understandably wary of these new "diaries".

At this point, Valerio Castronovo, a Professor of Modern Italian History at the University of Turin, weighed into the debate. "Lots of Mussolini diaries have surfaced over the past 20 years and none has proved genuine," he warned. Similarly, the editorial team at **L'Espresso** newspaper came forward to say that the paper had been offered the very same journals for sale over two years earlier. They had refused to buy them, suspecting they were fake, and now submitted the pages to a historian named Emilio Gentile. Gentile noted glaring historical errors, including Mussolini apparently celebrating his birthday on the wrong day.

Gentile also noted large sections had been copied and pasted from a variety of old newspaper articles – with many of which he was familiar. Roberto Travaglini, President of the Italian Graphologist Association, was given the diaries to study over a period of several weeks alongside authentic documents containing Mussolini's "real" handwriting. After very little study, he declared definitively that the diaries must have been forged – "there were too many elements that did not match up".

So many people wanted to believe the Dell'Utri diaries (or wanted to make money out of them) that the delusion lasted much longer than it should have.

THE HITLER DIARIES

When scholarly integrity was sacrificed in the rush to achieve the "scoop of the century", all concerned, except for the forger, lived to regret it.

Once freed, Konrad Kujau would capitalize on his notoriety by selling his forged versions of famous paintings as fakes.

In April 1983, the German magazine **Stern** published the first instalment of something sensational. It had obtained Hitler's diaries: 62 books covering the years 1932 to just before his death in 1945. They appeared to provide a first-hand account of the war years from the perspective of the man himself. **Stern** had achieved one of the all-time literary scoops.

Or rather **Stern** journalist Gerd Heidemann had. He claimed to have traced the diaries to an East German hayloft, where they had been kept since an East German general found them in a crashed plane in 1945.

The diaries were quickly pronounced genuine by several weighty authorities, among them the historians Hugh Trevor-Roper, also known as Lord Dacre, Eberhard Jäckel, and Gerhard Weinberg. Huge serialization deals took place, not only with **Stern** which paid nearly ten million marks – or $5 million/£3 million for them – and **Newsweek** in the US, but also with the UK's **Sunday Times**.

Although the British paper paid a relatively meager $400,000/£203,831 for the rights, there was a problem lying in wait close by. Trevor-Roper was not only a highly respected historian and author of **The Last Days of Hitler**, but a director of Times Newspapers Ltd. He was sent to Germany to scrutinize the diaries, and did so. He was convinced of their authenticity, but was not allowed to consult with any other experts, because he was bound by a confidentiality agreement with **Stern**.

The first thing that struck Trevor-Roper was the sheer volume of material, much of it dull. He decided it could not have been created out of the imagination and existing sources. He knew Hitler's handwriting – and this was it. They had to be real, he concluded, stating that a forgery on this scale would be "heroic and unnecessary".

Then, just two days after Trevor-Roper had published an article in **The Times** announcing his position, a news conference in Hamburg was called. Now he was not so sure, he admitted. He was unable to establish a proper link between the crashed plane and the supposed diaries. Most sensationally of all, he announced: "I must say I regret that the normal methods of historical verification have been sacrificed to the requirements of the journalistic scoop."

The journalist Philip Knightley remembered how the news had reached

Gerd Heidemann of Stern magazine, being pursued by journalists.

the **Times** offices a couple of days before this. Frank Giles, editor of **The Sunday Times**, was on the phone to Trevor-Roper, and there was a sudden change in his tone of voice. "Well, naturally, Hugh, one has doubts . . . but I take it that these doubts aren't strong enough to make you do a complete 180-degree turn on that? Oh. Oh. I see. You are doing a 180-degree turn . . . "

Soon afterwards, expert chemist Dr Julius Grant tested the diaries: the paper, glue, and ink were all modern. In fact, the diaries were school notebooks aged with tea. Further scrutiny followed: the diaries were peppered with historical inaccuracies. Much of the material was copied from Hitler's speeches, augmented with what appeared to be more personal comments. Serialization in **The Sunday Times** was canceled and a front-page apology was issued.

So what had happened? **Stern** journalist Gerd Heidemann came clean. The "diaries" had actually come from Konrad Kujau, a dealer in military memorabilia in Stuttgart who also went by the pseudonym "Peter Fischer". In 1985, both were found guilty of fraud and forgery and sentenced to four and a half years in jail each.

Heidemann had an intriguing past, too, as it turned out. He worked for the secret police in East Germany, and was still doing so when the forgeries were being created.

Trevor-Roper died in 2003. His reputation never quite recovered after the extraordinary episode of the authentication of the Hitler diaries.

THE RIPPER LETTERS

Jack the Ripper is the most infamous serial killer of all time – and his crimes are made all the more intriguing and horrific by the fact that he was never caught.

It was in the last few years of the 19th century that Jack the Ripper stalked the stinking, dark, foggy, already sinister streets of East London. Prostitutes were his chosen victims.

The first was Mary Ann (Polly) Nichols, killed on 31 August 1888. Since she was a prostitute, the police considered her to be more expendable than most. Still, her murder was shocking. Not only had she been repeatedly stabbed in the abdomen, but her throat had been cut so deeply that it exposed her vertebrae.

There was worse to come. On 8 September, another prostitute, Annie Chapman, was found. Her throat had also been cut, her body was mutilated, and her uterus had been removed. Three weeks later, on 30 September, Elizabeth Stride was added to the list, followed immediately by Catherine Eddowes whose body was discovered on the same day as Stride's and whose whose kidney and nose had been removed. Then followed Mary Kelly on 9 November 1888.

There was also a lot of written correspondence alleging to be the work of the Ripper. Such mystery surrounds the case that it is impossible to prove what is genuine and what is a hoax.

The "Dear Boss", "Saucy Jacky", and "From Hell" letters are the best known. Many believe the "Dear Boss" letters are genuine because, received by the Central News Agency on 1 October, the first of them seems to pre-empt the Stride and Eddowes murders – right down to the cutting off of part of Eddowes's earlobe.

Very soon after, the "Saucy Jacky" postcard was sent. Written in a similar hand to the above, and sent to the Central News Agency, it was sent immediately after the double murder: "number one squealed a bit couldn't finish straight off. ha not the time to get ears for police . . . " It was also signed "Jack the Ripper".

The "From Hell" letter was sent to George Lusk, president of the Whitechapel Vigilance Committee, on 16 October, along with half a human kidney preserved in wine. The kidney was very like the one removed from Eddowes, although its origin was not proved. The letter said, "I . . . prasarved it for you tother piece I fried and ate it was very nise." He signed off "Catch me when you can".

Police were sent several rhymes. One began: "Eight little whores, with no hope of heaven, Gladstone may save one, then there'll be seven."

Such were the plausible letters. Perhaps 200 were almost certainly fakes, some sent by newspapermen desperate for a story. One was sent to a local newspaper, threatening two witnesses: " . . . Now I known you know me and I see your little game, and I mean to finish you and send your ears to your wife if you show this to the police or help them if you do I will finish you . . . "

Some claim to be telling the police the Ripper's address: "What fools the police are. I even give them the name of the street where I am living. Prince William Street." Others are long on gore but even shorter on spelling and grammar than the originals: "the left kidny i was goin to hoperate agin close to you ospitle just as i was going to dror mi nife along of er bloomin throte . . . "

There was the famous Goulston Street Graffito, discovered on a piece of leather and sloppily transcribed on to a wall by a local, then, bizarrely, corrected by a policeman: "The Juwes are the men That Will not be Blamed for nothing".

Finally, a letter was "discovered" in a sealed envelope in the British Public Record Office in 1988. Many believe it was placed there recently. It begins: "So now they say I am a Yid when will they lern Dear old Boss! You an me know the truth dont we. Lusk can look forever hell never find me but I am rite under his nose all the time."

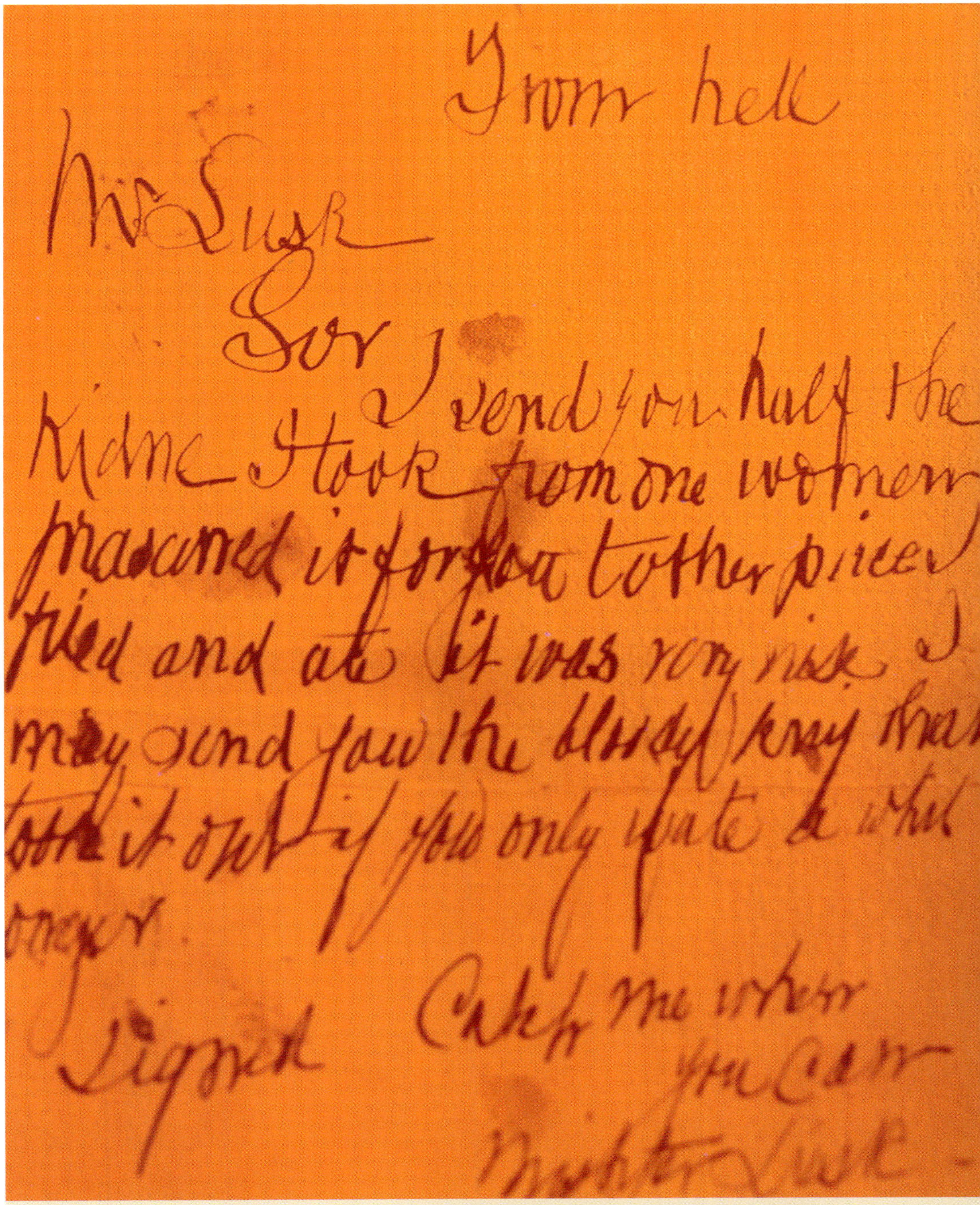

From hell

Mr Lusk

Sor

I send you half the Kidne I took from one women prasarved it for you tother piece I fried and ate it was very nise I may send you the bloody knif that took it out if you only wate a whil longer

signed Catch me when you Can Mishter Lusk

The Ripper's letter "From Hell" came with half a human kidney preserved in wine.

LINCOLN'S FAKE LOVE STORY

The letters supposedly sent between Lincoln and his lover and the magazine editor who was slow to back down.

The sculpture of Abraham Lincoln inside the Lincoln Memorial, Washington D. C.

It was 1928, and the editor of America's **Atlantic** magazine, Ellery Sedgwick, was receiving a visitor with a very interesting haul indeed. The visitor, Wilma Frances Minor, explained that the cache had been in her family for some time, and had now made its way to her.

What Wilma Minor brought to Sedgwick was a collection of various types of documentation. Most importantly, there were letters between Abraham Lincoln and his humble lover, Ann Rutledge. Legend had it that Lincoln's famous melancholies were the result of his intense devotion to Ann, whom he had lost to typhoid in 1835.

Also included within it was a detailed diary written by Ann's cousin Matilda Cameron, and various other documentation that seemed to support the notion of a relationship. Minor had written an account of the love story, incorporating all the material, and she wanted it serialized.

Sedgwick claimed that he was skeptical at first, so he asked the experts: a chemist and a historian. The first was able to confirm that the paper was the right age to be authentic; the second, Ida Tarbell, felt that it was indeed Lincoln's handwriting.

The lure of the scoop won the day, and a deal was done. Minor received the then huge sum of $6,500/£3,300 for a three-part serialization. Doubt was buried in all the bravado. "No reader will be more incredulous than the **Atlantic** when the collection was first brought to our notice," said Sedgwick. "Very gradually, as step by step we proceeded with our inquiry, conviction was forced upon us."

So what was in the letters? Certainly, they seemed to confirm the notion that Rutledge was ill educated and perhaps devoted too:

> my hart runs over with hapynes when I think yore name. I do not beleave I can find time to rite you a leter every day. stil I no as you say it wood surely improve my spelling and all that . . . I dreem of yore . . . words every nite and long for you by day. I mus git super now. all my hart is ever thine.

For his part, Lincoln was quite the besotted elegant swain:

> My Beloved Ann:
> . . . I am borrowing Jacks horse to ride over to see you this coming Saturday . . . I feel unusually lifted with hope of relieving your present worry at an early date . . . with you my beloved **all things are possible**. now James kindly promises to deliver into your dear little hands this letter. may the good Lord speed Saturday afternoon.
> affectionately A. Lincoln

The series was entitled "Lincoln the Lover" and so obsessed was the magazine with the story that it broke the rule made at its inception that it would carry no illustrations, and printed facsimiles of the letters.

Immediately the first part was released, it was denounced a fake. Ambitious young Lincoln expert Paul Angle scrutinized the material and found a catalog of problems with it. Among these was the fact that Kansas is mentioned twenty years before it actually existed, and Lincoln calls himself "Abe" – a shortening he hated. Ann and Matilda repeatedly get the name of their teacher wrong. Matilda gets the "last boat from Springfield" when Springfield is not on a river.

It took time for the editor to let go of his find. When he was on holiday, his staff hired a handwriting expert to look at the material. It was pronounced a forgery. They also obtained a sample of Minor's mother's writing which bore a stronger resemblance to it. But Sedgwick clung on to his belief. On this occasion, his philosophy that "An editor . . . should have an open mind, always steering closer to credulity than to skepticism," had not served him so well.

"The first concern of every forger is to secure old paper." This particular paper had "a suspicious resemblance to the flyleaves of old books." Paul Angle

THE FAKE HOWARD HUGHES BIOGRAPHY

How the paths of two playboys crossed and then they came to blows – and yet never met.

Howard Hughes was the kind of guy that men everywhere dreamed of being. Rich beyond imagining, a playboy, a Hollywood icon, even an aviator. But the mythologizing did not stop there. Toward the end of the 1960s, Hughes began to withdraw from the outside world, becoming a recluse.

This, of course, fed the fascination further. What had become of him? Had he had some kind of a breakdown? Was he even still alive? When in 1970 Hughes moved from living in a hotel in Las Vegas to living in one in the Bahamas, the media response was frenzied. Here, clearly, was a man with pulling power.

In fact, Hughes was not the man he had been. He had shut himself away and become obsessed with germ contamination. He had cut himself off from his first wife and his health had deteriorated further. He was vulnerable.

And it was this strange mix of mythology and vulnerability that attracted Clifford Michael Irving to Hughes's situation. Irving was an ambitious young writer with several literary successes behind him and something of a playboy himself. He had married a series of glamorous women, and – by his own description – was "living the good life on Ibiza".

Howard Hughes in aviator mode.

When Irving sent letters from "interview locations" around the world, he was actually visiting his mistresses.

The story goes that Irving was waiting in Mallorca to get across to Ibiza when he ran into an old friend, the writer Richard "Dick" Suskind. They got talking and the discussion led to the subject of Hughes. Irving claims he had a "wild idea" – he would tell his publisher that Hughes wanted him as his biographer. He would even forge letters from Hughes using the sample of his handwriting that had appeared in a recent **Newsweek** article. Suskind would conduct the research. Hughes would never come forward, Irving thought, he was too reclusive, ill – possibly dead.

Suskind agreed, and the publishers, McGraw-Hill, were taken in. Irving agreed with them that the biography would be based on interviews with the subject, and that Irving would be paid $100,000/£50,000 and Hughes $400,000/£200,000. Irving pushed the sum up to a total of $765,000/£382,500. Signatures were forged on contracts. A Swiss bank account was opened by Irving's new wife Edith to receive

Clifford Irving saw the faking of the Hughes biography as an exciting challenge rather than a criminal act.

the publisher's checks for Hughes. They were on their way.

And the signs were that they might pull it off. A forensic document analyst declared that the handwritten documents were genuine. They even got their hands on the manuscript for a book about one of Hughes's former managers and lifted information from that. More handwriting analysts confirmed that the documents were real. And then the great coup.

Howard Hughes himself rang the journalist Frank McCulloch, in a rage about the book. McCulloch, in two minds, read the manuscript. This put him in one mind. The person who phoned him was an impostor. This book was the genuine article.

Then on 7 January 1972, the beast in his lair really stirred. Hughes arranged a phone conference with seven journalists and said he had never met Irving. Hughes's lawyers filed suits against all concerned, and Swiss authorities investigated this bank account named "H. R. Hughes" – which Edith had opened under the name Helga R. Hughes. The Irvings denied all. This voice on the phone must have been an impostor.

Eventually they confessed, and the state charged Irving, his wife, and Suskind on 14 criminal counts, including possession of forged documents, intent to defraud, grand larceny for stealing from McGraw-Hill, perjury, and conspiracy. In the end they served two and a half years, two years, and five months respectively. The publishers got their money back.

OSSIAN – THE FAKE POET

In the 18th century, a Scottish schoolmaster, poet, and translator capitalized on the fashion for all things ancient by creating a Scottish Homer.

James MacPherson or Ossian the undiscovered poet?

In the 1700s, the fashion was for harking back to ancient times in order to establish fundamental, universal truths about the world. Collectors were plundering Egypt and Greece for ancient relics – and literature translated from ancient languages into English was all the rage.

In 1761, James MacPherson, a school master and poet from Inverness-shire, Scotland, announced that he had discovered an epic poem written by the 3rd-century poet Ossian. In December of that year, he published his translation of the poem: **Fingal, an Ancient Epic Poem in Six Books, together with Several Other Poems composed by Ossian, the Son of Final, translated from the Gaelic Language**.

"Ossian's" **Temora** and **The Works of Ossian** followed, in 1763 and 1765 respectively. Opinions differed as to the authenticity of the works. Several Irish historians smelt a rat immediately, because some of the Gaelic names were wrong, there were problems with the chronology, and MacPherson's story did not quite add up. Still, for a good number of experts, the fact that Ossian was a hoax did not detract from the fact that MacPherson was a gifted poet, and, for them, his Ossian "translations" demonstrated his talent.

Samuel Johnson was among those who thought MacPherson was a phony. In **A Journey to the Western Islands of Scotland**, published in 1775, he said that he thought MacPherson had found fragments of poetry and stories and woven them into his own romance. And indeed it had all the drama, and requisite big, sweeping themes, of heroism and love doomed from the outset.

"Alone I am, O Shilric!
alone in the winter-house.
With grief for thee I expired. Shilric,
I am pale in the tomb.
She fleets, she sails away;
as grey mist before the wind . . . "

As if to confound the mystery, there is a place in Co. Antrim, Northern Ireland, called Ossian's Grave.

MARGARET SELTZER

The young Californian whose autobiography turned out to be a work of pure fiction.

Margaret Seltzer, real name Margaret Jones, was born in 1975 into a well-off, white family in Sherman Oaks, California, and went to an expensive private school. As a teenager she would hang around outside a rough school in a neighboring area where she met some local African-American gang members and this "opened her mind". She later moved to Oregon where she enrolled on a creative writing course while continuing to work with local community groups to stop gang violence.

On her visits home, Seltzer continued to meet up with former friends and began taking notes. She took these to her creative-writing classes and referred to them as "writings about her family". Her professor was impressed. He called a writer friend who referred Seltzer to her own agent in New York. On the basis of 100 pages of these "autobiographical notes", the agent sold the work to a division of Penguin in the United States for "less than $100,000". An editor spent the next three years helping Seltzer to complete her "autobiography".

The book eventually appeared, amid huge publicity, as **Love and Consequences: A Memoir of Hope and Survival** under the pseudonym Margaret Jones. It described her experiences growing up as a half-white, half native-American foster child amongst the gangs of south central Los Angeles. Seltzer wrote about her foster mother, Big Mom, and her African-American foster brother, Terrell, who was in a gang called the "Bloods" and was shot dead outside the family home.

The huge publicity caught her out. Her own sister was amazed to see Margaret's photo in a **New York Times** interview and called the publishers to enquire further. Seltzer immediately admitted that the entire book was fabricated and the publisher had no choice but to recall all copies and refund all purchases. Her editor said that she was stunned and that Seltzer had been very naïve. Seltzer's sister, meanwhile, pointed out that the editor should have at least done some basic fact checking. Another case of believing what you want to believe.

Margaret Seltzer was finally found out by her own sister.

FAKE MANUSCRIPTS

A trend has developed for failed novelists and other disgruntled literary types to send famous works to publishers and agents as new submissions, in an attempt to deceive them.

Although not everybody knows it there is a recognized procedure when approaching a literary agent or a publisher with a manuscript or proposed book. Individual publishers' and agents' websites and/or entries specialist reference books are usually very specific about this, yet it doesn't stop the pile of unsuitable material gathering on their desks.

It will be some variation on the following: send us a – brief – covering letter, a synopsis, a chapter breakdown, and a sample chapter or chapters – usually the first one, two, or three. Often they clearly stipulate "no unsolicited manuscripts".

This doesn't stop people sending them, however. A staggering number of people work away at home on creating whole books. Often they are immensely long. And often these secret authors do not have a clear plan for them.

It is impossible for publishers and literary agents to do justice to every single manuscript sent to them by every person who disregards the guidelines.

If they pluck up the courage to send them off, the vast majority are destined for the slush pile, where manuscripts can wait forever to be read. If this seems harsh, remember that even the tiniest literary agency will receive an average of thirty unsolicited manuscripts a week. That's one and a half thousand a year. Then there's the agency's existing authors to look after too. Even those who do follow the rules are sending their precious creations to people pressed for time.

Yet in recent years, a favorite occupation of failed novelists has been to type out the opening chapters of classics – most recently by Jane Austen – and submit them as original material to literary agents and publishers. These fakers follow the rules, note. No sending of whole manuscripts for them.

One such was David Lassman, director of the Jane Austen Festival in Bath, UK. He submitted **Northanger Abbey**, **Pride and Prejudice**, and **Persuasion** to 18 publishers and agents. As an extra nudge for those in the know, he called **Pride and Prejudice** "First Impressions", the novel's original title, and signed them "Alison Laydee", a nod to Austen's pseudonym A Lady.

The punchline is that only one, an editorial assistant at UK publisher Jonathan Cape, recognized Austen's words and accused him of plagiarism. Apparently Penguin, who publishes the classics, said it "seems like a really original and interesting read" but didn't ask to see any more of it; and respected UK literary agency Christopher Little, which represents J K Rowling, said it was "not confident of placing this material with a publisher".

Opinions differ as to exactly what this proves. Presumably for Lassman, whose attempts to wow the agents and publishers with his own original fiction had failed, it demonstrated that that the publishing world didn't recognize real talent when it saw it.

To others, such as blogger Jean Hannah Edelstein, Lassman was not so big and clever. It was neither original as a stunt – the **Sunday Times** had just done it with books by V. S. Naipaul and Stanley Middleton – nor surprising in its outcome. Lassman should get real, was the message. Edelstein had worked in the publishing industry and sent standard rejections to cranks, and had she received this she would have assumed he was one. Others claimed in this day and age Austen would have been rejected because her novels would now be considered old-fashioned and lacking in originality.

The only certainty is what we all knew already: that the publishing industry is a tough and frustrating one, and that getting published is almost invariably a slog. Whether or not Lassman feels he has made his point, he remains an unpublished author. There is an irresistible tendency among unpublished novelists to rage against the publishing machine – a machine which, of course, merely consists of a set of individuals as brilliant and flawed as any other.

Engraving after Jane Austen.

THE FAKE SHAKESPEARE

This is the sad story of a neglected son who went to extraordinary lengths to gain the attention of his father – and was still crushed ultimately.

The reconstructed Globe theater, London, original home of Shakespeare's plays.

William Ireland was born in the mid-1770s. He was the son of the Earl of Sandwich's ex-mistress and Samuel Ireland, a cultivated man of many talents. William's father was an architect, a writer, and a painter. Unfortunately for William, he was not one of his father's enthusiasms. His father thought him dull and lazy.

What William's father was passionate about, though, was Shakespeare. He had an insatiable appetite for anything to do with his hero, and clearly believed that those close to him should benefit from his enthusiasm, too. Samuel would spend evenings in their home just off the Strand in London reading the works of Shakespeare to his family.

One of the consequences of Samuel's lack of interest in William was that he failed to notice that his son was also something of a poet. Not only that, but Samuel had told William the story of Thomas Rowley, who had forged poems of a 15th-century priest, and William had become fascinated by the story.

Eventually, starved of attention, William decided to see if he could pull off a forgery or two of his own. The reception of his initial attempts was encouraging. Samuel was taken in by his son's two tentative creations. The first, William said, he had found in a book that used to belong to Queen Elizabeth I. It appeared to be a dedicatory letter from the author. The second was a letter from Cromwell to a high-ranking official named John Bradshaw.

Spurred on by obtaining the approval of his father for the first time, William became more ambitious. Next he presented his father with what appeared to be a mortgage deed made between Michael Fraser and his wife, and John Heminge and William Shakespeare. Samuel Ireland was ecstatic.

William was flying. He had achieved longed-for recognition from his father. Of course he was not about to stop there. He then spun his father a yarn which potentially allowed the deception to go on indefinitely – with as many resulting "finds" as William dared to produce. He claimed to have met an eccentric, secretive aristocrat – "Mr. H" – in a coffee house. Mr. H, he said, had a chest full of documents that did not interest him.

He wrote more letters from Shakespeare which his father's eminent friends declared could only be the work of a genius. Understandably buoyed up by such endorsements, William decided it was time to try his hand at some poems and plays. Initially, the reception for these alleged "lost" plays of Shakespeare was encouraging again.

On 15 December 1795, Richard Brinsley Sheridan, the manager of the famous Drury Lane Theatre in London, agreed to show the first of these plays: **Vortigern and Rowena**. There were rumblings of doubt in London's theatreland about whether these newly unearthed documents were genuine, but the show went on.

William Shakespeare's signature – the real one!

For the first two acts the doubters appeared to be silenced. Then came the third act. One or two of the actors had been miscast, which did not help William's cause, making the clumsiness of some of the language all the more pronounced. The audience was soon in uproar. The public had rejected the play. It was the end of **Vortigern** and, William assumed, the end of him.

Samuel was so pleased with William's earliest "finds" that he gave his son the pick of the books in his library.

Still refusing to disclose the identity of Mr. H and unable to tell his father the truth, he told his sisters the story. They passed it on to Samuel who, despite their imploring him to look at the facts, would not believe that his son was capable of such masterful forgery. It was easier for him to believe the lie than to believe in his son. Samuel Ireland maintained that the works were those of William Shakespeare until his dying day in 1800.

LIFESTYLE

Here are the fake lives and fake deaths. Here, too, are those who make money from faking evidence of lives (fakealibi.co.uk, signature and autograph forgers, even crop circle makers). Some are just old-fashioned opportunists, capitalizing on some similarity between themselves and a well-known figure (Uday Hussein or Steven Spielberg's son).

Then there are those who feel that they have no choice but to change identity or fake – or even instigate – their own death. "Canoe man" John Darwin, and MP John Stonehouse, were both running away from financial difficulties. Stonehouse also wanted to marry his lover, while Darwin emerged from hiding for fear of his wife taking a lover. One compulsion overtook another for him. Donald Crowhurst, meanwhile, felt compelled to enter a grueling, non-stop, round-the-world yacht race that he was too inexperienced for, in an unseaworthy vessel, again due to his financial affairs. Tragically, the race only entangled him further. It is believed that he thought the only way out then was to take his own life.

So all human life is here, from the pathetic but intriguing (Anna Anderson, the fake Anastasia) to the lucrative but mundane (the makers of fake jeans, watches, perfumes, and handbags), with nipped and tucked gangsters (John Dillinger), pretend eminent archeologists (Shinichi Fujimura), and fake Viking cartographers in between.

Then there is that most fashionable, threatening, and escalating of crimes, identity theft, made easier in recent years by advances in technology and the guile and enterprise of those who have learnt how to exploit it to their own criminal ends. Beware – the hackers may well have your number.

THE FAKE RUSSIAN PRINCESS

How two impostors stirred up a Russian royal family and its acolytes – and kept the world guessing until the end.

Anastasia was the youngest of four daughters of the last Tsar Nicholas II of Russia. Born on 5 June 1901, she was close to her sickly baby brother Alexii, and not considered so beautiful and charming as her three older sisters.

In 1917, Lenin's Red Army arrested the family. For a year they were incarcerated at a country house in Siberia. Then Lenin had the entire family murdered. Eleven guards opened fire and kept shooting and stabbing with their bayonets until the family was wiped out.

Or perhaps not the entire family. In 1991, the skeletons of the Romanov family were dug up – and all but two were identified. Popular legend has it that the two missing skeletons were those of Anastasia and Alexii. Had the littlest been saved or escaped somehow? Why would the guards have let this happen? Where were they? Rumor abounded. Many claimed that Anastasia was alive and well, living as a Soviet woman.

People then began to come forward to claim they were the princess. Since World War II there have been around ten claims in all. The best known and most plausible of them were those of Eugenia Smith and Anna Anderson.

The Alexander Palace, residence of the Romanovs.

Smith, also known as Eugenia Drabek Smetisko, wrote **Autobiography of HIH Anastasia Nicholaevna of Russia**. The most compelling – although by no means conclusive – evidence that she was the missing princess came after she had submitted the manuscript to publishers, telling them she had been given it by Grand Duchess Anastasia.

The publishers made her take a lie detector test, which she failed. Then she changed her story, claiming that she was, in fact, the Grand Duchess Anastasia. She took a lie detector test again – and passed. It was good enough for the Manhattan party set, who welcomed her with open arms.

Two anthropologists who compared her features with a photo of Anastasia, a handwriting analyst, and a cousin and former playmate of Anastasia's were less easily persuaded. All of them remained unconvinced that she was the missing princess. More doubt was cast on her claim when she refused the offer of a DNA test in 1995. She died in 1997.

Anna Anderson came forward in 1921. Her story was so compelling that not one but two feature films were made about it: **Anastasia** (1956), starring Ingrid Bergman, and a remake in 1997.

Anderson was a troubled soul, whose story emerged after she had made a failed suicide attempt in Berlin in 1920, jumping off a bridge into the Landwehr Canal. Eventually, she said that she had been on her way to find her "aunt" Princess Irene, sister of Tsarina Alexandra. A passer-by took her to a mental hospital where doctors reported finding several bullet wounds and lacerations.

It was not until 1921, however, that she began to claim she was the princess. She had passed out during the shooting,

Those close to the real Anastasia noted that Anderson only spoke German. The Romanov princesses had all spoken Russian and English.

she said, and been shielded from further gunshot wounds by the body of one of her sisters. She had then been rescued by a soldier named Alexander Tchaikovsky and taken to Bucharest by him, where he fathered her child. Tchaikovsky had then been killed in a street brawl.

Many of Anastasia's friends, family, and close associates visited Anderson in order to decide once and for all whether she was the real thing. None could confirm for sure that she was the princess and several – including her supposed grandmother – denied it. Perhaps those who gave her more support did so out of compassion. She cut a pretty pathetic figure.

It had long been supposed by the skeptics that she was actually Francizka Schankovska, a Pomeranian factory worker. After her death, a DNA test showed that she was not a royal Romanov but that there was, indeed, a match with the Schankovski family.

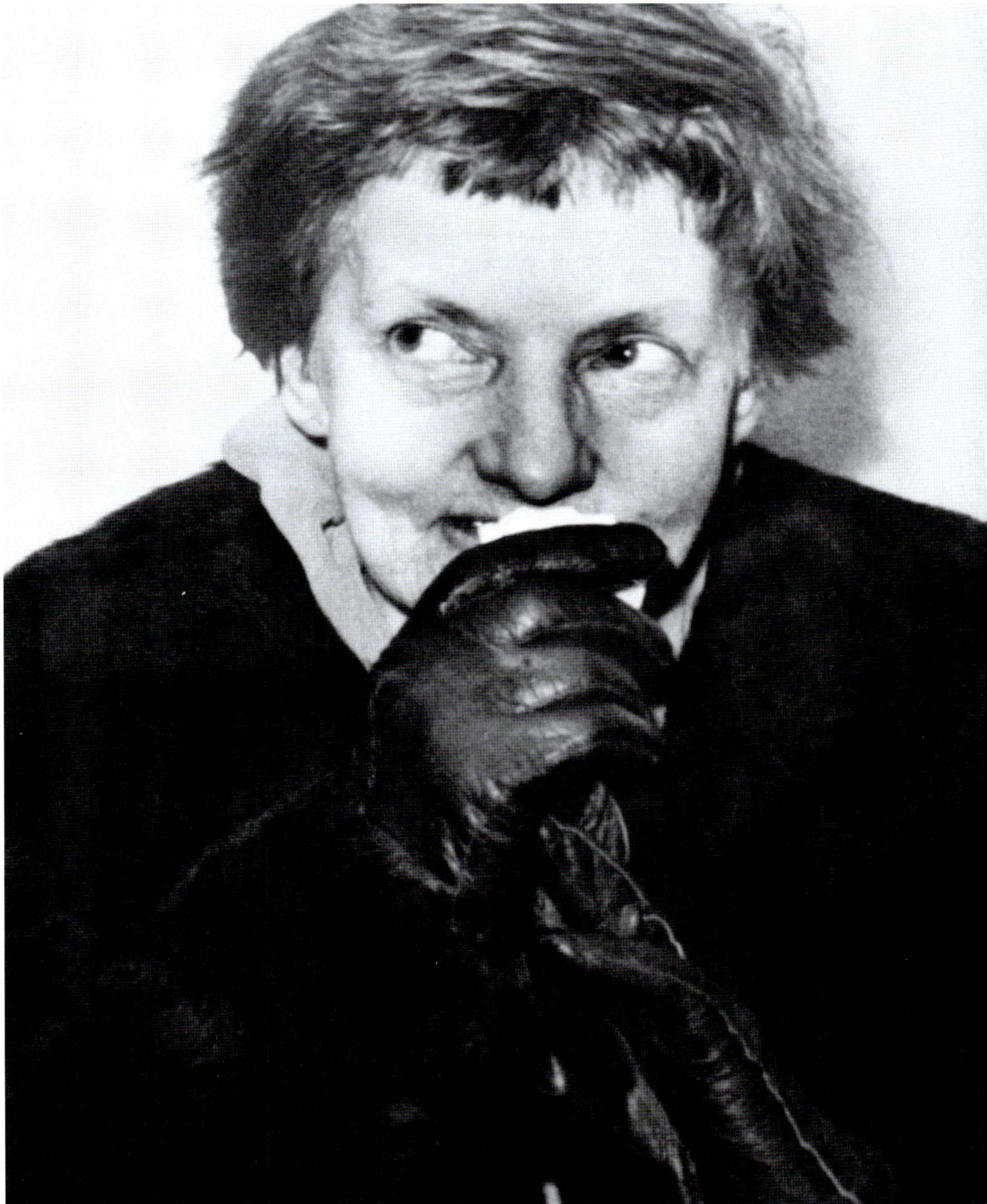

Anna Anderson was the most convincing of those who claimed to be Anastasia.

MARY BAKER

Nineteenth-century exotic princess is revealed to be a local farm girl in disguise, who takes gullible aristocrats for a ride.

On 3 April 1817, a humble cobbler in Gloucestershire, UK, came across a half-crazed woman in exotic clothing, wandering the streets and unable to understand English. The cobbler's wife took the poor soul to the local "Overseer of the Poor" who handed her to the local magistrate, Samuel Worrall.

The Worralls sent her to an inn where the only food she recognized was a pineapple. She ate it and went to sleep on the floor.

Concerned, Mrs Worrall took the woman back to the Worrall mansion where she attempted to communicate. All she discovered was that the woman was called Caraboo. Despairing, Mrs Worrall accompanied Caraboo to her husband's office in Bristol, a major international port.

All manner of foreigners came here but none could identify Caraboo's mother tongue. Eventually, a Portuguese sailor called Manuel Eynesso declared that this was not just a lady but the Princess Caraboo from Javasu in the Indian Ocean. She had been captured by pirates, he said, who held her enslaved until she jumped overboard in the Bristol Channel and swam for her life.

The Worralls were captivated and, for nearly three months, Caraboo lived with them and did all the things that wild natives do – swam naked in the river; prayed to a god called Allah Tallah; and had her illustration drawn for the **Bristol Journal**.

And so she was undone. A certain Mrs Neale bought the paper and informed the Worralls that this was no Princess but Mary Baker, the daughter of a cobbler from Devon. Her language was invented and her costume a sham. The English newspapers were delighted and exposed, not Baker, but the Worralls for being such fools.

Shamed, the Worralls sent Baker to Philadelphia. Having met Napoleon on St Helena, she returned to Europe in 1821 and was eventually buried in an unmarked Bristol grave in 1865. Her life was eventually commemorated in a successful 1994 film starring Phoebe Cates as the fantastic liar.

A scene from the film Princess Caraboo, starring Phoebe Cates.

SPIELBERG'S NEPHEW

Iranian refugee poses as the 14-year-old nephew of a famous film director and his fellow teenagers are only too happy to ride in his sports car.

Much of Anoushirvan D. Fakhran's early life remains shrouded in mystery, but we know that he was born somewhere in Iran around 1973. He later traveled to the USA and, once there, was amazed to discover that he bore a physical resemblance to one of his adopted country's most famous film directors. Fired up by this coincidence, he changed his name to Jonathan Taylor Spielberg and set off to forge a new life for himself. In 1998, armed with a fake reference from "the Beverley Hills School for Actors", he marched into the Paul VI Roman Catholic High School in Fairfax, Virginia, and enrolled on the school's register. He soon began attending one or two classes every week, claiming to be just 14, though he was, by this stage, roughly 25 years of age.

Fakhran impressed his friends with his fast cars and supposed jet-set lifestyle.

With his constant allusions to his Hollywood chums, he was the talk of the small-town school. He told his fellow pupils that his attendance was poor because 'his famous uncle was making a film' and, though he failed to hand in any coursework, he did spend lots of money on his new friends and he drove a very impressive BMW with personalized license plates marked "SPLBERG". The principal, it is reported, allowed him to park this in his own private space. Admittedly he did look a little old but he wore the school uniform as required and no one questioned his presence.

It was only after several months, when staff became concerned at his poor attendance, that they finally contacted Steven Spielberg to warn him about his nephew's educational "issues". They were informed that the director had no such relative.

On being arrested, Spielberg Jnr. said that he did it: "just for fun, to get the experience I never had". He received an 11-month suspended jail sentence and an order to attend mental health counseling.

WEARSIDE JACK – THE HOMICIDE HOAXER

It takes a sick mind to play jokes on the police when they are hunting a mass murderer – especially when it leaves the killer free to strike again, and again.

For five years a serial killer terrorized the town of Bradford, in West Yorkshire, England. A spate of knife attacks from 1975 to 1980 left 13 women dead – most, but not all, were prostitutes. Police issued warnings to women to take care and never go out alone. Such was the brutality of the attacks the murderer was dubbed the "Yorkshire Ripper".

The killer was so sure he would never be caught that for a full year, from March 1978 to June 1979, he taunted West Yorkshire police with letters and a cassette tape, all posted from Sunderland. His confident boast – "You are no nearer catching me now than four years ago when I first started" – delivered in a Wearside accent, sent a chill down the spine.

With such a distinctive voice surely the man would be easy to find among the people of West Yorkshire? Six years after the attacks started, the Yorkshire Ripper was caught. But he was not from Wearside, the Sunderland region of north-east England, but Yorkshire. His name was Peter Sutcliffe and in 1981 he received 20 life sentences for 13 murders and seven attempted murders. He was a truck driver –

from Bradford. So who was Wearside Jack? It seemed that the letters and tape were part of a macabre practical joke.

It would be nearly 25 years before the police had the answer. For all that time detectives had hung on to the tape, the letters and, most importantly, the envelopes they came in. They hoped the evidence would lead them to the man responsible for wasting their time and resources and delaying the hunt for the real Yorkshire Ripper.

In the 1970s, forensic science could do little to help. But in the 1990s came DNA fingerprinting and a breakthrough. The hoaxer's DNA was in the saliva he left as he sealed the envelopes. In 2005 the police found a match and arrested John Humble. The following year, the 50-year-old chronic alcoholic from Sunderland received an eight-year jail sentence for perverting the course of justice.

Humble, who was 22 at the time of the offenses, was fascinated by the original "Jack the Ripper" who had brought terror to the streets of Victorian London a century before. It was the similarity in the methods

Police had come close to finding "Wearside Jack". During house-to-house inquiries they spoke to John Humble's neighbors, but not the man himself.

The real Yorkshire Ripper, Peter Sutcliffe, leaving court in 1983.

of the two killers that had earned Peter Sutcliffe the name "Yorkshire Ripper".

Humble was never able to explain why he had done it. Yet the hoax was meticulously planned and carried out. Two letters and the tape were sent to Assistant Chief Constable George Oldfield of West Yorkshire Police, who was leading the hunt for the killer. The other letter was sent to the **Daily Mirror** newspaper.

Humble's letters seemed to fit the profile of a demented psychopath perfectly, and voice experts were able to pinpoint the accent they heard on the tape to the Castletown district of Sunderland.

In 2003 police decided to end the investigation into Wearside Jack. Yet one final trawl through the DNA database in 2005 scored a hit. Humble had been arrested three years before for a minor offense. A sample of his DNA was taken and placed on file. It was his undoing. Humble was convicted and later lost an appeal against his sentence.

Police would receive heavy criticism for putting so much faith in the authenticity of the letters, especially the tape. They had been so sure that the man they were looking for came from Wearside that other suspects interviewed over the crimes – including Peter Sutcliffe himself – were released purely on the grounds that they had the wrong accent. This was a fatal mistake, for it left Sutcliffe free to kill again, several more times.

JOHN DILLINGER – GANGSTER

Notorious American conman avoids the Great Depression by turning to crime – with the aid of plastic surgery.

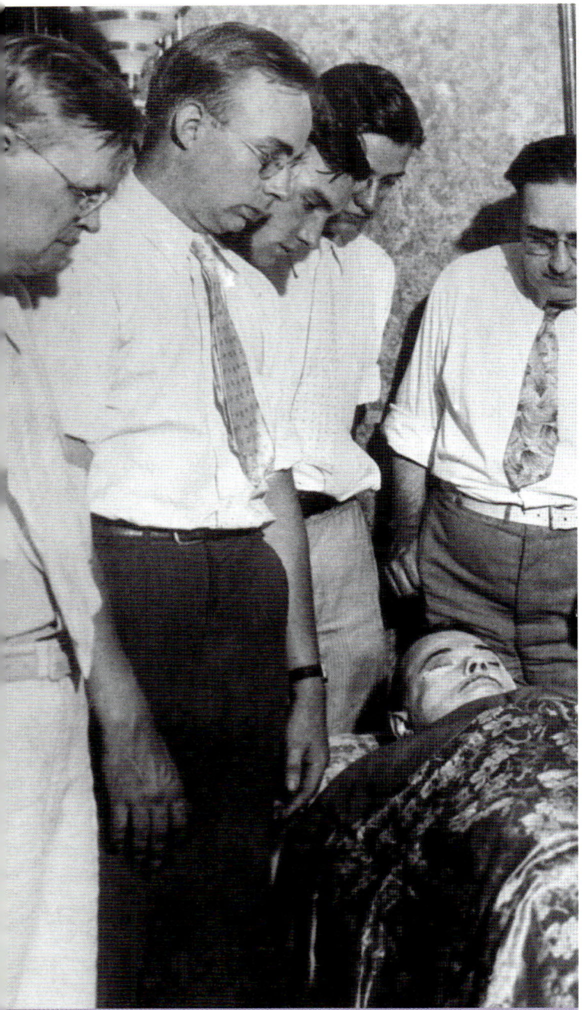

John Dillinger lying in state, 1934.

John Dillinger was born on 22 June 1903, in Indiana. He enlisted in the US Navy but deserted and returned to Indiana where he got a job and married a local girl. The mundane nature of this life did not suit him.

He decided to turn to crime, making friends with other, more experienced, criminals. On one occasion, having just been released from prison, he went back to help an entire gang of his fellow criminals escape. These men became known as the "Dillinger Gang".

They set up a series of daring bank raids. In one, Dillinger pretended to be a sales representative for a bank alarm manufacturer. He marched into a bank and demanded to examine its security system. The bank manager simply let him get on with it. On another occasion, he pretended to be the director of a feature film that happened to be set in a bank. A crowd of gawping onlookers stood and watched the "filming" while Dillinger and his pals made off with the entire contents of the safe. In March 1934, he effected a legendary escape from the top-security prison Crown Point by hand-carving a replica gun out of a bar of soap. Dillinger used this to threaten the guards, driving away in the local sheriff's own car. The Department of Justice offered a $20,000/£10,000 reward for his capture. That April, the "Dillinger Gang" settled in at a lodge hideout in Wisconsin where the owner's wife wrote to the FBI via a US Attorney's office in Chicago. The FBI botched the subsequent raid. The entire gang escaped.

It was then widely reported that Dillinger had attempted to elude police by undergoing plastic surgery to change his appearance, and had run away to South America to retire. Sources close to Dillinger said that he had the shape of his chin modified and his cheekbones slightly altered as well as having his hair dyed and his hairstyle changed. This seemed to work temporarily.

Three months later, Dillinger was hiding in Chicago, working in an office with an assumed identity and an altered appearance. In July, however, he was ambushed and shot dead outside the Biograph cinema, having just finished watching a gangster film.

Masses of people gathered at the morgue to catch a glimpse of one of America's "Most Wanted". With his changed appearance, some even said that the real Dillinger had escaped and was living happily in Argentina. Dental records proved otherwise. To this day, his gravestone is vandalized by people who want a piece of John Dillinger.

THE BODY DOUBLE OF SADDAM'S SON

Former schoolfriend of the son of Saddam Hussein is picked to be his double and spends his life fending off assassination attempts intended for another.

In the mid-70s Latif Yahia was at secondary school with Saddam Hussein's eldest son, Uday, for around three-and-a-half years. Both were in their early teens. Though many of their contemporaries commented that they looked somewhat alike, they were only casually acquainted – particularly since it was not a good idea to attempt to hang out with Uday. Uday would often bring his girlfriend into school with him and, on one occasion, Latif noticed that a teacher reprimanded Uday for this inappropriate behavior. That teacher never appeared in class again. Everyone learnt pretty rapidly not to cross paths with Uday.

Eventually Latif ended up at the same university as Uday, though in a different faculty. During his military service at the time of the Iraq-Iran war, which lasted for most of the 1980s, Yahia received a letter requesting him to appear at Baghdad Palace within 48 hours. He was driven straight to the Palace where he was introduced to Uday and told that, since their voice and eyes were relatively similar, he was now being awarded the dubious privilege of being Uday Hussein's body double. Yahia initially rejected the offer, but was soon sent to think over his decision in a tiny prison cell. Having carefully reconsidered, he allegedly underwent extensive plastic surgery on his teeth and his chin to enhance his natural physical similarities to Uday. He also needed to wear platform shoes as he was considerably shorter than Saddam's son.

Over the next few years, Yahia survived 11 assassination attempts but, in December 1991, finally managed to flee his native country. He lived in hiding for the next few years until the US and UK invaded Iraq in 2003 and he could safely emerge in public. He recounted his experiences in his book **The Black Hole**.

Latif Yahia – or is it Uday Hussein?

STEVEN JAY RUSSELL

Highly articulate American confidence trickster passes himself off as company manager, medical doctor, and his own parole judge – and almost always gets away with it.

Born in 1957, as Steven Jay Basham, Russell was adopted as a baby by a family in Virginia Beach. He had a perfectly suburban upbringing and later became a happily married family man and local police officer.

Using the professional resources available to someone employed in the police force, he began searching for his birth mother and colleagues reported that he soon became very proficient with the national identity database. He retired from the force and convinced a local businessman that he had an advanced degree in food services, getting a well-paid job in his company. Russell was eventually dismissed, not only because his qualifications were questioned but because it was revealed that he had been charged with lewd homosexual conduct. This setback did not deter him and he was subsequently able to get jobs at two other respectable companies, convincing them, too, that he was a qualified food services expert by using expertly faked identity cards and degree certificates.

His behavior then became considerably more unpredictable as he began to assume several identities over the next few years, using at least 14 different aliases. He posed, variously, as a doctor, a handyman, and a police officer in order to gain access to people's homes and goods. Russell was extremely good at his new profession. He was caught a number of times but only received brief sentences. On each occasion he managed to escape and, on each occasion, reputedly chose to escape on Friday the 13th.

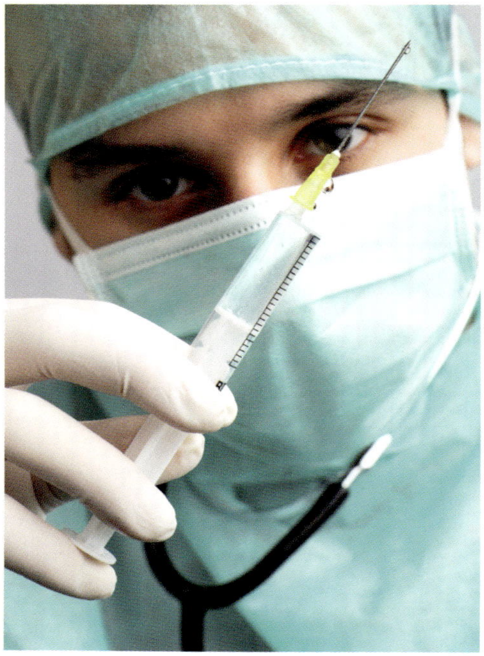

In May 1993, Russell emerged from a Texan jail and, under false pretenses, got a new job as the Chief Financial Officer of a Medical Management company where he immediately set about the serious business of defrauding the company of thousands of dollars. Imprisoned yet again, he found some kind of consistency in his life by meeting a boyfriend in prison with whom he became heavily involved.

Three years later, however, Russell was back inside. Never one to give up and wanting to get back to his partner, Russell impersonated a bail judge and ordered his own bond to be decreased from $900,000/£450,000 to $45,000/£22,500, which he easily met. On handing over this amount of money, Russell was subsequently released. It was only once he had left the prison premises that his guards realized that Russell had been impersonating the judge himself the entire time. He was re-arrested in Florida just 10 days later. Back inside, he began attending prison art classes. No one noticed that during the classes he was removing all the green pens. He used these to dye his uniform green and then walked out of the prison posing as a doctor.

Steven Jay Russell made a mockery of the legal system and even managed to impersonate a judge.

Five years later, he posed as a millionaire and attempted to defraud a bank into giving him a huge loan. On being arrested, he feigned a heart attack and was taken to hospital. Here he managed to acquire a phone and call his own guards pretending to be an FBI agent, instructing the guards to release their prisoner. They immediately did so though he was later recaptured.

Back in prison, Russell began visiting the library to read up on the symptoms of AIDS. He used laxatives to make it look as if he was suffering from the disease and then faked a medical certificate to that effect. On being released into medical care, Russell switched identities and posed as the doctor in charge of the case, immediately telling the authorities that his patient had died.

Russell was eventually re-arrested later that year and was sent back to his Texan jail where he is now serving a 144-year prison sentence.

JOHN STONEHOUSE – DEAD MAN WALKING

The extraordinary story of the UK Labour MP who faked his own drowning in Miami before setting off to Australia to marry his mistress.

The John Stonehouse affair of the mid-seventies came as a shock to the British public and political establishment alike. First, there was his "death" – by drowning, it was assumed – when he disappeared on 20 November 1974 while swimming off Miami Beach. Only a pile of his clothes was left. Most presumed had had committed suicide. He was just 49 years old. Despite there being no body, obituaries were written.

The John Stonehouse affair turned into a media frenzy.

They were nowhere near complete.

Only two months later, Stonehouse was found in the seaside resort of St Kilda, Australia, living under a false name – Joseph Markham – the name of the dead husband of one of his constituents, although his false passport bore the name J. D. Norman and he gave police the name Donald Clive Mildoon. Bizarrely, Melbourne police had placed the newcomer under surveillance because they thought he might be Lord Lucan, an even more famous Englishman who had disappeared under mysterious and suspicious circumstances just a few months earlier.

It emerged that Stonehouse had arrived in Australia on 27 November 1974, a week after his disappearance, before going away again and traveling between Singapore, Denmark, and Lebanon. He returned to Australia on 10 December. Despite the fact that he still had a wife in England, Barbara, his plan had been to marry his former secretary and mistress Sheila Buckley, a 28-year-old divorcee.

But it didn't end there. Stonehouse was also fleeing the British Department of Trade and Industry, who were investigating his business affairs. It emerged that Stonehouse

The resort of St Kilda, Australia, one of John Stonehouse's hideaways.

had been involved in a string of unsuccessful fraudulent businesses before he had fled the UK on what appeared to be a business trip to Miami. There was a delay. Australia was reluctant to deport a British MP.

Then Stonehouse was sent to England where, in August 1976, he was tried, conducting his own defense. He was convicted of no fewer than eighteen counts of theft, fraud, and deception involving more than $380,000/£190,000. The trial took 68 days. Stonehouse received a sentence of seven years. Incredibly, the Labour party did not expel him from their ranks, but he resigned just before his trial anyway, and joined the English National Party. After he left prison, he joined the Social Democratic Party.

Having been on remand in Brixton Prison, Stonehouse served his time at Wormwood Scrubs Prison, where he became notorious for complaining that the workshop where he worked played pop music on the radio. The mistress, Sheila Buckley, had also been involved in the fraudulent activity. She was tried and convicted – and sentenced to two years.

In 1979, several years early, he was released from prison after having suffered three heart attacks while incarcerated. He had open-heart surgery and, once recovered, began several years of work as a fundraiser for London charity Community Links.

Ultimately, Stonehouse was running away from himself, and the pressures of the political spotlight.

He divorced his first wife and eventually married Sheila in 1981. He already had three children with his first wife and one with his second. Having written three thrillers, he died of a heart attack in April 1988.

In 2005, a psychiatric report previously kept secret by Harold Wilson's government was released. It was the basis of a five-hour interview with Stonehouse following his arrest in Australia, and in it he claimed that he became A. J. Markham as a "safety valve" when the stress and disappointment of being John Stonehouse became too much. We know that Stonehouse had spent months rehearsing the role before his "disappearance". The psychiatrist was of the opinion that he took the action he did because he wanted to enjoy the feeling of being an honest man.

JOHN DARWIN – CANOE MAN

The story of a man who faked his death by canoe and then lived in hiding while his wife spent the life insurance.

At the end of 2007, the world was stunned by one of those news stories that unfolded in front of its eyes and seemed to get better and better, and more and more unbelievable, with every passing day.

So far as anyone knew, John Darwin – a 52-year-old teacher and former prison officer – had been drowned in 2002 in a canoeing accident off the Cleveland coast, north-east England, half a mile from his home.

Then he walked into the police station on Savile Row, central London, looking tanned, refreshed, and healthy. "The guy can't remember anything about what's happened or why he's come forward," said Inspector Helen Eustace, of Cleveland Police. "He has no memory at all. He has obviously been somewhere for the last five years and a lot of questions need answering."

Indeed, some had felt questions needed answering five years earlier, when his wrecked red canoe had washed up on the beach without him. Rescuers had expressed puzzlement that someone could get into difficulties in such calm weather conditions. One member of the emergency services described the sea as "smooth as a millpond".

John Darwin.

"To be honest, I don't believe he ever got wet," said Darwin's aunt Margaret, 80, before the Panama episode emerged.

Perhaps more surprisingly, those close to him felt there had been something slightly suspicious going on, too. In fact, Darwin's own father, 90-year-old Ronald, remarked to a newspaper, "I always said to the police that there might be more to this than it appeared at first. When his canoe was found but he wasn't, it just didn't seem right."

Still, there were emotional reunions to be had before questions were answered and his poor sons, Anthony (29) and Mark (31), were shocked but elated. Then, just two days later, the dramatic turnaround. When confronted with a recent picture of herself with her husband in Panama, Anthony and Mark's mother had to admit the whole thing had been a ruse. Understandably, the sons were baffled and upset. They described themselves as having been through a "rollercoaster of emotion".

"My sons are never going to forgive me," observed their mother, who had just moved to Panama in a hurry, having sold the family home. "They are going to hate me."

This from the woman who had talked five years earlier about wanting to see a body, so she could move on. The same woman who was described by a neighbor as the "dominant partner" now had to explain away the fact that she'd spent her husband's life insurance – or at least half of the $100,000/£50,000. The other half was withheld from her because there was no body. It later emerged that a secret hideaway had been built into their house, which Darwin had lived in for quite some time.

Darwin was charged with making an untrue statement in order to obtain a passport and obtaining $50,000/ £25,000 from an insurance company by deception. His wife was accused of dishonesty in obtaining mortgage funds of $274,000/£137,000 and $50,000/ £25,000 in life insurance. She was described by Hartlepool police as being very co-operative, in what they called a "surreal investigation".

Nobody is quite sure why the couple created the scam, although it is thought that the financial difficulties that Darwin was experiencing with his home rental business might have been a factor. What Darwin's fellow prisoners wanted to know was why he gave himself up when he did. Presumably his claim to solicitor John Nixon that he was worried about his wife and was missing her failed to convince them.

And it seems they were right. Darwin allegedly told the police that he was worried she was having an affair and was going to leave him penniless.

Sunset over sailboats in Panama City harbor – Darwin had been hiding in the Central American country for five years.

HACKERS AND IDENTITY THEFT

Impersonation frauds have a long history, but the online age means they are now more dangerous to the victim and more profitable for the criminal.

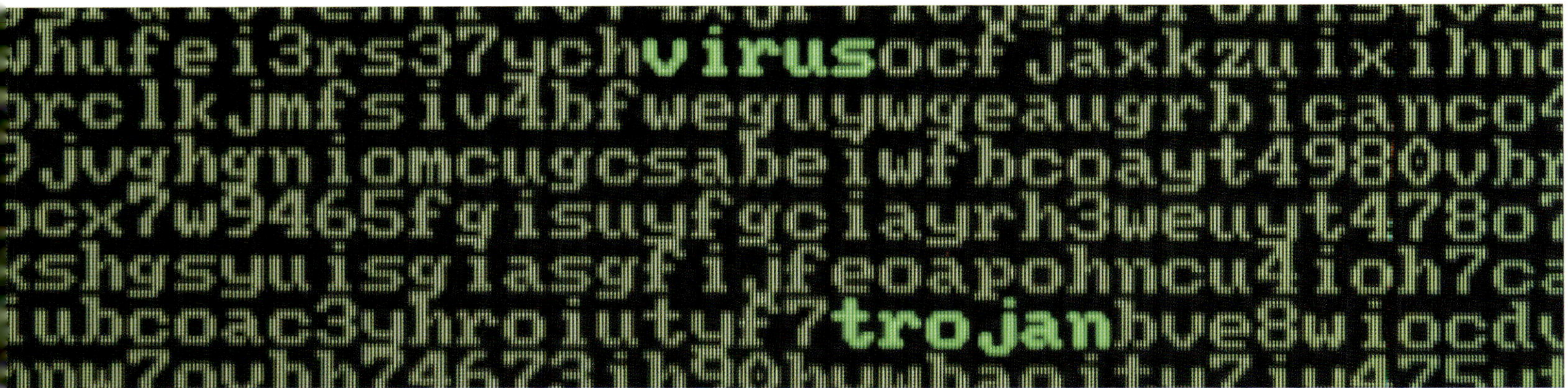

Hackers are expert in the art of infecting computer systems on a worldwide scale.

Now dubbed identity theft, the practice of pretending to be somebody else to gain money, goods, or services fraudulently has been made a lot easier by the web and the internet. Internet banking, internet shopping, and internet services are becoming increasingly common. To make an illegal profit, the hacker needs to acquire only that information which is necessary to gain access to a person's online accounts.

Some crooks gain this information by "phishing" or by distributing hoax surveys that ask for the data, but there are more sophisticated methods. Keyloggers, for instance, are malicious programs that are sent to infect computers. They record what keys are pushed. If the address of a bank's website is entered, the program then records the next string of keys pushed – these are most likely to be passwords – and transmits them over the web to the criminal's computer.

Since 2003 there has been a rise in "botnets". These are programs that allow criminals to take over a computer and use it to launch frauds and deceptions without the computer's owner being aware of the fact. The police and security organizations trying to track the fraud will trace it to the "bot" or "zombie", but not to the actual criminal. In 2007 it was estimated that there were about 1 million "bot" infected computers worldwide, though not all of them were active.

Celebrities are often at more risk than more humble folk. They are not only richer, and so worth more as victims, but some of their personal details are in the public domain. In 2001 Abraham Abdallah was arrested and charged with identity theft involving figures such as Steven Spielberg, George Soros, Ross Perot, and Oracle boss Larry Ellison. He was caught only when success made him greedy and he tried to transfer $10,000,000/£5,000,000 from the account of businessman Thomas Siebel.

FAKEALIBI.CO.UK

A service, used in the main by adulterers, which, as the name suggests, offers pretend alibis to those who want to be where they shouldn't.

The existence of Fakealibi.co.uk confirms what a strange and sometimes unsavory world we live in. Since 2004, for a fee, the company has been essentially backing up the lies of those who want to remove any danger of their nearest and dearest finding out the truth about them.

Fakealibi.co.uk may send an invitation to a law conference to a solicitor who wants to spend time with his mistress. They may fax hotel booking confirmation to someone who wants to mislead their spouse about a trip abroad. In each case there will be a phone number on the document. If the partner's intuition leads them to call the number, the person who answers will pretend to be from the fake destination.

It claims to have over 21,000 happy customers. A job such as faxing hotel details and providing a phone number just in case will cost about $700/£350. They also give fake job references.

The company appears to be relaxed about what it does. It uses the accessory's perennial excuse: these people are already having affairs. It draws on those cases of people who are in unhappy arranged marriages, or in long-term partnerships where the other half of the couple is ill.

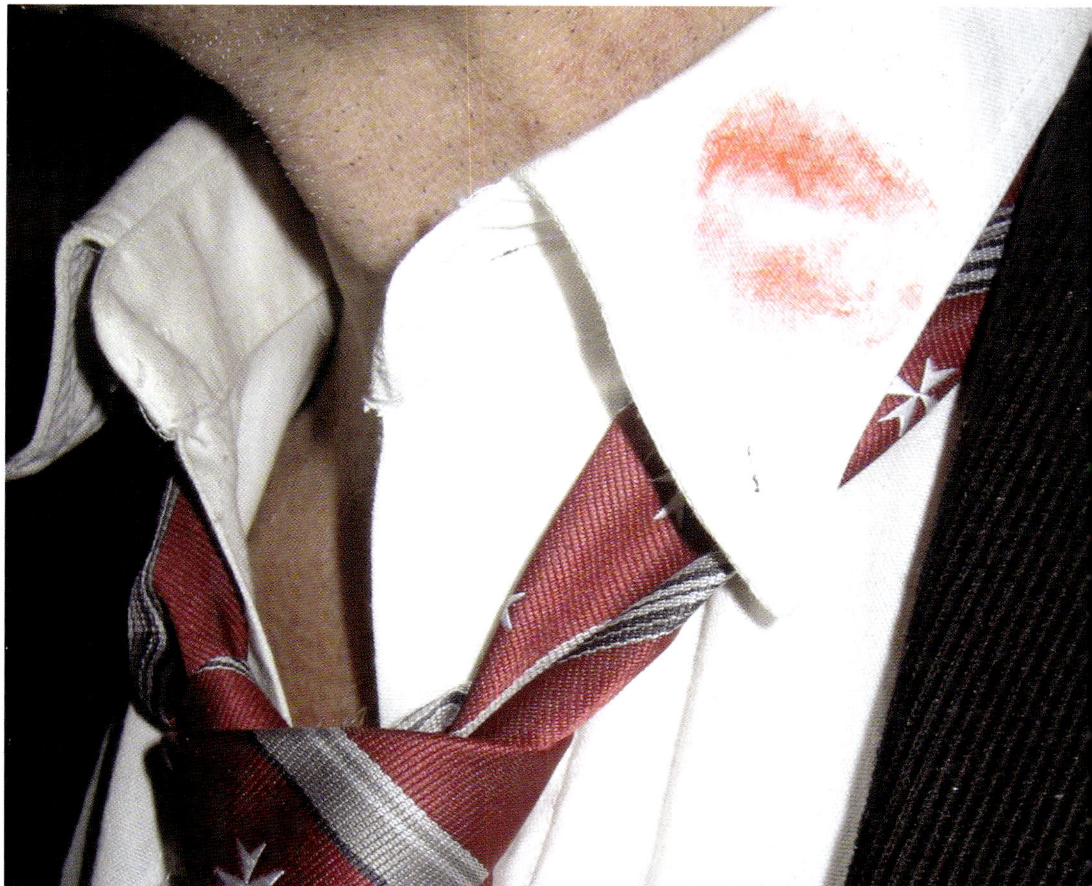

Where do you want to be, and when? Fakealibi.co.uk can help you.

Solicitors in general take a dim view of the service. Whatever their personal feelings, their immediate concern is that the company could end up facilitating a crime, however inadvertently.

FAKE PASSPORTS

Easy to fake and even easier to obtain, a counterfeit EU or US passport becomes a quick way to a home, social benefits, and even sudden wealth for forger and recipient – unless you get caught.

The market for passports is worth $2.5 billion/£1.25 billion a year. Not surprisingly, therefore, the forged passport has a long and colorful history.

In the UK, the Home Office's official policy is that any stolen passport must be reported to Interpol immediately. New-style passports are designed to be much more difficult to copy since they now have holographic images securely stored inside them in chips. There are still, however, more than 100 million people entering and exiting the United Kingdom every year and it would be almost impossible, therefore, for immigration officers to spot every single fake passport.

New biometric passports have a tiny black security chip embedded in them.

Potential customers can access counterfeit documents for little above $500/£250 through newspaper advertisements, internet sites, or advertising cards stuck up on shop windows. Stolen passports, on the other hand, are generally removed from their owners in Eastern Europe and then merely have a new photograph added. This type of fake would never pass the test of a holographic border scanner but would be perfectly effective for a few months while the recipient fills in a job application, applies for a new home, and opens a bank account.

In 2003, two Algerians called Baghdad Meziane and Brahim Benmerzouga became the first members of al-Qaeda to be jailed in the UK. It was widely reported at the time that both these men had entered the country on forged passports and the police finally woke up to the widespread nature of the industry. After some initial investigations, daily news reports of forged passports began to emerge, with most experts coming to the conclusion that Thailand was, at that time, the export center of the global fake passport industry. The Thai government, it appeared, had not appreciated the perils of such industry until after various terrorists had been arrested.

In 2005, with the Thai police on a higher alert, a UK citizen was arrested at Bangkok airport with 452 fake blank passports in his luggage. He was about to board a plane to the UK. Mahieddine Daikh, who had only actually been a naturalized British citizen for two years himself, was arrested in a midnight sting while en route from Koh Samui to Amsterdam. He claimed that he had bought the passports from an unnamed Pakistani man in Koh Samui for about $6,000/£3,000 but that he had been told he would receive about $30,000/£15,000 when he handed them over to his contact in London. A British Embassy official who examined the passports said that he was incredibly impressed with their quality. If truth be told, he could not immediately say which, if any, were fakes.

In the USA, meanwhile, Jocelyn Kirsch and Ed Anderton had begun living the high life, having stolen the passports and identity documents of not one, but nearly all, of their friends, relatives and acquaintances. They met in September 2006 and began broadcasting their flamboyant relationship almost as soon as they got together. Just three months later, Jocelyn, a student, and Ed, unemployed, declared that Jocelyn's rich dad had given them some money, so they packed their Gucci matching luggage and set off on a European shopping holiday. On their return, they rented an ultra-modern apartment, which friends reported was strewn with designer clothes and furniture. In her International Relations class, Jocelyn showed so much potential that her professor nominated her onto a University panel about globalization where she sat next to the special guest, Prince Charles. She introduced herself as "an immigrant from Lithuania" and kept everyone entertained for hours. Unemployed Ed, meanwhile, fetched her packed lunches and apparently even took an economics exam on her behalf.

Ed and Jocelyn's former friends managed to cash in on the scandal by hiring agents and selling their memories, and photos, of the notorious couple.

Fatally for the couple, however, he also accompanied the love of his life on a 2007 trip to have luxury hair extensions put into her hair. On leaving the well-known salon, Jocelyn wrote two relatively small cheques to pay for the seven-hour appointment. These both turned out to be forged and the furious hairdresser rang the mobile number that the pair had left to demand immediate payment. Apparently believing themselves untouchable, the couple sent a threatening text message. The hairdresser immediately reported the matter to the local police.

When the police broke into the couple's flat they were astonished to discover an extensive identity-theft operation,

complete with industrial ID counterfeit machine, computer spyware, and lock-picking tools. They had, apparently, used the spying software to log into the computers of every apartment in their luxury block. They had then used professional lock-picking equipment to break into their neighbors' apartments and steal necessary papers to set up false passports with which they subsequently set up credit cards, bank accounts, and duplicate driver's licenses. They had used these in turn to raise, and spend, about $100,000/ £50,000 in less than a year.

FAKE AUTOGRAPHS

The market for forged autographs has never been larger – or the profits greater for the con artists who create them.

Since the days of silent movies, autographs have had their problems. The chances were that if you were lucky enough to get hold of a film star's autograph it was the genuine article, but even then he or she might have used a stamp for speed, which is not quite the same thing – whether it was handled by the star or not.

Then cinema exploded in terms of its popularity, and the autograph hunter had to be more wary. In an attempt to keep up with demand, assistants were hired by stars

Crowds rush to get hold of a real Kennedy signature – in this case Robert F. Kennedy.

such as Walt Disney, sometimes for the sole purpose of signing autographs. This was the world of appearance – the game was to keep the publicity machine moving. Never mind if a little deception was involved along the way.

Megastars from other spheres adopted the same approach. It was said that a person in the know could tell whether JFK's autograph was signed by secretary one, secretary two, or secretary three. In the swinging sixties, Beatles and Rolling Stones fans would have to hand their autograph books in at the stage door, and after a short wait, they would be handed them back, complete with signatures. Of course, these were often scribbled down by assistants. These autographs pose particular problems for autograph collectors today.

Now, decades on, autographs form a multi-million dollar global industry – and spotting the difference between an expert fake and the hastily scribbled, upside-down real thing is extremely difficult. So, if you weren't witness to its signing, how can you tell whether your autograph is real or not?

A certificate of authentification alone is not enough. Look out for authentification from a recognized body such as the Universal Autograph Collectors' Club registered dealer program or the Autograph Fair Trade Association Limited.

If it is signed on paper or card, feel the surface of the paper. The autograph should be raised. A perfectly flat autograph is likely to be one of several copies. Autographs written on a shirt or cap are not so easily authenticated in this way, because the ink tends to soak into the material.

If it is a team shirt, look for the size and style of signatures. A genuine collection of autographs will be different sizes and different ways up, and the spacing between names will be uneven.

The number of autographs available is also something of a giveaway. An autograph dealer is unlikely to have several David Beckham signatures available at once – if they're genuine. Celebrities often try to sign only one autograph at a time or personalize the message, in an attempt to avoid people profiting from them.

Look out, too, for signs of a stamp being used. If it has, a microscope will reveal more ink at the side of the letters than in the middle, these are known as "tramlines". Under a microscope, a real signature will be uneven, creating "bridges" and "tunnels" in the ink. If a machine has made it, the ink will be smoother.

For an Elvis autograph, expect to pay upwards of $500/£1,000 – anything less is most likely a fake.

Only buy autographs over the internet if you are an experienced collector. The online marketplace is awash with unscrupulous "dealers" more than happy to take your money and supply you with worthless fakes in return. If you must buy online, heed all the above advice, and take some tips adapted from the Top Ten Rules of expert collector Garry King:

Don't buy from anyone who uses the "Private" option. What have they got to hide?

- Check that the seller and the location are in the same place
- Check the dealer's reputation – obviously
- Watch out for a dealer who is selling several big names at the same time, at well under market value.

DESIGNER HANDBAGS

Prada, Gucci, Burberry, Fendi – everyone wants a classic designer bag. And they can get one, provided they don't mind if it's one of the thousands of mass-produced fakes that flood the markets daily.

When it comes to fake goods, handbags are a counterfeiter's dream. They are easy to replicate and poorly paid workers prepared to make them are equally easy to find. In fact, today's fakes are so convincing, even the professionals have trouble telling them from the real thing.

So, how do you know what is authentic? The price, for a start. You can be confident that the new Louis Vuitton bag you spot for \$100/£50 is a fake; the real thing will retail at at least \$500/£250. And then there's the sale venue. It may sound obvious, but you will not find a new Gucci bag being sold at an online auction or out of the trunk of a car. Another important clue is the point of origin tag. Your coveted Chanel will not be "Made in Taiwan." Louis Vuitton's leather goods are only manufactured in France, Spain, and the United States.

It seems that more and more of us are happy to buy fake handbags, knowing they are just that. Yet should we be so pleased with ourselves? Counterfeit fashion items are almost always produced by underpaid, underage workers in relatively poor conditions, particularly in the Far East and Eastern Europe.

Our handbag obsession shows no sign of letting up.

Worse still, terrorists, gangs, and organized crime syndicates all profit from selling counterfeit merchandise. Sometimes, designer knockoffs are lined with hard drugs and used for smuggling. There is even evidence that the bombing of the World Trade Center in 1993 may have been funded in this way.

But the fashion houses have been fighting back and an increasing number are turning to the courts in an effort to stem the rising tide of cheaper counterfeit products that are causing their sales to fall and denting their brand image.

Yet spotting the fake is still a problem for the designer brand, and an expensive one too. When retailer Daffy's sent their fake Jackie O Gucci bag to Gucci to be repaired, the designer returned the item fixed, with no comment. Even Gucci hadn't recognized the fake.

DESIGNER JEANS

When it comes to judging the fake pair of designer denims from the real thing, the devil truly is in the detail.

For more than a century, jeans were low-price, hard-wearing clothes for the working man. In 1978, however, the Nakash brothers launched their "Jordache" line of high-quality, high-price jeans, cut specifically for the female figure. Suddenly, faking jeans became a profitable business and large numbers flooded the market.

Noticing the high sales that Nakash were achieving, other companies moved in to promote women's jeans. These included Sassoon, Gloria Vanderbilt, Calvin Klein, and JouJou. Most of these upmarket labels produced high-quality garments with attention to detail unknown in traditional men's jeans. Soon, men wanted the better quality product, which was by 1979 known as a "designer jean", so men's versions began to be produced.

It was in late 1979 and early 1980 that the first fake designer jeans began to hit the market. These came overwhelmingly from the Far East and, like most fakes, entered the market through market stalls, temporary traders, and informal sales. The fakes mimicked the cut and design as well as the labels of the real thing, but were made with far inferior materials and by workers in rushed conditions, who paid little attention to quality. In about 2002 a new wave of fake designer jeans hit the market, most now apparently originating from China, and the numbers available increased dramatically after 2006.

Denim – it's all about the label.

When trying to assess if a pair of designer jeans is genuine or fake, it is best to look at the detail. It is here that the fraudster will fall down, as details cost money to reproduce. For instance, genuine True Religion jeans have labels that state they are "made in USA", while most fakes read "made in U.S.A.". A genuine seller will not object to a buyer having a look at such details – or sending you a photo if the sale is on an internet auction site. Only the seller of fakes will not agree.

DESIGNER PERFUMES

The rapid recent rise in the demand for fake fragrances has gone hand in hand with our craving for celebrity-endorsed products.

Perfume is one of the easiest luxury items to fake.

For many centuries, the majority of perfumes were made by individual craftsmen for their local market. That began to change in the 19th century when companies such as Guerlain and Penhaligon produced and marketed mass-produced, standardized fragrances. By the 1930s, Chanel, Dunhill, and others had joined in. This production of highly priced, quality perfumes led to a growth in counterfeits, but they remained a tiny section of the market and were produced in generally small numbers.

It was the introduction of celebrity -endorsed fragrances that both revolutionized the perfume industry and opened the door to forgery on a massive scale. Celebrity perfumes began in a small way in 2002 and by 2004 were still accounting for only 1 per cent of the perfumes market. But a big push by advertisers led to a 2000 per cent rise in two years and by 2008 they accounted for around 25 per cent of all perfume sales.

These products, with their emphasis on name and packaging, were almost ready-made for the counterfeiter. Perfumes are generally sold in cellophane-sealed packets so the purchaser does not actually smell the product before buying. All the forger needs to do is get the packaging correct and sales are almost guaranteed. Good fakes may mimic the bottle inside the packaging as well and some have been known to have fragrances that smell similar to the real thing. But instead of lasting a full day the fake will wear off after less than an hour.

It is not just that the buyer gets an inferior product – in some cases they can also be dangerous. In 2005, one batch of counterfeit perfume caused intense itching. Other fakes have led to rashes and skin discoloration – though most of these have fortunately been only temporary.

In the EU, seizures of fake perfumes rose by 300 per cent in 2002. By 2007, the market was thought to be worth around $400 million/£200 million.

FAKE WATCHES

Each year, websites shamelessly advertise any number of fake brand-name watches while the world's street traders display all the latest designer models.

When it comes to watches, there is little that counterfeit agencies can do except supply public information about the ways in which the fake goods might be identified. Until recently, US government advice merely suggested that if the bargain was too good to be true, then the consumer should be wary. But in the 1990s, more pragmatic guidelines were issued to help consumers decide if they were being ripped off.

The first guideline is to examine the watch's caseback. Take the case of the Rolex, the counterfeiter's favorite watch. Rolex has never made a watch with a transparent back, through which one can see the inner workings. Counterfeiters are very keen on these because they're cheap and they look impressive. If you can see the mechanism, therefore, it's a fake.

A genuine Rolex will also have its coronet symbol micro-etched into crystal just below the 6 o'clock mark and it will always hold a hologram sticker of the Rolex Crown just above the case reference number. It is also worth testing to see if a watch is genuine sapphire crystal by checking its surface tension. When held under water, a fine film of liquid should collect on the ultra-smooth surface.

If this doesn't happen, then no crystal has been involved in the process.

When Rolex hired its own private detectives to visit the local flea market in Fort Lauderdale, Florida, in 1985, they purchased two fake watches for $27/£13.50 each from a trader named Torkington. Three weeks later, another 742 replica Rolexes were seized on a raid in the same market. The District Court dismissed the incident, saying that no one could reasonably believe that a real Rolex cost $27/£13 but the Court of Appeal reinstated the fine and ordered that Torkington and his accomplices be sent to prison.

A customs agent drives a steamroller over 17,000 fake designer watches.

THE "FAKE KIDNEY" TV SCAM

The plight of kidney patients who are desperate for a donor organ makes a suitable subject for a documentary – but a game show? Viewers in the Netherlands certainly thought so.

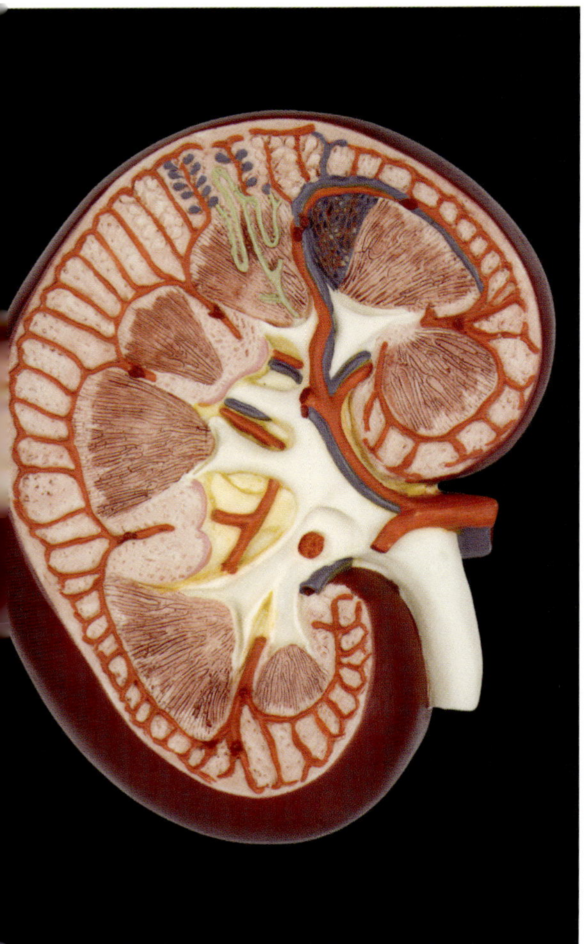

Could a kidney really be sold on TV?

In 2007, millions of viewers tuned into the **Big Donor Show** to see Lisa, a dying 37-year-old kidney donor, and to vote for which of three patients would become the lucky recipient of Lisa's kidney. The show drew widespread criticism even before going on air. Dutch broadcaster BNN had to field thousands of complaints and Dutch embassies around the world were besieged by irate callers.

Politicians were united in calling for the show to be scrapped. Presenter Patrick Lodiers denied that program-makers Endemol were playing God. These were the same program-makers who had created the famous **Big Brother** reality TV series, which began in the Netherlands in 1999 and was then exported successfully all over the world. But a reality organ transplant show? Surely that was in the realm of the ridiculous.

"Think of it as playing Santa Claus," said Lodiers, with cheerful enthusiasm. Only when the time came to announce the "winner" did Lodiers reveal their secret – it was all an elaborate stunt.

"We are not giving away a kidney here," Lodiers told viewers. "That is going too far – even for us!" In fact, "Lisa" was revealed to be an actress by the name of Leonie, and although the recipients were real renal patients, they were all also in on the hoax.

The program had been made not as a cheap publicity stunt but to highlight the chronic shortage of kidney donors. Once the aim was revealed, politicians began to backtrack, with Dutch culture minister describing the show as a "fantastic stunt".

The program had been made as a tribute to Bart de Graaff, founder of public service broadcaster BNN – Bart's Neverending Network – who had died of kidney failure five years before, at the age of 35, following an unsuccessful organ transplant.

A former actor, Bart de Graaff was well known for his provocative program-making aimed at a youth audience, and for tackling controversial subjects such as teen sex and drug-taking in an explicit way. Presenter Sander Lantinga once streaked at a Wimbledon tennis match for the BNN show **Try Before You Die**.

The car accident that caused de Graff's kidney failure also led to a growth disorder that left him looking like a prepubescent boy – something he used to his advantage in programs.

FAKE FERRARIS

How Chinese car manufacturers vie to produce the most authentic copies of desirable western models.

In 2002, the Chinese automobile industry began copying Citroën ZXs. A group called J. M. Star proudly announced that they had managed to copy the design of the French classic and were planning to sell it on their burgeoning home market as a model called a Fukang. J. M. Star then sold the company to the Geely Group who made their own copy of the copy, called the "Maple Whirlwind". This "Whirlwind" was, in turn, copied by several other companies and the publicity surrounding this incident apparently left Chinese consumers not outraged but gasping for more.

Advances in computer programing meant that local designers were able to "reverse engineer" almost any model. In other words, as soon as they had relevant drawings, they could use advanced analysis software to produce their own versions. And it soon transpired that the most desirable vintage car on the market was a Ferrari 330P4 (1967), of which there were only four in the world.

A team of highly gifted engineers soon set to work to imitate the distinctive "Enzo Red" exteriors from cheap fibreglass. They then purchased old Toyota bodies and "remodeled" them into classic Ferrari styles. Now, for around $10,000/£5,000, consumers were able to purchase a car which would have fetched around $130,000/£65,000 at auction, had it been genuine.

Italian police display the handiwork of the fake Ferrari gangs.

Meanwhile, over in Sicily in early 2008, police smashed a counterfeiting ring and arrested 15 people for attempting to do almost exactly the same thing. These red Ferraris looked, to the uninitiated eye, like genuine model 328 GTBs – a car that had ceased to be produced in the late 1980s. But they were, in fact, made up of bogus parts and put together in a factory in Palermo by "extremely able" body shop mechanics.

In all, 21 cars were confiscated while 14 had already been sold to Ferrari enthusiasts who knew they were fake – but didn't care. Looking "real" was really what mattered.

EBAY & COUNTERFEIT GOODS

The growth of eBay and similar web-based auction sites offered to solve one of the perennial problems of the counterfeiter – that of credibility.

Fake goods have traditionally been the preserve of market stalls, temporary shops, and door-to-door salesmen. Customers, however, have long been aware of these outlets for counterfeits and have become accustomed to treating them with suspicion. As a result, the prices that fake goods command in such circumstances have been low and profits – though worthwhile – correspondingly meager.

However, using eBay, a gang selling fakes could masquerade as an individual clearing out a house of unwanted goods, or as a legitimate small trader. Behind the anonymity of the eBay website, the dishonest trader could find it much easier to mislead the public and so obtain higher prices for fake goods than would normally be the case.

The internet auction sites are, of course, aware of the problem, though they often disagree over the scale of the fake sales.

eBay's early attempts to deal with forgeries was by way of its Feedback system. At the end of each transaction both buyer and seller are able to rate the service offered by the other, and leave a comment of up to 80 characters. This enables a buyer who has purchased a product in good faith, only to find it is counterfeit, to rate the seller badly and leave a warning for other buyers. Buyers are recommended to check out a seller's ratings before bidding for high-price items.

The Feedback system is recognized as being effective against individual rogue traders, but has its weaknesses against gangs. An organized gang could set up a false identity, carry out a large number of bogus transactions with other false identities to establish a high-grade rating and then begin selling counterfeits in large numbers. After a week or so of intensive trading, the gang would close down the identity, bank the money and disappear before the complaints came in.

The auction sites have moved on to posting advice, reviews, and guides to help buyers spot fraudulent dealings. By 2008 there were around 5,000 separate pieces of advice on eBay about how to identify and avoid fake items.

The companies whose goods are being pirated, however, have frequently claimed that the auction sites are not doing enough. They have responded by action of their own. They monitor sites to try to identify sellers that pose as private individuals but are in fact selling hundreds of items. The companies will then alert the police.

There have been some impressive successes. In 2004, employees of the jewelry company Tiffany's bought 200 "Tiffany" items at random from eBay, finding that over 150 of them were fake. The police were alerted and most fakes traced back to a single address. The property was raided and

Ebay is now one of the leading outlets for counterfeits. Up to 95% of items in some categories are fakes.

found to contain many hundreds of fake Tiffany items. The owners were arrested and convicted of trading in fake items.

In 2007, Louis Vuitton and Dior Couture launched legal action in France against eBay, claiming to have identified over 90 per cent of their items sold on the site as being fakes. The lawsuit claimed the auction site was not doing enough to stop the sale of counterfeit goods and the designer brands received massive damages. A similar court case in Germany launched by Rolex ended with a decision that eBay was not responsible for individual sales of fakes, but was liable if, having been warned a buyer was dealing in fakes, it did not take steps to block future sales.

The legal arguments continue, of course . . . as do the sales of counterfeit goods, from handbags to pet food, and TVs to prescription medication. It's true what they say: "you can get anything on eBay". Whether it is genuine or not is another matter.

The Tiffany lamp – a favorite with brand counterfeiters.

FAKING SIGNATURES

Reproducing the handwriting of another person is a great art. Throughout history, there have been better and worse artists. There are even machines . . .

Signatures may be faked legitimately as well as for other, devious reasons. Many important, establishment figures rely on a machine, called the "autopen", for this purpose, which creates a facsimile of their signature. Film stars and captains of industry employ it if they want to give their correspondence the personal touch without committing to the time-consuming business of writing.

Most famously perhaps, the British royal family use an autopen to work their way through the Christmas card list. They used to change their autopen signature every two years. If they put a personal message in your card, however, consider this a good sign – a genuine signature probably follows it.

Autopens pose an interesting problem in terms of authenticity, because technically the signatures they produce are not forgeries. They "remember" what is known as the "matrix" of a signature and reproduce it mechanically, sometimes even using the signatory's own pen.

Almost all US presidents since John F. Kennedy have used the autopen, and Kennedy began the practice of having several different autopen versions of his signature, thus overcoming its main problem: that it produces the exact same signature

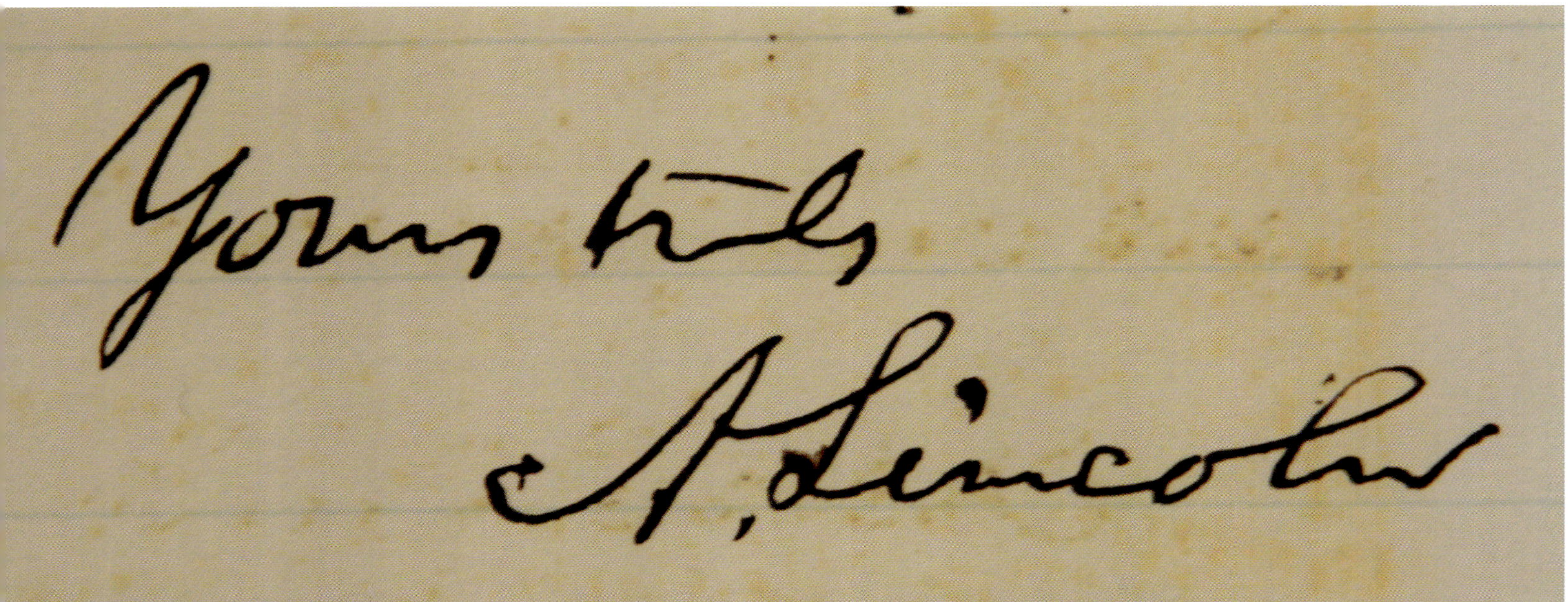

Joseph Cosey was skilled at forging Lincoln's signature. This one is the real thing, however.

each time and no two real signatures are exactly the same. Now everyone uses several different writing patterns.

There are other ways of identifying autopen signatures, however, just as long as you possess a magnifying glass. When you sign your name, the pen usually starts moving before – and, often, after – you start writing. An autopen signature, on the other hand, begins abruptly with a dot and ends abruptly with a dot. This can be seen most easily under a magnifying glass.

And, for autograph collectors at least, it's worth getting it right. An autopen card by the Queen and Prince Philip should fetch upwards of about $150/£75, one with genuine signatures about $800/£400. An autopen card "signed" by Princess Diana might make $400/£200 or more, a genuine signature more like $4,000/£2,000.

So, what of the more unscrupulous fakers of signatures? Perhaps the most infamous and talented forger of the early 20th century was Joseph Cosey, who forged the documents and signatures of several prominent American figures in amazingly convincing style – among them that most frequently forged of signatories, Abraham Lincoln.

Born Martin Coneely in Syracuse, New York, in 1887, Cosey was in trouble with the law from an early age. Having been discharged from the army for assaulting a soldier, he began stealing – which landed him in San Quentin Prison in California. Once released, in 1929, he embarked upon his career as a forger.

The real turning point came when Cosey saw a pay warrant dated 1786, signed by Benjamin Franklin, in the Library of Congress. He stole it and began practicing. Soon he was so good at forgery that he had replicated it several times and sold it to dealers.

Encouraged, he began to make a lot of money forging the signatures and documents of other icons, among them Thomas Jefferson, George Washington, Abraham Lincoln, Edgar Allan Poe, Mark Twain, Walt Whitman, Theodore Roosevelt, and Rudyard Kipling.

Although his work was not flawless to the very serious scrutinizer, his documents were particularly convincing because, like all good forgers, he used the right materials – old paper and writing implements, and the brown ink characteristic of the 18th century.

Then, in 1937, he was caught selling a forged "Lincoln" letter to a stamp dealer. He pleaded guilty, was sentenced to three years, and only had to serve one. When he was released he kept forging until his death in the early 1950s. Much of Cosey's work is still in circulation and still assumed to be genuine.

Throughout history there have been more forgers than we think. Only six examples of Shakespeare's signature are accepted as being genuine. All of them are in major institutions.

Signature expert Charles Hamilton said Cosey "whipped out his forgeries with great ease, never resorting to the amateur device of tracery".

FAKE FOODS

Faking foods is as old as the hills. Some deceptions are more detrimental to our health than others. All have come in for greater scrutiny during the past few decades.

In the War years, powdered egg was a common substitute for the real thing.

In the early 1700s, gin was laced with sulphuric acid or turpentine, while in the 1800s, coffee would be made to stretch with chicory powder – still used by some manufacturers, though openly now – or, less appetizingly, ground acorns, flour, or parsnip powder.

The tricks of food photographers are nothing new either. In the mid-1800s, market traders would use red paint on fish gills to make them look fresher and a layer of fat would "polish" meat that was past its best. Oranges were sometimes boiled to give them weight and a shiny appearance.

At least when modern-day advertisers paint wood preservative onto hazelnuts to make them look more hazelnutty, or make "ice-cream" out of icing sugar and dye, nobody is expected to actually eat the food. You'd struggle with the ice cubes – they're made of plastic – or the cookies – which are often huge and made of foam.

Of course wartime brought rationing, which resulted in a whole new phase of ingenuity in terms of food. Almost everything was made with turnips during WWI, including bread and coffee. You could also sample "mock hare" (beef and pork) and "mock crab" (shrimp and herring roe).

In the spring of 1942, America's Food Rationing Program was in motion. Food substitutions stepped in when staples were no longer available: cottage cheese, crows, frogs, locusts, and snails became substitutes for meat, while coffee was brewed from okra seeds that had been dried and browned, or from roasted acorns and wheat berries.

Post-war advertising had its desired effect on housewives, convincing them that what was cheap, modern and convenient was best. They seemed so understanding. Housewives were busy people with endless important domestic chores to perform. Who needed the added burden of baking apple pies when you could make instant whip in just one minute? As the advertising slogan had it: "Who'd ever think you could whip up this lovely sweet . . . in less time than it takes to lay the table?"

And we did all think it was lovely. By the 1970s, synthetic flavorings were everywhere, and everybody was excited. There was a new kind of career, you could be a "flavorist" and many considered themselves to be the artists of the taste world. Lime, coffee, and paprika could be imitated, and later more complicated tastes such as sausage. More and more chemicals were added, and the scientist became more excited still by their own cleverness.

By the end of the 1800s, honey was regularly being replaced by glucose – mixed with dead bee parts for added authenticity.

It was not until the 1980s that all this activity was questioned and the era of serious food scandals really began. In **The Beginner's Guide to Natural Living**, American author Larry Cook reveals the average additive consumption per adult, through flavorings and pesticides, is nine to ten pounds a year. By the time an American child is five years old, he will have consumed more than 7.5lb (3.4kg) of food additives through preservatives, emulsifiers, synthetic sweeteners, flavor enhancers, and artificial colors. In 1995, the world's flavors and fragrance market was worth $12 billion/£6 billion – food flavorings accounting for 40 per cent.

Now research seems to back up the growing tide of concern over additives designed to make food look like what it is not. In particular, new research warns against what are known as azo dyes. These food colorings are by-products of the coal tar industry and a link has been found between all of these products and hyperactivity in children. They are as follows:

E110	Sunset yellow. Coloring found in squashes.
E104	Quinoline. Yellow Food coloring.
E122	Carmoisine. Red coloring in jellies.
E129	Allura red. Orange/red food dye.
E211	Sodium benzoate: Preservative.

Synthetic colorings have been linked to hyperactivity in children.

FAKING PHOTOGRAPHS

The faking of photographs started off as a hobby but with the arrival of digital technology all manner of trick manipulation suddenly became possible – and profitable.

As early as 1821, an apprentice silversmith named Gardner visited the Great Exhibition in London where he was captivated by the work of the American photographer Mathew Brady. In 1856, Gardner moved his family to Washington, D.C., where he got a job at Brady's gallery and began taking photographs.

By 1825, Gardner had become friends with Allan Pinkerton, who was Head of President Lincoln's intelligence gathering operation. The pair came up with the idea of taking portraits of soldiers as they set off for the Civil War and Gardner soon became the War's most famous chronicler – but there was one snag.

Research later proved that Gardner's photos had been mocked up for the cameras and that he had used the same corpse in multiple locations. He thus became one of the first examples of a distinguished line of political image manipulators.

Photographic manipulation was used extensively in the Soviet Union after former Communist favorites fell out of favor with their leaders. Leon Trotsky, for example, suddenly disappeared from all official photographs after he was exiled in 1928.

Photo editors are increasingly aware of the perils of digital manipulation, which is now available to almost any amateur enthusiast.

In modern times, a wider variety of methods have been used – though not necessarily more complex. In 1933 a surgeon, Dr. Robert Kenneth, supposedly photographed the world-famous Loch Ness monster in Scotland, from half a mile away. This resulted in several explorations with high-tech sensing devices. On his deathbed, Kenneth confessed he and a friend had rigged up a toy submarine as a hoax.

With the arrival of the digital age, stand-ins are no longer required. Re-imagers can create and manipulate images using a range of widely available digital tools. As a result, the authenticity of any image is no longer guaranteed. In the field of forensic imaging, for example, police investigators must routinely ask if a photograph of a blood stain was digitally altered in order to deceive. These days, say inspectors, it is almost impossible to define an "original" photograph. Research suggests that color analysis may be one of the only true indicators of image tampering since color analysis normally involves scaling, enhancement, or blurring, all of which involve color alteration. This can only be detected, however, by specialist methods.

The famous 1930s faked photograph of the Loch Ness monster.

A memorable case of controversial photo manipulation occurred in 1982 when editors of **National Geographic** magazine moved two Egyptian pyramids closer together, in order to make them both fit on the magazine's vertical cover. This visual trick led to a debate on the ethics and appropriateness of photo manipulation in journalism. The argument in that particular instance was that the editors had depicted something that did not actually exist and had presented it as fact. In the United States, the National Press Photographers Association has set out a Code of Ethics in order to promote the accuracy of published images.

In 2004, the editor of the UK's **Daily Mirror** newspaper was fired after admitting that photographs of British soldiers abusing Iraqi prisoners in Abu Ghraib prison had been faked. The newspaper said it had been the victim of a "malicious hoax". Yet basic editorial research could soon have established that the backdrop for the photos was Lancashire rather than Iraq, and that details of the uniforms and weapons were wrong.

In 2006, a rather more high-tech attempt to dupe the media was made by Lebanese photographer Adnan Hajj, who was taking photos of the Israeli army's air strikes on Beirut. He digitally manipulated the images to make the damage on the ground look far more extensive than it actually was and then sold the pictures to Reuters News Agency for mass syndication. The deception was discovered within hours, not by editors, but by eagle-eyed bloggers on the Internet.

The truth is that technology has not only made it easier to fake photographs, but has also made it simpler for the amateur sleuth to detect the fraudsters.

THE COTTINGLEY FAIRIES

A series of photographs of fairies apparently taken by two young cousins in the idyllic English countryside were supposed to prove the existence of the magical creatures – but later turned out to be fakes.

Elsie Wright was born in 1901, the daughter of one of Britain's earliest qualified engineers. Her cousin, Frances Griffith, was six years younger and was born in South Africa but came to live with Elsie, in Cottingley, Yorkshire, at the start of World War I. Elsie's father had a very early plate camera that Elsie often borrowed and, one day, she came back from Cottingley Beck, a wooded area behind her house, with an exciting new series of photographs. In the first one, Frances is looking into the camera as a troupe of fairies dance on the branches of a tree. The second shows her cousin playing with some fairies.

Conan Doyle: Fooled by the fairies.

Elsie's father was skeptical about the whole adventure but her mother was swept up in the new vogue for spiritualism and, in August 1919, attended a meeting at the local Theosophical Society. She mentioned the photos to her fellow participants and the reaction was immediate. She was asked to reprint the photos for the Annual Theosophist Conference later that year.

There she met Edward Gardner, who was considered an expert in the field. Spiritualism (and the possibility of communicating with the recently deceased) had become hugely fashionable after the end of World War I and one of its leading adherents was the author Sir Arthur Conan Doyle, who had coincidentally been commissioned to write an article about the existence of fairies for **Strand** magazine's Christmas issue.

Conan Doyle made contact with Gardner and borrowed Elsie's prints. The issue of **Strand** appeared in December 1919 and sold out within days. Conan Doyle sent Gardner to Cottingley in July 1920 to conduct further investigations while Conan Doyle himself left for a lecture tour of Australia. Gardner reported that the Wright family seemed upright and honest and that he had supplied each girl with a camera and 20 photographic plates, encouraging them to collect further proof. During August 1920, Elsie and Frances took four more photos of fairies and the plates were sent to London packed in cotton wool by her father, though he said that he found it hard to believe that as distinguished an author as Conan Doyle could have been taken in "by our Elsie and her at the bottom of the class!"

But Gardner was elated, and Conan Doyle viewed the fairy photos as a huge gift for the spiritualist cause. On his return, he wrote another **Strand** article, though the public mood had modified and there was now a growing feeling that Conan Doyle was a credulous old man. In August 1921, however, he organized another expedition to Cottingley with a clairvoyant called Geoffrey Hudson. No photographs were taken and Elsie and Frances appeared to

Frances stated that she thought that Sir Arthur Conan Doyle must have "wanted to be taken in" to believe their story.

have become fed up of the whole business.

After studying art and photography, Elsie emigrated to India while Frances got married and moved to Ramsgate. Both managed to avoid publicity for the next half century but, in 1971, a BBC documentary revived interest in the whole affair by interviewing Elsie, who said that she was finally prepared to talk since Mr. Gardner had died the previous year. She was still not prepared to admit that she had lied but seemed to concede that a few facts had been falsified. Another documentary in 1976 interviewed Frances, who also neither admitted nor denied the allegations.

In 1981, and nearing their deaths, the cousins eventually admitted to a magazine that the photos had been faked using cut-out cardboard drawings stuck together with hatpins. Elsie said that, having fooled the creator of Sherlock Holmes, they were too embarrassed to admit the truth.

Frances Griffith with the fairies, photographed by Elsie Wright in Cottingley, July 1917.

FAKE INSURANCE CLAIMS

Criminal gangs make millions from staging fake car crashes and then submitting fraudulent insurance claims, in an almost risk-free scam.

Evidence suggests that the most common type of fraudulent car insurance claim in the world involves fake crashes during which the criminals deliberately stage an accident with an innocent motorist and then put forward claims for replacement vehicles and fictitious injuries.

In April 2008, police arrested a number of people in Hyderabad, India, for claiming fake accident insurance on a huge scale. Dr. Surender Reddy, an orthopedic surgeon, and N. Rami Reddy, a lawyer, devised a scheme in which they paid people to pose as drivers of vehicles that had been in accidents. The doctor would then issue a fake accident certificate, claiming serious injuries, while the lawyer registered the claims in a local court. It soon appeared that Reddy and Reddy had worked this trick on dozens of previous occasions.

Frayed tempers and another collision on the roads – but is it real or staged?

In another case, Karen Hacking, from Lancashire, UK, was driving home when she stopped at traffic lights. The car in front moved off when the lights changed and, as she too moved forward, the car in front slammed on the brakes. She shunted into the car's back bumper, causing slight damage. The driver and the passenger got out, staggering and clutching their necks. Both demanded that the police and an ambulance be called. When the police arrived they were suspicious and kept watch.

"I saw the two of them return to the car wearing hospital neck braces," said the officer in charge. "They were laughing when they took off the braces and threw them in the car. The accident was a total fake."

In the US, in May 2008, The Allstate Insurance Company, one of the biggest car insurers in the world, decided it had had enough and informed 45 doctors, lawyers, and street-level workers in Los Angeles that they were being sued for $107 million/£53.5 million for what the company contended was their part in orchestrating scores of fake crashes. It is the biggest suit ever filed in connection with fake auto accidents.

Investigating lawyers in the UK, meanwhile, estimate that 30 per cent of car insurance policies end up being handed out to fake claimants. It is very hard for police to investigate such crimes and the market is now worth up to $4 billion/£2 billion a year, with a large proportion of scams being worked by professional syndicates.

The first impact of such crimes is on the price of insurance policies but there are also significant implications for public safety. Proof, however, remains a difficult area and police are reluctant to prosecute where a conviction is unlikely.

Of course not all fake insurance claims are motoring ones. In October 2002, Linda Hayes of Burlington County, New Jersey, submitted about $42,000/£21,000 worth of false insurance claims after a burglary at her home. She said that lots of her valuables had been stolen and even falsified documents to prove that expensive goods had been removed that she hadn't even owned.

The Coalition Against Insurance Fraud estimates that, in 2006, a total of about $80 billion/£40 billion was lost in the US due to insurance fraud. And according to the Insurance Information Institute, fraud accounts for about 10 per cent, or $30 billion/£15 billion, of losses in the property and casualty insurance industries. Health care is equally vulnerable. The National Health Care Anti-Fraud Association estimates that 3 per cent of US health care industry expenditure is due to fraudulent activities, amounting to $51 billion/£25.5 billion, while other organizations put it at 10 per cent.

Many leading insurers now have their own detective units and are hiring lawyers specializing in "white-collar crime".

DONALD CROWHURST – THE FAKE YACHTSMAN

The tragic story of an inexperienced yachtsman who felt he had no choice but to enter, then fake, an around-the-world race.

Donald Crowhurst had high hopes but his lack of experience let him down.

The Golden Globe Boat Race was inspired by legendary sailor Francis Chichester's round-the-world voyage. He had completed the journey in 226 days, receiving the knighthood for his achievement. The newspaper that sponsored Chichester's voyage now wanted to be associated with the first non-stop single-handed circumnavigation of the globe. No sailing experience was required of entrants, and competitors could set off any time before 31 October 1968.

There were nine entrants, and it was billed as a test for the world's greatest yachtsmen. Several big names were involved, but Donald Crowhurst was not one of them. In fact, he was something of an underdog, who was to sail an unproven type of boat, a 40ft (12m) trimaran which he christened **Teignmouth Electron**. Potentially, these could be quicker than traditional boats, but if overloaded they could be slow and were problematic when attempting to sail close to the wind.

Crowhurst had designed a buoyancy aid to help him, which he meant to manufacture on completion of the race.

Having received the £1,000 consolation prize for second place, Nigel Tetley did up his boat and then, less than a year later, committed suicide.

He had persuaded a local businessman, Stanley Best, to sponsor him, but this was conditional: if Crowhurst did not finish the race, he would have to pay for the boat himself.

So the inexperienced Crowhurst had a great deal invested in this race. Not only was he relying on the new design in more ways than one, but his business was in trouble and he needed the prize money. First prize was a trophy, but it was the prize of $10,000/£5,000 – the equivalent of tens of thousands of pounds today – for the fastest circuit, that he had his eye on.

Crowhurst set sail from Teignmouth, Devon, England, on 31 October 1968. This was the latest he was allowed to leave and he was ill-prepared. He had been short of time as the race drew near and was hoping to complete work on his safety devices en route. It is said that he broke down in tears with his wife the night before leaving, because he knew the boat was not ready but he was unable to see any way out of his desperate situation.

Crowhurst's boat and equipment were problematic from the start. What he sent back to land, however, were confident reports of steady progress. When there was silence, his position was simply inferred from earlier reports. What was actually happening was that Crowhurst was spending a lot of time doing complex mathematics to calculate his false reports. At least he was still afloat. Four competitors had turned back before reaching the Indian Ocean.

Then his boat started leaking. Should he confess all or plough on and risk his life in an unseaworthy vessel? He stayed in the Atlantic, just north of Brazil, for three months – cutting off radio contact and filling in his fraudulent logbook every day. He dropped anchor at an Argentinian port to make vital repairs – strictly against the rules.

But his problems did not end there. Robin Knox-Johnson had completed the race and won the trophy, but slowly. According to the information he had given the world, Crowhurst was in sight of the $10,000/£5,000! Close scrutiny would follow in that case, which he knew he would not withstand. Chichester had already expressed doubts about Crowhurst's reports. Still, perhaps he could just get away with coming second to Nigel Tetley, the other frontrunner. He decided to go slowly across the Atlantic.

But he hadn't reckoned on Tetley, who pushed his boat – another 30-ft (9.144-m) trimaran – so far to "catch" Crowhurst that it ended up sinking. Tetley had to abandon ship on 30 May, 1969. Crowhurst was in the lead. But after all that solitude and pressure, his sanity was deserting him. His logbooks became rants and raves. On 10 July 1969, **Teignmouth Electron** was found empty, drifting aimlessly at sea. To this day it is assumed her captain had taken his own life. Robin Knox-Johnson was awarded the £5,000 and gave it to Crowhurst's wife and family.

A trimaran, as sailed by Crowhurst.

FAKE QUIZ SHOW CONTESTANTS

With the rise of television, quiz shows became so popular that the temptation for producers and contestants to rig competitions was at times overwhelming, leading to a number of scandals.

Quizmaster Jack Barry congratulates Charles Van Doren (right) on his win.

During the 1950s, television suddenly became one of the Western world's prime sources of entertainment. Within less than a decade almost everybody had bought a set and the quiz show genre, with its huge prizes, immediately blossomed. In 1955, a radio quiz show called **The $64 Dollar Question** transferred to US television as **The $ 64,000 Dollar Question** and Revlon, the show's sponsor, saw the potential for huge commercial rewards.

One of the first winners was Dr Joyce but she wasn't attractive enough to be associated with a make-up company and Revlon encouraged the producers to give her a series of questions about boxing – about which she knew nothing.

Meanwhile, Charles Van Doren, a handsome English Professor at Columbia University who was earning a meager salary wrote to the producers of a show called **Twenty-One**. Van Doren was exactly the sort of contestant they were looking for. Their reigning champion was plain and the producers needed someone more charismatic.

In January 1957, therefore, Van Doren made his first appearance on the show and won. Ratings immediately began to rise. By the middle of February, Van Doren had earned almost $140,000/ £70,000 and appeared on the cover of **TIME** magazine. In March of that year he eventually lost to a lawyer called Vivienne Nearing, whose husband Van Doren had defeated in an earlier episode. Still, he was hugely charismatic and the producers of NBC News immediately offered him a contract as a "cultural correspondent".

His defeated competitors, however, were suspicious and, in November 1959, Van Doren was called before the House Sub-committee on Legislative Oversight and asked if he had been given the questions and answers – in advance. He testified that he had asked not to receive any prior assistance but that the producers had insisted, telling him that this was common practice. The deception was not actually illegal so no one was charged but his integrity, and that of the producers, never recovered. The original incident still provokes such interest that in 1994 it was made into a successful feature film directed by Robert Redford.

Several decades later in the UK, the TV channel ITV broadcast a quiz show called **Who Wants to Be a Millionaire?** The show was hugely, and immediately, successful. In September 2001, it featured a new contestant.

Charles Ingram was a British Major who had served as a peacekeeper in Bosnia. He was eminently respectable and, during the first day's broadcasting, appeared to be a pleasant, unassuming person. During the second day, however, Ingram suddenly had a fabulous run of correct answers and won the top prize of $2 million/£1 million.

When Charles Ingram won his $2 million/£1 million, it had only ever been done once before on the show.

Major Ingram seemed rather unhappy for someone who had just become a millionaire but the show's host, Chris Tarrant, was convinced that the Major was genuine and immediately wrote out a check.

Just a week after Ingram's victory, however, a fellow contestant contacted the producers to say that the Major had behaved peculiarly during the recording, particularly with regard to his eccentric coughing pattern. The prize money was withheld and investigations began. It soon emerged that a third contestant, Mr. Whittock, had audibly coughed at 19 crucial moments during the recording of the show and that these coughs may have been coded signals to assist Major Ingram with his responses.

In court a jury heard Whittock claim he suffered from an itchy throat and that his timely coughing had been "pure coincidence". He had not, however, coughed when answering his own questions. Whittock also said that he was merely a "serial quiz show loser" when he had, in fact, won several quiz shows. The jury found Ingram, his wife Diana, and Whittock guilty, sentencing them to two years suspended and costs totaling $130,000/£65,000. Ingram resigned from the army and he and Diana were later declared bankrupt.

Major Charles Ingram with his wife Diana arriving at court in 2003.

THE TRAVELING STONES

The most successful spoofs are those that people really want to believe. If a trickster hits the target then the finest scientific minds can be duped – and refuse to believe otherwise.

William Wright (1829–1898) was a respected news reporter who wrote under the name "Dan DeQuille". His close friend and former colleague was the comic novelist Sam Clemens – better known as Mark Twain. They both enjoyed writing hoax news stories, which Wright called "quaints". Wright thought his bogus **Traveling Stones of Pahranagat Valley** would be the best one yet – and he succeeded beyond his wildest dreams.

The story, first published in 1865 in Virginia City's **Territorial Enterprise** newspaper, told of a prospector who chanced upon some cobble-size loadstones, rich in magnetized iron, while searching the remote Pahranagat Valley, in south-east Nevada.

According to the report, "When scattered about on ... a level surface, within two or three feet of each other, the stones immediately began traveling toward a common center, and then huddled up in a bunch ... "

The tale reappeared in **The Big Bonanza** (1876), an otherwise genuine history of Nevada prospecting, also written by DeQuille.

The story drew scant reaction at first, but then interest began to grow. The famous circus impresario P. T. Barnum became interested in the story and offered Wright $10,000/£5,000 to take his "rolling stones" on tour. Letters began arriving by the sack-load requesting samples of the stones. One was from a group of well-respected German physicists who were investigating electromagnetism. They felt sure "the eminent physicist Herr Dan DeQuille" had made the breakthrough that they were seeking. They refused to accept Wright's denials, believing he wanted to keep all the glory.

Yet more letters came. Wright began referring writers to "Mark Twain, who probably has. . . 15 or 20 bushels of assorted sizes." This didn't work. After 15 years the joke was wearing thin and Wright had no option but to come clean: "We solemnly affirm we never saw or heard of any such diabolical cobbles." He pleaded for the letters to stop: "We are growing old and want peace!" Clearly, some hoaxes just work too well.

THE POODLE SHEEP SCAM

No one could be easier to dupe than a wealthy socialite desperate to keep up with the latest fashion trend – unless, of course, it's a newspaper journalist.

Western journalists rubbed their hands with glee when they heard of wealthy Japanese women being duped into buying lambs, believing they were the latest must-have pet – miniature poodles. According to the **Sydney Morning Herald**, "flocks of sheep" were being imported from the UK and Australia to be sold via the Internet. Up to 2,000 people had been persuaded, said the London-based **Sun** newspaper.

Journalists claimed the story came to light when a movie star complained her new pooch wouldn't bark or eat dog food. It gave headline writers a chance to come up with quips like, "When it comes to pulling wool over the eyes . . ." But it was the reporters who were feeling "sheepish" when the scoop was revealed to be a hoax.

Faith in the story rested on the mistaken belief the Japanese do not eat lamb and so wouldn't know a sheep when they saw one. In fact, they are major sheep farmers and would have seen pictures of lambs from childhood, as research would have revealed.

Is it a poodle, or a sheep? The Japanese certainly weren't sure . . .

The origin of the lambs' tale remains a mystery. But it came to public notice when actress Maiko Kawakami heard the story from her hairdresser and repeated it, to much hilarity, on a talk show. The story was relayed to news agencies and passed on to the international press, where the tale grew bigger in the retelling. Foreign journalists followed the hoax mindlessly – like sheep. This was just one of many "urban legends" about the gullible rich, buying unlikely animals in the mistaken belief that they were a new breed of pet. The most famous previous example was when a wealthy US tourist sold a rare breed of pointy-nosed wire-haired Chihuahua – which turned out to be a rat. That, too, was a shaggy dog story.

THE DEVIL'S HANDS

The self-taught Japanese archeologist who planted many of his finds – until he was found out by a photographer in 2000.

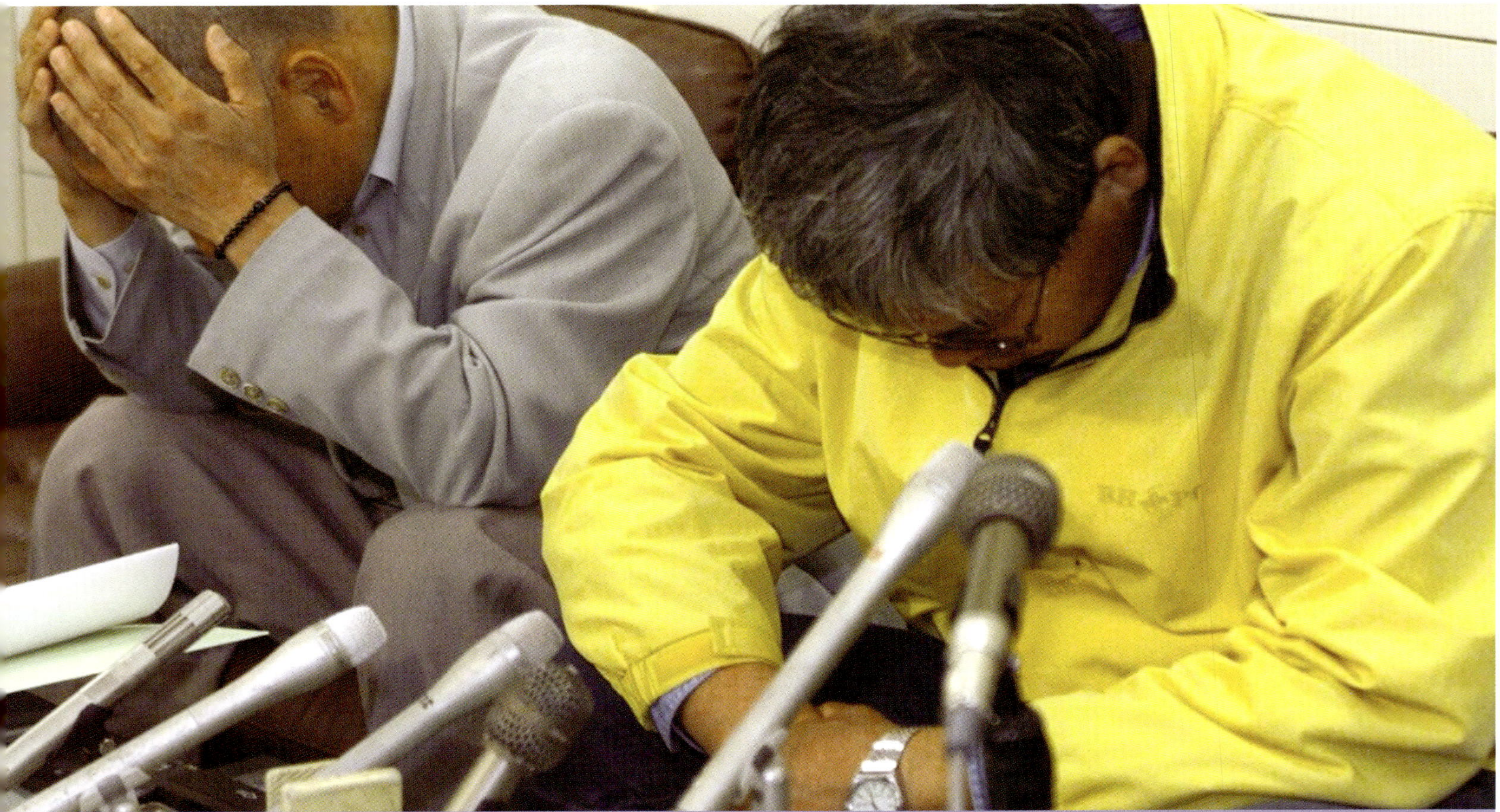
Fujimura (right) hangs his head at a press conference in 2000, after admitting to mass forgery.

Shinichi Fujimura was a phenomenon in Japan, where archeology is particularly popular, and prompts a great surge in tourism wherever finds are made. Over nearly 20 years he had gained a reputation as one of the leading archeologists there. This was no mean feat, since Fujimura had received no formal education in the discipline. He began as a self-taught hobbyist searching for early Japanese artifacts.

Then, in 1981, he made the first of a number of headline-grabbing finds. He found stoneware that was estimated to be over 40,000 years old. Overnight he became a celebrity, and more and more opportunities presented themselves to him. He went on to work at around 180 sites over the years. His incredible ability to make older and older, and more and more important, finds earned him the nickname "God's hands".

Fujimura consistently made the front pages of newspapers, and all over Japan, the textbooks were being rewritten to incorporate new information brought to archeology via its hero. Stone Age Japan was now a serious era for study, although it was not a sphere without problems. Organic material can be studied using radiocarbon dating, but stone is more often analyzed using uranium/lead and potassium/argon dating techniques. These are known to be notoriously unreliable.

It was 2000, and the town of Tsukidate, nearly 200 miles north-east of Tokyo, had been enjoying a successful archeological dig for quite a while. Many important finds had been made, and the eminent Fujimura, by now senior director at the Tohoku Paleolithic Institute, had joined the team. Before long, it appeared he had made another of his miraculous discoveries.

Fujimura had already announced that his team had found ancient stone pieces – some of them adapted by humans for scraping or cutting, and holes thought to hold pillars or columns which supported very early huts or tent-type structures. The dwellings were even older than Japan's oldest existing huts at Chichibu, north-west of Tokyo. Toward the end of October, he said that he believed the stones and holes were more than 600,000 years old. This made them among the first pieces of evidence of human habitation anywhere. Fujimura was suddenly world famous.

Then the bombshell. Two weeks later, Japan's **Mainichi Shimbun** newspaper ran three photos on its front page. They appeared to show Fujimura digging holes at Tsukidate and burying artifacts. A press conference was held later which aired on national television. During it, the distinguished 50-year-old, his head bowed in shame, confessed to having visited the Tsukidate site in the early hours of the morning and buried the relics, as well as having planted many other of his other supposed "finds" over the years. Among them were 29 artifacts dug up earlier that year at the Soshinfudozaka dig in Shintotsugawa, in the north of Japan. Clearly, the authenticity of material found in every one of the sites that he had worked at was now called into question. The paper observed: "Japan's research over the Paleolithic period may be forced into a fundamental review."

"I have nothing more to say except that I am deeply sorry for what I have done," Fujimura said. "I fell victim to temptation. I am speechless when I think about how I can apologize."

At the Tsukidate site, as a result of the dig there, the locals have created a special drink known as Early Man.

His colleagues were livid. He had clearly exploited the problems inherent in dating stone artifacts. Japanese publishers set to work correcting all their Stone Age archeology books.

It appeared from the press meet that Fujimura's motivation was not money; he said he had been forced to use material from his own collection in an attempt to produce older and older "finds". It seemed to be about fame and ambition. He wanted to be known as the archeologist who had discovered the oldest stoneware in Japan, he said.

THE VIKING DECEPTION

The 15th-century version of the world map that changed the face of modern archeology – but which was later conceded to be a forgery.

In 1957, an alumnus of Yale University who had become an antiquarian book dealer offered to sell his former college a map that appeared to be the earliest European document ever to record the existence of America. It showed the territory of Greenland (Vinland) and Newfoundland, at the tip of North America. The dealer declined to say where, or how, he had acquired the document and it was strangely bound together with a codex called the "Description of the Tartars", which was a memoir written by an Italian monk describing a trip he had made to Mongolia in 1245 and relating the early history of the Mongol people.

Yale administrators were intrigued but mystified and asked the well-known art collector, Paul Mellon, to buy the map for them. He agreed, on condition that its provenance was verified by two well-known British Museum curators. The research took years but, by 1965, they had concluded that it was genuine and Mellon bought it for the Yale library.

The following year, an entire conference was organized at Washington's Smithsonian Museum to discuss the various implications of the map. By the mid-1990s the map was reputed to be worth $25 million/£12.5 million.

Historians, scientists, and linguists have devoted themselves to the analysis of the Vinland Map.

Yale, where the saga began.

Doubts over its authenticity remained, however, particularly when the dealer admitted that he had told "certain untruths" during the purchasing process. Even into the late 1960s, therefore, radio-carbon dating investigations continued. Physicist Douglas Donahue and chemists Jacqueline Olin and Garman Harbottle concluded that, while the parchment dated from around 1440, the entire map had been coated in an unknown substance in the mid-20th century. In itself, this was inconclusive, as the coating could have been the result of an earlier, misguided, attempt at restoration or, in a more sinister development, part of a deliberate forging process.

Having exhausted the possibilities of the paper, ink samples were sent for analysis to the British Museum. None of the museum researchers had ever seen such a chemical composition. In 1972, Yale sent more ink samples to a forensic specialist who concluded that it contained titanium dioxide, which had only been manufactured since 1923.

In 1985, however, the University of California concluded that the titanium might have been due to contamination by the tests themselves and, in 1991, further microsamples were taken which demonstrated that the manufactured samples were not synthetic at all but possibly made from animal skin, again throwing the research into confusion.

Finally, in July 2002, a brand new technique called Raman spectroscopy confirmed that whilst the Tartar Codex contained genuine medieval ink, there was indeed titanium on the map, almost certainly confirming it as a forgery.

The Vinland Map, showing what is believed to be the earliest cartographic depiction of North America.

The matter was then handed over to map historians who immediately noticed that it was similar to a map produced by an Italian called Bianco in the 1430s – it even cut off Africa at exactly the same place as Bianco's, because of a fold in the page. Cartographers pointed out that the person who drew the map must have known where the fold would be.

Linguists, meanwhile, commented that Leif Eriksson's name, written on the map in 17th-century Latin, includes dipthongs. These would have been unheard of in the 15th century. Similarly, at the 1966 Vinland Conference, it had also been pointed out that one caption referred to "regionumque finitimarum" (the neighboring regions), a phrase that was only previously known to have appeared in the work of a scholar called Luka Jelic – who was not born until 1863. Yet later discoveries proved that Greenland, and Newfoundland, had already been settled by the Vikings.

The debate over the authenticity of the Vinland Map continues. It is generally accepted now to be a forgery, but its origins remain a mystery.

100

FINANCE

Finance draws fakers and forgers like wasps to a honey pot. If there's money to be had you can bet someone is hatching a devious plan to get their hands on it. Ever since the credit card was invented, crooks have found ways to use it to their advantage. As the banks invent new safeguards to protect clients, so fraudsters devise ways to beat the system.

Then there are the true artists of the conning trade – selling the Eiffel Tower for scrap metal. Surely no one would fall for that? All fakers and forgers know that there's no shortage of suckers – and you never give them an even break. Some fraudsters show such gifted salesmanship, such as selling bogus shares in non-existent companies, that you wonder why they don't use their talent to turn an honest profit.

Of course, big money is to be found on the stock exchange. Financiers are gamblers, quick to react to market changes. It's a jungle out there, make a killing or get wiped out yourself. This is the perfect hunting ground for fakers, forgers, – and hoaxers. Get the timing right, and a well placed tip-off (death of a dot com billionaire perhaps?) will send share prices tumbling.

What if the rumors are bogus? Not a problem, providing you're the one spreading them. Some people use fakery for fun, others for malice – but most for profit. In this section you'll read examples of all three. But they all have one thing in common – the potential consequences can be devastating. If you want a guiding hand through the maze of financial scams and hoaxes, infamous fraudster turned advisor Frank Abagnale (see page 110) will be only too glad to help you – for a fee of course.

CREDIT CARD FORGERY

A piece of embossed plastic is remarkably easy to forge, despite the increasingly complex anti-fraud devices and tactics being used by credit card companies.

Credit cards are such a ubiquitous part of modern life that it can come as a bit of a surprise to find they were invented only in 1950. That was when Diners Club was established by a group of American businessmen to enable them to buy meals in restaurants without needing to hand over cash. In 1959 the American Express card was launched as the familiar embossed plastic card. At first the bill on all types of card had to be paid in full at the end of each month, but by the 1970s it was possible to carry debt over from one month to the next and so the modern credit card came into being.

Close-up of a security chip on a credit card.

Although the convenience of credit cards to the user was immediately obvious, the vulnerability of the system to fraud soon became apparent. Before long, the earliest and most simple credit card fraud was being employed. This involved pickpockets stealing cards, then using them to buy products. An early security measure was to add a paper strip to the card on which the owner could sign their name – and then ask them to sign the credit card bill when making a purchase. Thieves who could fake a signature were still able to use stolen cards, so credit card companies then introduced phone numbers for cardholders to call if the card was stolen so that it could be canceled. These days additional security features on most credit cards include a personal identification number (PIN) which is set personally by the card-holder for extra security, an electronic microchip, a magnetic strip on the back and a hologram on the front.

Taken together, the various security measures above have made it increasingly difficult for criminals to gain much advantage from merely stealing a credit card. Rather more profitable are those other widespread fraud and forgery techniques that go by names such as "skimming" or "phishing".

Skimming is when a dishonest employee of a legitimate trader copies details of a credit card when taking a payment. This typically happens when the credit card is taken out of the sight of its owner on a pretext, then run through a machine that copies its electronic components. Skimming may also happen when a cardholder uses a cash machine, whereby a device is fitted on to the cash machine that reads the card as it is inserted.

The criminal then manufactures a fake card and loads on to it all the electronic data that has been skimmed. Skimming is difficult for a holder to detect, but credit card companies find it relatively easy to detect the point at which a card was skimmed and can take action against the trader.

Phishing is an email technique that involves the criminal emailing a person and disguising the email to look as if it is from their bank or credit card company. The email usually makes a spurious claim that requires the cardholder to send the bank details of the card. If the holder replies to the email with this data, it allows the criminal to produce a false card.

Card criminals fit devices to cash point machines that read the card's details.

It is estimated that in the UK forged cards produced by skimming and phishing cost credit card companies around $240 million (£120 million) in fraud.

Even easier for the criminal is to use the data from a skimmed or phished card to buy products over the internet or by mail order. In these circumstances no actual forged card is needed, only the data. In both cases, the criminal will often make sure that the forged card works by making a small donation to a charity website. If the payment goes through, the criminal knows that the card works. However, credit card companies are becoming wise to this scam, and have come to recognize a small charity donation as signaling the start of a fraudulent spending spree. They will sometimes contact a cardholder to ask if a high-value purchase made immediately after a small charity donation is genuine. Often it is not.

FRANK ABAGNALE – THE GREAT CON ARTIST

The poor boy who became the world's greatest con artist, pulling off a series of scams so audacious that Steven Spielberg made a film about him.

Frank Abagnale.

The signs were there from the start. Even as a boy, born in 1948, Frank W. Abagnale bought things using his father's credit card and then sold them for cash. Then when he was 16, so the story goes, the judge at his parents' divorce hearing tried to make him choose between living with his father and his mother. He ran away.

His destination of choice was New York. Physically he was tall and, amazingly, his hair was beginning to go prematurely grey. On his driving license he changed a digit from 4 to 3 and suddenly he was ten years older – and his job prospects improved markedly.

There was no doubting it, Abagnale was, and remains, a scam-minded man. Having opened a bank account, he had the idea of printing his account number in magnetic ink on the deposit slips available on the counter. It had to be worth a go. Every time someone used a slip to make a deposit, the money went straight into Abagnale's account. He made over $40,000/£20,000 in this way. By the time the bank discovered the scam he had changed his identity.

But the most audacious scam of all was when he passed himself off as a pilot – never, thankfully, actually having to fly a plane, but hitching a ride with genuine Pan Am employees and enjoying the airline's hospitality in terms of food, drink, hotel accommodation. This is one of the most memorable scenes in Spielberg's **Catch Me If You Can**.

Frank continued to aim high. Having forged a Harvard law diploma he passed the necessary exams and landed himself a position in an attorney general's office. He was supervisor in a hospital for a time, lectured in sociology at a college, and passed himself off as a stockbroker. Perhaps his cheekiest move of all was to pose as an FBI agent.

To gain his pilot ID, Abagnale contacted an ID card company requesting a sample of their work with his details on it. No one asked any questions.

Steven Spielberg and his wife Kate Capshaw at a special screeing of Catch Me If You Can.

And he amassed money. Lots of it. Perhaps $2.5 million/£1.25 million. According to the man himself, it was all about supporting a lifestyle that allowed him to get girls. The fact that he had defrauded people in every state in the USA and in a staggering 26 other countries was just an unfortunate side effect of this five-year mission. He was just 21 years old.

But Frank's time was up. An Air France employee recognized him from a wanted poster and he was arrested in 1969. A five-year stretch in French, Swedish, and US prisons followed. But the audacity did not stop there.

For the past thirty years, Abagnale has turned establishment. He has written books, most recently on fraud prevention, and has been advising the world on fraud and identity theft. The latter, he believes, is the crime of the future. He is a frequent guest on US talk shows and in 1989 even co-hosted a show called **Crimewatch Tonight**.

He has an extremely slick website which announces the amazing truth:

> Mr. Abagnale has been associated with the FBI for over 30 years. He lectures extensively at the FBI Academy and for the field offices of the Federal Bureau of Investigation. More than 14,000 financial institutions, corporations, and law enforcement agencies use his fraud prevention programs. In 1998, he was selected as a distinguished member of "Pinnacle 400" by CNN Financial News.

It goes on to say that he believes punishment for fraud and recovery of stolen funds are so rare that prevention is the only viable course of action.

Interviewed by a US magazine, he once said that he still gets ideas for scams but, being a respectable family man, he doesn't act on them these days.

FAKE MONEY

Counterfeiting money is a cat-and-mouse game that has been around for hundreds of years and will no doubt always be with us.

Counterfeit French 10-franc coins.

"When it comes to counterfeiting," says Robert R. Shannon, researcher at the University of Arizona, Tucson, "you have to fool some very clever people."

It wasn't always such a sophisticated art. Counterfeiting notes began in earnest in the British colonies in the mid-1700s, when paper money was introduced. In those days, since many colonists were illiterate, extremely rough and ready fakes would suffice. All one really needed was a printing press.

On 1 May 1758, an Englishman by the name of Vaughan was the first to be hanged for forgery of bank notes. He had hired a number of engravers, each of which created a portion of a note. He then joined these together and posed as a wealthy man. Until one of his employees informed on him.

Back in the U.S.A, after the failure – due to counterfeiting – of the Continental Congress's currency, it was left to private banks to issue currency. Around 1,600 banks did so, producing over 7,000 different types of notes. Before long, more than a third of Ameriacn currency was fake.

By 1862, this had increased to at least half of US currency. **The New York Times** claimed that 80 per cent of banknotes were fakes. Counterfeiting, it announced, was "undermining our morality as a nation." The situation was so bad that the Secret Service was formed in order to tackle forgers.

One of their first targets was the infamous William E. Brockway, New York's "King of Counterfeiting" who was in charge of a ring which, between 1850 and 1890, was responsible for producing hundreds of thousands of fake bills. Eventually the Secret Service caught up with Brockway.

Artful, but on a smaller scale and more subtle, was German immigrant and sign painter Emanuel Ninger. He was a one-man band who drew his fake notes by hand on top-quality bond paper which was not the same as that used for currency, but close enough. This he cut to size and then "aged" with coffee. It is, of course, much easier to pass on an old-looking note than a new one.

He then traced the pattern of an original note onto the paper, carefully going over it with ink once he had completed it in pencil. He used a fine brush to recreate the colored threads found on real bills. It was

Ninger's notes are prized by collectors, but not traded openly because treasury departments have the right to seize all counterfeit notes.

a time-consuming business, but it did not go unnoticed and he kept his anonymity. Every week he would leave his farm in New Jersey and make small purchases with his notes in New York. By 1892, the **New York Times** was admiring his "particularly fine counterfeit of a 50-dollar bill". It had been scrutinized by bankers and "received the respectful consideration it deserved."

Faking coins has an even longer, and equally fiddly, heritage. Villains would saw gold coins in half, scrape out the gold, fill them with base metal, and then solder them together again. But they would then either be the wrong size or the wrong weight. Bankers replied by creating slots that measured the size of coins, and then they would weigh them. And so it went on.

No such craft is necessary for today's counterfeiters. The descendant of the early faker's printing press is one of their most useful tools: the scanner. Even as recently as 1990, a 600 dpi (dots per inch) color scanner might have cost you $20,000/£10,000. Now you can get a 4800 dpi scanner (i.e., one giving much more detail) for $500/£250. Hundreds of billions of dollars now circulate worldwide, and those who are in charge of foiling the fakers know this dialog will never end. "With enough money, counterfeiters can do anything," says Shannon. "If a group wants to invest $1 million to make phony currency, they can simply buy intaglio presses and print exactly the same currency printed at the U.S. Treasury Department's Bureau of Engraving and Printing."

A fake $100-bill found at the Korea Exchange Bank headquarters in 2005.

BOGUS LOTTERY SCHEMES

Fraudulent schemes all over the world fool gullible members of the public into thinking they have won a lottery fortune

Genuine Big Game Lottery tickets being sold at a store in Chicago.

The arrival of the Internet has made it alarmingly easy to prey on naïve members of the public by sending out spam emails that suggest to the innocent that they have become suddenly wealthy. Many of these messages inform people that they have won amazing prizes in lotteries they didn't even know they had entered. Prospective victims will generally receive a letter or an email stating they are the winners of a lottery, even though they had not bought a ticket. To make this claim seem more authentic, the forgers will often also attach some kind of certificate or communication with apparently official verification. Such attachments include certificates from the IRS (Internal Revenue Service) in the U.S.A. and from the Metropolitan Police in the U.K. The Metropolitan Police, indeed, have issued an official statement to the effect that they would never support or provide evidence for any lottery wins. In the UK, the fraudsters then demand a fee to release the winnings.

In the U.S., meanwhile, a common strategy is to send random pop-ups to people across the country. These inform people that they have won a huge amount of money and invite the credulous to send off postage and administration charges in order to claim large but unspecified financial rewards. None of these "winnings" ever appear, while the fraudsters make off with the hefty administration charges.

When these bogus lotteries first appeared, unsuspecting folk all over the world immediately fell for the scams but, as the public became more used to seeing such messages pop up regularly on their screens, the scams themselves had to become more sophisticated in order to continue to deceive. In one scheme, for example, fraudsters sent out thousands of messages informing members of the global Internet community that they had won a FIFA-sponsored lottery inspired by the 2010 Football World Cup in South Africa. These bogus notifications contained not just virus attachments, intended to steal the computer users' identities, but specifically requested bank details in order that the FIFA money be paid directly into winners' bank accounts. Anyone unsuspecting person who sent their details, however, soon found that, rather than winning prizes, their accounts were promptly emptied of all their savings by a gang of highly professional computer experts.

Police spokespeople could only say, not unreasonably, that if computer users suddenly discovered that they had won a considerable amount of money, they should be extremely suspicious as it was almost certainly not true.

In the U.K., a scheme was set up in 1999 to distribute nearly $6 million/£3 million pounds of money raised from the National Lottery. Individual awards would be limited to $10,000/£5,000 and they would be given to small-scale but deserving local causes. A highly organized team of fraudsters then immediately sent in a whole range of genuine-looking applications for a wide variety of community enterprises – $1,000,000/£500,000 was claimed for "sports" programs; $400,000/£200,000 for "heritage projects" and nearly $2 million/£1 million for the promotion of local community cohesion. Since the idea of the fund was that it should be easily accessible and not hampered by bureaucracy and red tape, most of these bogus applications were successful. A huge chunk of the fund thus disappeared forever.

The scam was eventually discovered in 2005. The government wasn't keen to go into details, in case this encouraged other fraudsters to try the same trick, but did reveal that all applications had seemed "really genuine" and that the scam had only been uncovered when a whistle-blower at the Big Lottery Fund told them that it had been going on since the scheme's inception in 1999. Nineteen men and one woman were arrested and the scheme was suspended.

A real ticket from the New York lottery.

There is little the police authorities can do to protect people, except to tell them to be wary of anything that looks too good to be true.

BILL GATES ASSASSINATION HOAX

Is Bill Gates the world's most hoaxed man? It can be hard to tell with the spoofer's Number One target. Not everyone sees the funny side, though...

When you're the richest man on the planet, hoaxers regard you as fair game. There are entire websites devoted to making up crazy tales about the Microsoft chairman, Bill Gates – including that he is not the world's wealthiest man!

Most spoofs are just harmless fun, but sometimes they get rather out of hand. In 2003 jokers at the online gaming website CG-Rom set up a spoof web page modeled on the CNN News network site, which regularly updates its website with the latest business news stories. Financiers keep a close eye on the news so that they can react to events and keep ahead of their competitors. The spoofers knew this was ripe for a set-up.

The hoax CNN website led with the shock announcement that Bill Gates had been gunned down by a lone assassin while attending a gala charity event in Los Angeles. Most people who saw it realized it was not to be taken seriously. But not everyone in the world understands western humor.

South Korean news agencies discovered the website and immediately alerted the country's three main TV stations, MBC, YTN, and SBS, all based in the capital, Seoul. The broadcasters lost no time in going live with the news. Would his death rock the global electronic industry so vital to South Korea's economy?

The shock announcement triggered a wave of panic selling: in a few hours of frenzied activity the Korean stock exchange dropped 1.5 per cent and lost a staggering \$3 billion/£1.5 billion. For those bankrupted in the pandemonium, the joke was not so funny.

This was not the first Gates' assassination story. A highly realistic film of the "killing" was made by US humorist Brian Fleming and posted on his website, complete with **LA Times** banner heading, and photograph of the body. It also linked to a website giving excerpts from a realistic-looking document called **The Garcetti Report** – purportedly written by Los Angeles County District Attorney Gil Garcetti – into the "Murder of William H. Gates III". The report claimed the killing occurred on 2 December 1999.

The earliest-known Bill Gates stock market hoax concerned an alleged Microsoft "hostile takeover" of the Catholic Church. It included a quote from Gates promising "to make religion easier and more fun for a broader range of people." Those participating were promised exclusive electronic rights to the Bible.

One of the longest running Gates hoaxes, invented in 1997 by Bryan Mack, an Iowa computer science student, is based on the old chain mail letter ploy. Victims receive a personal invitation to take part in research for Microsoft's browser software Internet Explorer. Simply forwarding the offer to try the "Microsoft/AOL/Intel

There's one born every minute... A year after the CNN Gates' death hoax was first posted, a Hong Kong-based paper, *China Daily*, published it again!

email beta test" to contacts would earn the lucky participants $245/£124 a time.

According to Mack, that hoax started as "a joke between a couple of friends." But once spoofs start they are difficult to stop. The Gates name has such caché that few can resist and the hoax is still doing the rounds today. Luckily it is harmless: entirely virus-free, unless you include spreading "red face syndrome", a condition experienced by those who discover they've been had.

One hoaxer even tricked Gates. On 1 April 2002, Quebec radio "shock jock" DJ Sebastien Trudel phoned Gates posing as Canadian PM Jean Cretien, inviting Gates to a Montreal strip-joint. Even when the bogus premier cursed his own PC – "Damn computer! Who's the idiot that invented it!" – Gates didn't smell a rat. Eventually Trudel owned up: "[Gates] did not seem angry but he did not find it funny!" he said.

One hoax even claims the "Millennium Bug" was itself a hoax engineered by Bill Gates to punish the bullies who picked on him at school. Clearly preposterous . . . or is it?

Bill Gates contemplates another hostile hoax at a Microsoft press conference, 1997.

BOILER ROOM SCAMS

A film lifting the lid on Boiler Room scams was released in 2000, yet this brand of financial fakery still appears to be thriving all over the world.

We are all, to some extent, at the mercy of the money markets.

The Boiler Room scam is a process whereby a "company" of stockbrokers is set up, with the sole intention of selling worthless or non-existent shares to unsuspecting clients. The success of the scam is heavily reliant on the effectiveness of the sales people involved, who must convince investors to part with thousands of pounds with a cold call.

You might think that no one would fall for such an outrageous and apparently transparent lie, but these outfits are extremely sophisticated. Not only are lists of enthusiastic investors in the stock market used as a basis for calls, but the "brokers" are rigorously trained – in particular to deliver their persuasive script – and often believe they are working for a legitimate company – at least initially.

One such "broker" mentioned to a friend that he would like a job in finance and in the sun. Soon after, his "friend" had fixed him up with a job at "Windsor Advisory Services" which operated out of Barcelona. He was not aware that he was doing anything illegal for the first few months, he told the UK's **Guardian** newspaper: "[and by then]… I was … so used to big money that I put my scruples aside."

Still, his patter had always been misleading. "I would always start off by telling cold call targets that they had responded to a marketing survey in the past year – never true, as we got names and numbers from UK shareholder lists." His other technique was to make sure targets had a pen and paper to hand, so they could write down the huge profits that were to be made, thereby reinforcing them. This "… also put you in charge: you were dictating to them."

This "broker" allegedly gave up because he started to feel sorry for the victims –

A Boiler Room scam will target investors in one country from a location well removed from that country, which considerably aids the deception.

one was 90 years old – although this is unconvincing, since he went on to work at another boiler room company. Perhaps the rumors circulating at the time that the big boss would soon be unable to pay the brokers had more of an effect.

"Brokers" might be able to make $10,000/£5,000 or more a month – real money, which enables them to support an extravagant lifestyle – the cars, the drugs, the women – however fake the foundation upon which that money has been earned. It is easy to see how you could feel like the "real deal" when you can lead the same life as him – and use cocaine to alleviate any doubts.

So who are the losers? The FSA (Financial Services Authority) carried out a survey on UK boiler room scam victims and found that, on average, they were losing $39,333/£20,000 each to the con men. Most victims were men over 50 living in London and the South East, and claimed to be experienced investors.

In the US they like to do things big, of course. As long ago as 2000, the **New York Times** magazine was reporting boiler room scams worth $50–$100 million/£25–£50 million, the first of which was a "joint venture" between five mafia families. Managing to miss the point in spectacular fashion, such cases have resulted in huge competition between lawyers, each vying to handle the biggest "pump and dump brokerage" case in history.

Frenetic buying and selling on a Stock Exchange floor.

But spare a thought for the innocent stockbroker. One posted a comment about the 2008 Gunter case – where a US father and daughter relieved 15,000 UK residents, most of them pensioners, of a relatively modest $4,600/£2,300 each – on the web. "I find it a shame that these boiler rooms soil the name of the industry," he said. "A huge number of people that invest . . . do so on the back of unsolicited calls, which are genuine and hopefully end up earning them money." He almost sounds naïve.

FAKE BANK WEBSITES

Modern society is awash with con artists setting up fake bank websites which dupe individuals into parting with personal banking information.

Data protection is one of the fastest growing industries in the world, and for good reason.

The scam has been around for some years, originating in West Africa, but in 2007, figures suggested that, between 2004 and 2006, there had been a threefold increase in "pirate" bank websites. It is a truly international crime, in that companies committing the fraud operate all over the world.

One trick is to pose as an online payment system such as Paypal, sending an email saying that the system has gone down and your bank details are needed for clarification. The con artists are sophisticated. They may mention that this is for security reasons, to make you feel safe. All the correct financial services logos will be on the documents.

In the US in 2007, $3.2 billion/£1.6 billion was lost to online banking fraud, affecting 3.6 million adults. In the UK, there were 14,156 fake bank websites in 2006, up from 1,713 the previous year. The rise is expected to continue.

So far, banks have always paid back defrauded customers promptly. However, the scale of online fraud is now so large that banks such as the Bank of Ireland have started to say that this may not always be the case.

Consumer groups are up in arms, but in a sense you can see the banks' point. Before this, they paid up because fraud demonstrated that there was a hole in their security system; if people are being tricked into volunteering their own details, this is not the banks' fault.

The advice is this: however convincing their website is, whether they ask for it via email or telephone, never tell anyone your PIN number. And if they ask for it, they are not who they say they are.

In webspeak, sending out emails en masse on the assumption that a handful will respond is known as "phishing".

PHANTOM PROPERTY

Property fraud is a highly lucrative business – the stakes are high and even experienced investors can be dazzled by the potential profits.

In May 2008, Norman Schmidt of Colorado was sentenced to 330 years in prison for a property fraud that netted him around $38 million/£19 million from over 1,000 victims. Schmidt created an entirely fictitious property development using forged title deeds and photos of other properties and locations. Investors were promised a quick return. To give the scheme an air of reality the first few investors were paid handsomely using the income from later investors. As the number of investors boomed, but before the scheme was unmasked as a fraud, the criminal absconded with the money. A total of $18 million/£9 million was retrieved by investigators.

Another classic property fraud is to sell a plot of remote, undeveloped land on the promise that it will shortly appreciate greatly in value, due to the emergence of other developments nearby. During the 1930s Florida was developing rapidly and many areas of swampland became highly valuable house plots as roads were built. Criminals produced fraudulent road plans backed up by forged government authorizations in order to sell worthless plots of swamp for high figures. The scam still takes place. In 2006 Dudley Cohn was convicted of selling plots for $15,000/£7,500 that were worth barely $1,000/£500 each on the promise that a road would shortly be built linking them to the interstate.

But perhaps the most famous property hoax took place when Czech con man Victor Lustig convinced scrap metal merchant André Poisson in 1925 that the Eiffel Tower was going to be torn down. Lustig rented an office from the Paris City Council inside the City Hall, posed as the "Deputy director-general of the ministry of Posts and Telegraphs", and got hold of all sorts of fake ID, stationery, and other "official" documentation. Then this bogus Council representative sold the Tower to Poisson – and fled to Vienna with a suitcase stuffed full of banknotes.

WORLD'S BIGGEST DIAMOND

After enterprising British businessman claimed to have discovered, and attempted to sell, the world's biggest diamond in South Africa, the whole enterprise was revealed as a hoax.

A miner holds the Cullinan Diamond shortly after it was found in 1907.

In late August 2007, newspapers all over the world reported the discovery of the world's biggest diamond in the North-West Province of South Africa.

Since 1905, the Cullinan had been the largest diamond found in the world at 530.20 carats. This new rock was reputed to be twice its size. The diamond house selling the jewel was a company called Two Point Five and though its spokesman, a British businessman called Brett Jolly, was not prepared to reveal where or how they had found the diamond, he did say that the gem was being kept under armed guard in a vault in Johannesburg and that no one had yet decided what to do with it. Prospective purchasers should expect to pay around $30 million/£15 million.

In October, and nearly six weeks after Two Point Five's first announcement, Jolly was still refusing to state the name of the mine where the diamond had been found or to identify its owners. Ernst Blom, Chair of the South African Diamond Council and President of the World Federation of Diamond Bourses, said that he had repeatedly asked to gain access to the stone but that this had been denied and that the only photo he had seen showed a low-resolution image of a green, glassy crystal. Blom said that, from what he could see, the diamond was "a disgusting lump of resin".

Blom then asked Jolly for documents relating to ownership of the stone and its discovery but none of these appeared. Blom had never previously experienced such elusiveness and said that any legitimate operation would immediately have produced all such documentation.

Having refused to take Blom to the site of the discovery, Jolly then invited media organizations to pay him to take them there. Only one journalist agreed to these unusual terms and Jolly kept him blindfolded for most of their minibus journey. Toward the end, the reporter later said, a row developed between Jolly and one of his business associates, André Harding. Harding apparently won and the minibus then stopped in the middle of nowhere. Harding then pulled off the reporter's blindfold to reveal the stone. He also produced a "diamond tester" to prove its value though it appeared to the reporter that Harding had preset the device to flash to "diamond" before he had even got out of the van.

On the way back to Johannesburg, Harding told the reporter that he had been in the diamond trade for decades and that he was sure he was being followed by "government agents". He therefore kept the diamond, he said, in a safe welded to his car.

Shortly after reports of this bizarre expedition appeared, Ernst Blom openly declared that he was withdrawing from the verification process. A leading trade journal called **Mining Weekly Online** conducted a new interview with Jolly, during which he claimed that he had only just moved into diamond trading from property development, and that he earnestly wished that he had never got involved with the diamond in the first place.

Mining Weekly said that Jolly had offered the magazine the opportunity to examine the stone but only on condition that the magazine applied for permission to publish its findings. It was clear, by this stage, that Jolly suspected that his diamond was a fake. He told the magazine's website that, depending on the outcome of investigations, he was now preparing to lay charges of theft and fraud against Harding who had also offered to sell him the land on which the diamond had been "found".

The world's biggest diamond house, De Beers, was delighted. It owns the Cullinan and didn't want its iconic status displaced. "The search for diamonds is just so romantic," said its spokesman. Sadly, it was not so for Mr Jolly.

As events reached a head, Brett Jolly confessed to being "very confused" and declared that he "no longer cared whether it was a diamond or not".

SCIENCE & TECHNOLOGY

Throughout history, advances in technology have been blamed for all sorts of corruption – sometimes with good reason. Without film and stills cameras – and Photoshop – there would indeed be less scope for creating UFOs, ghosts, and fairies (although it should be remembered that it is not the box or the software itself that has the mischievous intent). One way or another, Orson Welles, Elsie Wright and Frances Griffiths, or any of the other fraudsters you can read about in the following pages would have created havoc, whatever the tools at their disposal.

Advances in science and technology may function as either the cause or the effect of scams. Cheap, very detailed scanners have assisted the forgers of banknotes immeasurably; bankers in the 1800s created slot machines to catch the fake coins of counterfeiters. The has provided countless opportunities for those on the make, and it is that beautiful thing to those who operate on the fringes of legitimacy – unregulated (witness the activities of the fake Viagra salesmen).

What the fakes and forgeries of science and technology highlight most of all, though, is humankind's ambition. In scholarship, where this is combined with inexperience and a willingness to cut corners, wholesale ruin of reputations is the only possible result. Such was the situation with the anthropologist Margaret Mead – who never knew it – and embryo researcher Hwang Woo-suk – who did, although at first he denied everything and claimed that his projects had been sabotaged.

Such blundering pales into insignificance, however, next to the wickedness of those who fake anti-malaria drugs – at the expense of thousands of innocent lives.

PILTDOWN MAN – THE FAKE MISSING LINK

The famous case of the fossil that appeared to provide the "missing link" between man and primates fooled the world for 40 years.

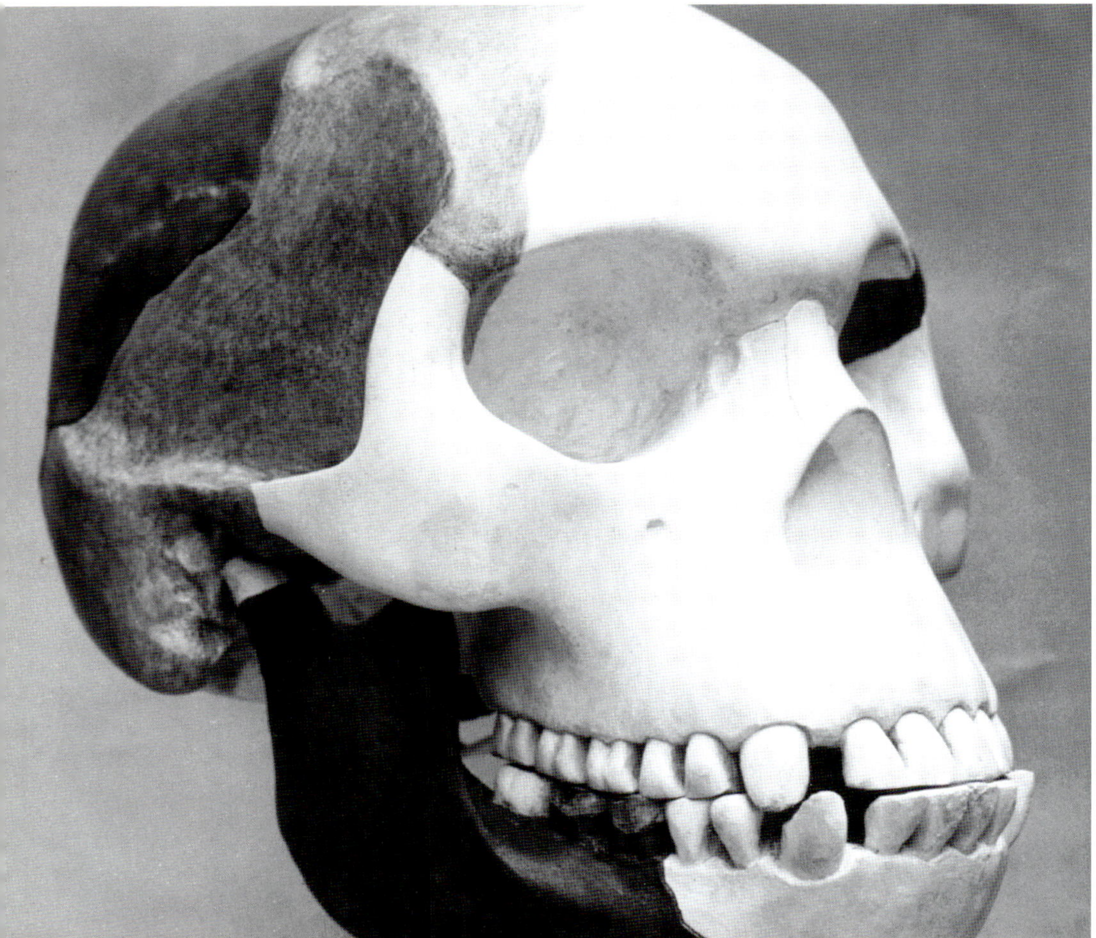

The cast of the first construction of the celebrated "Piltdown Man".

This hoax is so well known that the phrase "Piltdown Man" has now entered the English language, used to describe any questionable research.

It was 18 December 1912 and newspapers were carrying the kind of headlines that excite people the world over – headlines such as "Missing Link Found – Darwin's Theory proved". Charles Dawson, an amateur archeologist and solicitor, had just found the most important fossil in the world in a gravel pit in Sussex, south-east England. Keeper of Geology at the British Museum, Arthur Smith Woodward, assisted his friend Dawson with his finds.

Charles Darwin had brought the world his theory on the origin of the species in 1859. The 50 years since had been fraught with scientists trying to prove the great man right – or wrong – in thinking that human beings were related to primates. Now a skull and jaw fragments were being unveiled at the Geological Society in London which seemed to prove just that. Significant Neanderthal fossils had already been found in Germany and France, so the race was very much on. British scientists were elated to prove once and for all that human civilization began in earnest in the UK. The fossil was named **Eoanthropus dawsoni** in Dawson's honor.

It was claimed that the fossil was at least 500,000 years old. It might even have been closer to 1,000,000. Also found at Piltdown was what was thought to be a "digging tool" shaped like a cricket bat. Everything went quiet in Piltdown after Dawson died from septicaemia in 1916 and nothing new was found in either of the sites that had seemed so exciting only a few years earlier.

Many legitimate fossils were questioned in the four decades that followed, because they did not seem to fit with the skull found at Piltdown. Then, on 21 November 1953, the Piltdown finds were revealed to be fakes. The skull, which had been treated with chemicals to make it appear old, was not more than 500 years old. The jaw was that of an orangutan. A file had been used on the bones to get rid of any tell-tale evidence. The "cricket bat" digger was made out of genuine elephant fossil bone and shaped with a metal blade.

Still. Who was the forger? In the 1970s, the plot thickened further. A trunk was found that had belonged to a volunteer at the British Museum during Dawson's time. His name was Martin Hinton. In the trunk was a number of what looked like test fakes. Like the skull, these were bones that had been cut and treated to look very old. Of course the explanation may be perfectly innocent. In such a climate, Hinton may have been conscientiously trying to figure out how forgers set about creating their fakes. But the Piltdown Man, at least, was decades away from being discovered as a fake. Did he have something to do with the Piltdown Hoax? Or was it simply Dawson or Woodward? The mystery remains unsolved.

Unfortunately for more recent fossil fraudsters, they have been busted within their lifetime. One such was eminent German anthropology professor Reiner Protsch von Zieten. The professor's claim that he had been fortunate enough to "find" the elusive missing link skull – 36,000 years old, no less – in a peat bog near Hamburg was just the beginning. He went to make the rather extraordinary claim that modern humans and Neanderthals had not only co-existed but might even have had children together.

Professor Protsch was described as having a fondness for gold watches, Porsches, and Cuban cigars – but he was unable to work his own carbon dating machine. As investigations continued, an alarming catalog of all his untruths and inaccuracies emerged. Protsch's cover was finally blown when he was caught trying to sell his department's chimpanzee skull collection to the US.

Nearly one hundred years on from Charles Dawson's well-known "discovery", we are no closer to knowing the identity of the Piltdown Man forger.

THE MYTHICAL MUMMY

The mummified body of an ancient Persian Princess seemed like an archeological marvel. The find soon captivated the world's press – but the embalming was fake and hid a grisly secret.

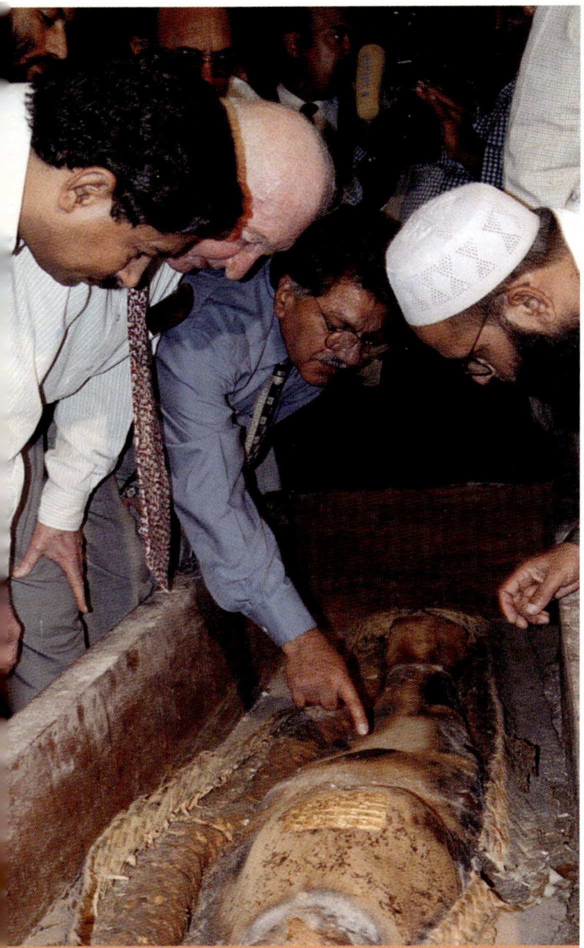

Pakistani officials examine the mummy.

When a 2,600-year-old mummy was suddenly discovered in Pakistan's south-western Balochistan province, close to the border with Afghanistan, the event nearly sparked a diplomatic row. Who had the right to this exciting find, which was certain to draw scientists – and tourists – from far and wide?

Pakistani police located the mummy in a wooden sarcophagus in October 2000, following a tip-off from an informer. Subsequent inquiries led them to the town of Quetta, and the home of Baloch tribesman Wali Mohammad Reeki. He explained that he had procured the mummy from an Iranian, Sharif Shah Bakhi, who chanced upon it in Iran, following an earthquake. They were trying to sell it on the black market for $11 million/£5.58 million.

The mummy certainly looked to be the genuine article. It was wrapped in bandages and resting in a wooden sarcophagus which was covered with religious images. So the mummy was immediately taken to the National Museum in Karachi where it was kept under the eye of the guards before being presented to the world's press.

Archeologist Ahmed Hassan Dani told journalists that a preliminary examination suggested the mummy was genuine, dating from 600BCE. He thought it was possibly the daughter of King Xerxes of Persia, according to cuneiform writing on a gold plaque found on the body. Or perhaps she was an Egyptian princess married to a Persian king and hence buried in the style of her own country.

The Iranian Cultural Heritage Organisation immediately laid claim to the mummy. Iran demanded the return of their royal heritage, threatening to mobilize Interpol. Afghanistan's Taliban government said their experts must get involved. While authorities in Quetta claimed the police raid had been illegal.

When the museum's curator, Professor Asma Ibrahim, carried out scientific tests on the mummy he was in for a shock. It was the body of a 21-year-old woman bludgeoned to death just two years before. Her internal organs had been removed and the corpse filled with powder to dry it out, prior to bandaging. It was not an ancient artifact at all, just a modern murder.

THE FAKE PHYSICIAN

Most people have faith in doctors. The more highly qualified they are the more we trust them. Dr Abrams relied on this to perpetrate the greatest medical fraud of all time.

Few medical practitioners have more impressive qualifications than Dr. Albert Abrams. Trained at the illustrious University of Heidelberg in 1882, Abrams was vice-president of California State Medical Society, professor of pathology at Cooper Medical College, and president of the San Francisco Medico- Chirurgical Society. He was also a quack.

In 1916 he launched a hitherto unknown treatment called the "Electronic Reactions of Abrams" (E.R.A.). This was based on his unproven claim that all diseases vibrate at their own unique frequency. This frequency can be detected in blood or hair samples – or even handwriting – sent via the mail.

Diagnosis and treatment were made using electronic gizmos called "oscilloclasts". They were not for sale but could be leased from Abrams. Thousands of "therapists" applied. They did not mind the high cost as there was bigger money to be made from patients. E.R.A was applauded in the journal **Physico–Clinical Medicine**, published by Abrams himself.

In a typical session, a specimen was placed on a sample holder (or "dynamizer") in the oscilloclasts. A connection then went from the machine to the forehead of a healthy person – "the reagent" – who stood on a rubber mat facing west. The practitioner diagnosed the disease by manipulating the reagent's abdomen.

Abrams assumed that those who used his therapy, rather than conventional medicine, were probably hypochondriacs with nothing clinically wrong with them. Diagnosis invariably revealed a number of diseases, often including cancer and TB but always syphilis. This guaranteed the patients' secrecy – even if they suspected fraud. Further adjustments to the machine brought about a long-distance cure.

By 1923, reputable medical journals were denouncing Abrams as a fraud, his claims demonstrated to be both false and intentionally deceptive. **The Lancet** mailed a sample of guinea pig blood to try to catch him out. The animal was indeed diagnosed with syphilis. But it all came too late. Abrams died of pneumonia in 1924 – a wealthy man.

Dr Abrams and his famous machine.

THE TASADAY TRIBE

A stone-age tribe discovered, complete with cavemen outfits and tools, in a rainforest in Philippines is revealed decades later to be a money-making enterprise by a local fraudster.

In June 1971, in the Philippines, a local official named Manuel Elizalde claimed that he had been led into the rainforest by a tribesman called Dafal who had introduced him to a tribe that had never previously had contact with the outside world. They called themselves the Tasaday.

The Tasaday Tribe was incredibly primitive. It consisted of seven men and six women who lived in caves deep in the jungle. They dressed mainly in leaves and wore their long hair tied back in ponytails.

Since they had no idea how to cultivate crops or rear livestock, they subsisted on a diet of fruit and vegetables as well as freshwater fish and crabs that they caught with their bare hands. They appeared to be astonishingly peaceful and their language contained no words for "weapon", "war", or "enemy". Ancestral lore had told the tribe never to leave the site and suggested that their savior would, one day, appear. They believed that with the arrival of Elizalde, the prophecies had all come true and they looked to him as their savior.

The Philippine President, Ferdinand Marcos, immediately declared that, unless the entire area was protected by the army, the tribe would be overwhelmed. So he posted soldiers outside the caves and all visitors to the camp had to apply for a permit from Elizalde. Very few were issued. Shortly afterwards, the **National Geographic** magazine ran several articles about the tribe and CBS broadcast a documentary about the discovery. Elizalde used the publicity to create a charitable foundation to preserve the tribe and celebrities queued up to donate funds.

Then a few slightly discordant things happened. One scientist, having been denied permission to carry out research, hung around outside the caves and claimed that he witnessed a member of the tribe smuggling in some sacks of rice. Another researcher said that he had spotted members of the tribe smoking cigarettes. Elizalde mocked all of these reports, stating that the researchers' accusations were nothing more than the jealous claims of the scientifically excluded.

In 1986, nearly 15 years after the Tasaday were first discovered, General Marcos' regime was overthrown and, suddenly, scientists had much greater access to outlying regions of the Philippines. A Swiss anthropologist called Osward Iten had been waiting to study the group for years and he joined up with a local journalist called Joey Lozano to make a documentary. The pair headed straight for the caves, which were deserted. They scoured the area and soon found the 'tribal members' less than a kilometer away, living in simple but modern huts, dressed in jeans and T-shirts and smoking.

Iten and Lozano were amazed. The tribe said that they were, in fact, members

The evidence was overwhelming. The whole charade would have been uncovered in a matter of minutes, if it hadn't been for Manuel Elizalde.

A member of the fake Tasaday tribe, apparently living in "Stone Age" conditions.

of two other local tribes and had been living in modern housing for decades. The two men showed them the article in **The National Geographic** and then recorded footage of the tribespeople laughing heartily at the illustrations. These clips were shown as part of an ABC documentary called **The Tribe that Never Was** and viewers were mesmerized. Why had no one spotted such an obvious hoax?

It emerged that, amongst other blatant clues, the Tasaday had been wearing commercially manufactured materials; had been seen with weapons made of foreign materials; had been openly trading with other local tribes for decades; and spoke a language that shared 85 per cent of its vocabulary with the other local tribes.

The reason that the hoax ran for so long was partly down to Elizalde himself, who was incredibly convincing, and partly due to the public's willingness to believe. Elizalde left the Philippines soon after the documentary was broadcast and took with him the entire $35 million/£17.7 million he had raised for the charitable foundation for the preservation of the tribal way of life. The local people appeared to have gained little, if any, benefit from the deliberate financial fraud while Elizalde took his millions and went to live in Costa Rica. Here he became a drug addict and died in squalor in 1997.

THE FAKE BIRD DINOSAUR

Greed, ambition, and mischief have all played their parts when human beings dig up artifacts, fossils, and bones. And nothing captures the imagination like dinosaurs.

In the 1800s, the dinosaur enthusiast Thomas Henry Huxley, who was a friend and distinguished colleague of Charles Darwin, sought to answer what was and remains one of the most pressing questions in paleontology: where do birds fit into Darwin's evolutionary tree?

He examined a new fossil from Germany, the Archaeopteryx, which was making waves in paleontological circles. The excitement was due to the fact that there were clear signs of feathers on the animal, making it the earliest fossilized bird ever found. But there was more. Huxley observed that the skeleton looked like those of the therapods – a family of meat-eating dinosaurs. Perhaps he had at last found a place for birds in evolution. Birds, he announced in the 1860s, came from dinosaurs.

Many dinosaur experts thought his claim was absurd. How could such a small, delicate, airborne thing as a bird have anything in common with those great lumbering giants of the earth, dinosaurs? What Huxley and those who supported him needed was solid evidence of some kind of link.

The fossil of the Archeopteryx.

Cut to China, 130 years on. Around 130 million years ago, the Liaoning region in the north of the country had been a wetland filled with wildlife, before volcanic eruptions covered the area, preserving many animals as fossils in its silt. Two fossils were found in Liaoning in the 1990s that seemed to help Huxley's case at last, although they did not prove it conclusively.

A fossilized animal they called Sinosauropteryx was found by Chinese scientists in 1996. This had a lot in common with other dinosaurs, but again appeared to have feathers on its body. Then, in 1998, another apparent relation of the dinosaurs was found, this time with what looked like even more distinct feathers. Other similar discoveries followed. The problem was, paleontologists were still not satisfied that these were "missing link" animals. Perhaps they were simply new species of bird. Or perhaps those weren't feathers at all.

Then it happened. In spring 1999, at the Tucson Gem and Fossil Fair in Arizona, a fossil showing true "transitional features" turned up. It had the skull and upper body of a bird, but the teeth and hands of a dinosaur. It also had the legs of a bird but the tail of a dinosaur. It seemed to capture the moment dinosaurs began to experiment with flight. The amateur collector who bought it certainly thought so: he paid $80,000/£40,000 for it. Not long after, the discovery was hailed with great fanfare in **The National Geographic**.

But paleontologists are not an easily convinced lot. Such was the potential importance of this fossil – apparently smuggled out of China, where such finds are classified as "national treasure" and not meant to be bought and sold – it was admitted to the University of Texas at Austin for examination.

The conclusion reached was that it was a composite, a "mosaic" carefully constructed using several different fossils: the front part was the skeleton of an ancient bird cemented on to a slab. It was a fake, reminiscent of that other famous "missing link" hoax the Victorian "Piltdown Man" (see p.126). It had doubtless been altered to increase its value on the underground market.

But fortunately for dinosaur and bird lovers everywhere, the story did not end there. The specimen still has implications for the evolution of birds. Dr. Timothy Rowe, of the University of Texas said, "Now

The "archeoraptor" was scrutinized using high-resolution Computed Tomography (CT) X-ray equipment, a technique more normally employed in medical examination.

. . . we can see that there is a new species of extinct bird present in the forgery and that it definitely deserves to be studied and described. The tail came from a different animal altogether," he added, "and it has already been described and named Microraptor. We may never know where the legs came from."

People hoping to find the link between birds and dinosaurs were, ultimately, disappointed.

THE MAKE-BELIEVE MERMAID

Showman P. T. Barnum, the king of "fakery", was famous for playing tricks on visitors to his museum but his "Feejee Mermaid" capped them all – he duped the public three times over.

P. T. Barnum with "Tom Thumb".

The build-up to the arrival of the great explorer and naturalist Dr. J. Griffin and his amazing discovery was relentless. For months, New York City newspapers were swamped with letters announcing the imminent appearance of Dr. Griffin of the "British Lyceum of Natural History" and his "Feejee Mermaid".

When Dr. Griffin finally turned up, in the summer of 1843, reporters besieged his hotel demanding to see the exotic creature he had brought. They were not disappointed and rushed off to file their stories. Lurid journalistic prose was accompanied by woodcut illustrations of a beautiful sea maiden – fair of face and bare of breast – provided by famous showman Phineas Taylor Barnum. That the image was half female and half fish simply added to the allure.

Soon the streets of New York were awash with pamphlets giving more information about these seductive sirens. Dr. Griffin gave lectures at the New York Concert Hall in which he described his voyages to "Feejee" and other South Sea Islands where mermaids abound. By the time the mermaid went on show at Barnum's American Museum in New York the excitement was at fever pitch. Ticket sales soared.

For Barnum, this was his greatest hoax ever – he had pulled off a triple sting. First, Dr. Griffin was entirely bogus – he was an accomplice of Barnum's called Levi Lyman. Second, the British Lyceum of Natural History did not exist, Barnum made up the name. Third, the exhibit was not a beautiful sea maiden at all but the withered upper body of a dead monkey stitched to a fish's tail – an ugly monstrosity.

Barnum was the master of showmanship. He had been a store owner and newspaper publisher in Connecticut before moving to New York in 1835 and turning his hand to variety shows, later buying a museum and renaming it "Barnum's". He combined his experience of sales and journalism to make the museum a success.

Many of the attractions were genuine, including the original "Siamese Twins", Chang and Eng, and the midget "Tom Thumb". Barnum also exhibited the world's biggest elephant, the very first "Jumbo". The

The "Feejee Mermaid" is thought to have been made by fishermen in the East Indies, to represent a spirit of the seas in their religious festivals.

authenticity of these attractions made it all the easier to convince the public that his bogus exhibits were genuine too.

On one occasion he claimed to have found a weed that would turn black people white. Another hoax involved William Johnson, an African-American of restricted growth and abnormally small head who Barnum described as a "man monkey" and the "missing link" in the evolution of apes to humans. To add to the myth, Barnum made up a gibberish "jungle language" for Johnson to speak.

P. T. Barnum was not the first person to attempt to make money out of the "Feejee Mermaid". An American ship's captain by the name of Samuel Eades had acquired the object from Dutch merchants in the Far East, having sold his ship to raise the $6,000/£3,000 he needed. Despite taking the mermaid on tour and even exhibiting her in London, Eades was never able to recoup the money he paid and died impoverished and in debt. On his death, the mermaid passed to Eade's son. He sold it for a pittance to a Boston showman called Moses Kimball, who ran his own museum of "weird and wonderful creations". Still, the "Feejee Mermaid" failed to make money until Barnum leased it from Kimball. It took all Barnum's skill as showman and hustler to make it a star attraction.

When the "Feejee Mermaid" was not on tour it was on permanent show in New York or Boston. It continued to draw the crowds until it was destroyed in a fire. Barnum never admitted duping the public, claiming his scams were "humbugs" to attract visitors to his museum. His "mermaid" was the most successful humbug of all.

Another famous mermaid – the Little Mermaid in Copenhagen, Denmark.

FROZEN FOLLY

Nothing captivates subscribers to **Discover** magazine quite like reading about a new find in the animal world – and the more bizarre the better. The April 1995 issue did not disappoint.

Few creatures are as bizarre as the hotheaded naked ice borer, scourge of the Antarctica. Readers of **Discover** were informed that the ferocity of these hairless, razor-toothed, mole-like creatures belies their minuscule size.

Hunting in packs, they slither through tunnels they've carved in the ice, silently stalking their target – a solitary penguin. Then, by heating a unique bony plate on their forehead, they melt the ice, causing the hapless bird to topple into their slushy trap. The ravening hotheads then devour their prey like a pack of pink piranha.

For many readers, neither the date of the issue nor the name of the alleged discoverer, Aprile Pazzo (Italian for April Fool) alerted them to the fact that this report might have been less than genuine. It drew the biggest response of any story in the magazine's history. Many readers wrote gushing letters asking for more information before realizing they had been suckered by bogus biology.

One enthusiastic response came from The Small Mammal Zoo and Discovery Center in San Francisco. Curator Shigatsu Baka announced that directors had set aside $2 million/£1 million for the construction of a special area where the ice borers could be housed. He had also asked the California Academy of Sciences to donate "some of the weaker members of their penguin exhibit" to the discovery center in order to sustain their little stars. The Academy had been "cool on the subject", however.

Most readers spotted the joke and joined in enthusiastically. One writer thanked Aprile Pazzo for explaining the disappearance of her ancestor, polar explorer Philippe Poisson. His last diary entry had read, "Saw three of the creatures today but failed to capture any . . . Their repulsiveness is formidable." As Aprile had pointed out, the 5ft 6in/ 167 cm. Poisson would have looked like a large penguin to the ice borers.

The new species was very similar to the naked mole rat, above.

THE BOGUS BUTTERFLIES

Linnaeus was the greatest scientist of his age who created the species classification system used in biology. Though even he could be fooled.

Carl Linnaeus (1707–1778) was a Swedish doctor and naturalist who devised the famous "Linnaean taxonomy" system used by biologists today. The system attributes a genus and species name to plants and animals in order to distinguish them from all others.

To carry out his task Linnaeus traveled all over Europe collecting plants and animals to study and classify. He also received specimens from other collectors from around the world. Some of the species differed from others in extremely subtle ways but there was not much Linnaeus missed – except, perhaps, for an entirely bogus species of butterfly.

In the twelfth edition of his groundbreaking work **Systeme Naturae** (1763), Linnaeus describes and names three yellow butterflies in the section headed "**America Septentionali**." One of them, the European brimstone butterfly (**Gomneptryx rhamni**) is entirely genuine. The other two were given as examples of a related but much rarer North American species, which Linnaeus named **Papilio ecclipsis**.

The main difference between them is that the European brimstone has plain wings whereas the North American variety had unusual blue patches or "eyespots" on its wings. On one of the examples, the eyespots are very noticeable indeed. It was only when the English butterfly collector John Curtis (1791–1862) studied the collection many decades later that the hoax was uncovered. Someone had carefully painted the eyespots on the wings.

Remarkably, Curtis suffered from poor eyesight for much of his life and was blind by the time he had died. But even he managed to spot the colorful subterfuge. It is not known exactly who perpetrated the hoax, but the pranksters must have gained great satisfaction from seeing their creation in print in one of Linnaeus's highly respected works.

The "fake" North American butterfly species, with its unusual blue "eyespots".

UNIDENTIFIED FLYING OBJECTS

Not many subjects excite such strong feeling and fierce debate as unidentified flying objects (UFOs), and none is so famous as The Roswell Incident of 1947.

The Roswell Incident is supposed to have occurred in June 1947, in New Mexico, USA. Apparently, that month, rancher Mac Brazel found sticks and metallic debris like tinfoil on his farm. Some weeks later at market, he heard of UFO sightings in the area and decided his strange finds might be worth reporting to the sheriff.

The sheriff's response was to tell Major Jesse Marcel, Roswell Army Air Field and Intelligence Officer. Marcel inspected the wreckage, and concluded that the debris was from a flying saucer. The very next day the headline in the **Roswell Daily Record** read: "RAAF [Roswell Army Airfield] Captures Flying Saucer on Ranch in Roswell Region." The airforce collected up the debris and took it in for examination.

Then they changed their story. The debris was part of a high altitude weather balloon or radar target, they said. Everything went quiet for 30 years. Then, in the 1970s, interest was sparked once more. A retired Florida professor claimed to have interviewed witnesses to Roswell, who said they had not only seen the UFO but had also witnessed its alien occupants.

Suddenly witnesses began appearing everywhere and stories, more or less plausible, abounded. Someone even claimed to have footage of an alien autopsy, which has since been widely discredited. Many people suspected a government cover-up and a top-secret project led by President Truman to recover and study all foreign or extra-terrestrial materials. More recently there has been a trend toward believing that there was indeed a government cover-up – but that what they were concealing was their own aircraft development program.

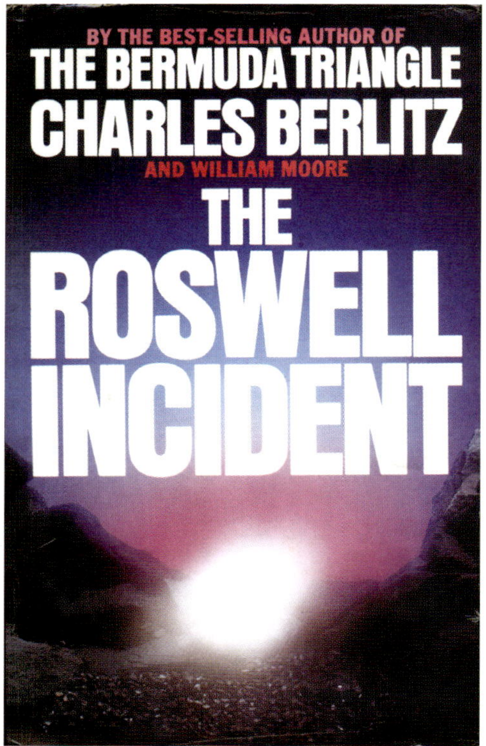

Berlitz and Moore's account of America's most famous UFO story.

Over thirty years later, on the night of 26 and 27 December 1980, the UK had its very own Roswell, although Americans were still central to the action. American Servicemen based at RAF Woodbridge and Bentwaters, Suffolk, reported seeing strange lights in nearby Rendlesham Forest.

Several airmen followed the various different combinations of lights – which they described as "weird phenomena". One of them, Deputy Base Commander Lieutenant Halt, gave a running commentary into his Dictaphone. Some of the lights were beams which appeared to originate from up in the sky; others were described as red, white, and blue.

The men then described seeing an alien spacecraft, triangular in shape. Locals Tony and Maureen Boreham claimed to have witnessed "this huge thing which was a mass of bright orange lights hovering above the trees". Maureen was sure it was a spaceship and described it as being "as big as a fairground ferris wheel". But former USAF Security Policemen, Kevin Conde, claimed the lights were the result of a practical joke he played on the airmen. "I drove my patrol car out of sight from the gatehouse, turned on the red and blue emergency lights and pointed white flashlights through the mist into the air," he said.

As with Roswell, many still think Rendlesham was a cover-up for suspect military activities. Some were as specific as to say that the RAF were developing stealth bombers. And as with Roswell, there are those who will swear to their dying day that there were UFOs in Rendlesham Forest that night.

If a poll conducted by the **Rendlesham News** is anything to go by, we – or at least the residents of Rendlesham – are protective of our UFOs. The paper posed the question "What happened in Rendlesham Forest in December 1980?" In response, 83 per cent (281 people) maintained there was a UFO; 5 per cent (18 people) thought there was no UFO, believing it to be a lighthouse or a police car or a tractor, and 12 per cent (40 people) believed the story was created as a distraction, possibly to cover up a military accident.

A nuclear physicist, a teacher, and an author published a book in 1980 claiming the Roswell debris was unfamiliar and surprisingly tough.

A local resident captures a "flying saucer" hovering over a field in Oregon, USA, 1951.

FAKE CROP CIRCLES

Crop circles are a mysterious and fascinating phenomenon. They have been around for millennia, and at least some of them are the work of fakers . . .

All sorts of crop circles have been recorded in all sorts of crops – and in grass as well as grain – all over the globe in all sorts of different ways throughout history. Among the earliest was one found in Lyon, France, in AD816. There were medieval crop circles too. One late-16th-century woodcut shows the devil mowing a field into patterns.

This is a good illustration of how an era and a culture expresses that which it most fears. In God-fearing medieval times, the devil is depicted as the hand behind the crop circles, although witches were sometimes blamed, or fairies. In more recent years it has been put down to UFOs and, more recently still, the weather or electromagnetic pollution caused by radio masts and mobile phones. None of which proves these are not to blame, where an explanation cannot be found, of course.

Crop circles have extraordinarily regular and beautiful patterns.

Some crop circles are certainly the work of hoaxers, though. David Chorley and Douglas Bower ("Dave and Doug") have claimed responsibility for a huge number of crop circles found in southern England from 1978 onwards. The whole idea started in a pub in Hampshire, they say. Ninety percent of UK crop circles – and some years as many as 98 per cent – are found between Dorset and Norfolk on what is known as the aquifer line. This is a layer of rock that can hold water.

"How To Make Crop Circles" on the file-sharing website YouTube gives an idea of both the methods used by fakers and their motivation for creating them. If you have a team of six people and a length of rope for measuring out your circle you are most of the way there. Much of the flattening out is trampling by feet, but people also roll around, or roll garden rollers on the crop. In fact according to the hoaxers, balls are

Crop circles are unlikely to be created by mini tornadoes, as some suggest – these move around and could not make such precise and regular patterns.

responsible for the "feathering" effect at the edge of circles which used to be felt by "croppies" to be an indication that a circle could not be manmade.

And why do they do it? As with most hoaxers, the thrill is in standing by while believers believe and find telltale signs of the circles' authenticity. Others find the creation of circles a kind of spiritual experience in itself. They are, in a sense, believers themselves. One such on YouTube views crop circles as "temporary temples". For some it is a money-making enterprise, pure and simple. They may be in cahoots with landowners who, charging "croppies" and regular tourists about $2/£1 a time, may make $60,000/£30,000 from a circle.

Not that believers will have it that the story ends there. They would say, "What of the circles that are never seen by people? What of the farmers who keep them quiet because they don't want the hassle? What of circles where there are no footprints?" Again an Internet trawl gives a good indication of the inexact science we are dealing with. The majority of those who discuss crop circles want them to be genuine.

Not so for one expert, Dr. Colin Andrews, who has been studying crop circles for 17 years. He estimates that 20 per cent are caused by small movements in the earth's magnetic field and the rest are manmade. The former are created when a small shift in the earth's electromagnetic field flattens the crops in its path, he believes. George Bishop, of the Center for Crop Circle Studies, agrees that this is possible, and might be why, in some circles, electrical equipment doesn't work properly.

But thankfully there will always be room for doubt, as circlemaker John Lundberg found out one night in Wiltshire. "It sounds embarrassing," he said, "but I have had a UFO sighting while making circles in Wiltshire."

THE FAKE RADIO BROADCAST

The radio drama whose trickery was so convincing that hordes of listeners believed they were experiencing an alien attack.

New Jersey residents really believed the aliens were coming to get them.

On Halloween night, 1938, listeners tuned into CBS radio station to be greeted by frenzied "newsflashes" about an alien invasion. In fact, what they were listening to was the 23-year-old Orson Welles introducing his live radio drama **War of the Worlds**, adapted from H. G. Wells's 1898 novel, and with the action uprooted from late Victorian-era Surrey to contemporary but remote Grovers Mill, New Jersey.

Yet those who switched on after the introduction thought they were listening to something far more sinister.

Welles's "Announcers" began to broadcast reports from various U.S. observatories that explosions of incandescent gas were occurring at regular intervals on Mars and then "moving towards the earth with enormous velocity".

In a dramatic masterstroke "Professor Pierson of the Observatory at Princeton University" – an actor – calmly reassured the public that the chances of living intelligence on Mars were a thousand to one, and dismissed intense shockwaves near Princeton as "merely a coincidence" and probably a large meteorite. Still, the "commentator", Carl Philips, persisted. This is an extract from the actual radio transcript:

> PHILIPS: And yet how do you account for those gas eruptions occurring on the surface of the planet at regular intervals?
> PIERSON: Mr. Philips, I cannot account for it.
> PHILIPS: By the way, Professor, for the benefit of our listeners, how far is Mars from earth?
> PIERSON: Approximately 40 million miles.
> PHILIPS: Well, that seems a safe enough distance.
> (OFF MIKE) Thank you.

Then, according to reports, a huge, flaming cylindrical object landed in Grovers Mill. The professor and the reporter Carl Philips made it to the scene. Just as the professor was beginning to doubt that this was a meteorite because it was not made of any terrestrial metal, its top unscrewed and a hideous monster emerged.

> PHILIPS: Good heavens, something's wriggling out of the shadow like a grey snake. Now it's another one, and another. They look like tentacles to me. There, I can see the thing's body. It's large, large as a bear and it glistens like wet leather. But that face, it . . . Ladies and gentlemen, it's indescribable. I can hardly force myself to keep looking at it. The

Many listeners to Welles's broadcast had idly flicked over from *The Charlie McCarthy Show* while one of the variety acts was being introduced.

eyes are black and gleam like a serpent. The mouth is V-shaped with saliva dripping from its rimless lips that seem to quiver and pulsate.

Indifferent to the white flag raised to it by officials, the monster proceeded to attack onlookers with a heat ray. Soon, around 40 people lay dead, their bodies "burned and distorted beyond recognition". Martial law was declared.

This was just the beginning. Soon after announcing there was no cause for alarm, senior official Captain Lansing spotted an alarming machine, a "shield-like affair rising up out of the cylinder".

It proceeded to wipe out the huge numbers of troops deployed to repel this enemy, horrified listeners heard. And cylinders were falling all over the country. In New York, boats overloaded with a fleeing population were pulling out from docks, they were informed. The scale of the response has been exaggerated over time, but the police were inundated with calls and some people fled, fearing for their lives.

So why did Welles do it? Mischief mainly. Just like the author of the novel he based his radio play on, H. G. Wells, Orson liked to stir things up. The great George Orwell wrote of how H. G. Wells delighted in unsettling respectable people. "Back in the 1900s it was wonderful . . . for a boy to discover H. G. Wells," Orwell wrote. "There you were, in a world full of pedants, clergymen, and golfers . . . and here was this wonderful man . . . who knew that the future was not going to be what respectable people imagined."

Orson Welles rehearsing the War of the Worlds broadcast.

LUNAR LUNACY

A world-renowned astronomer, famed for pushing back the boundaries of space science, would expect his latest amazing "discoveries" to be believed – no matter how fantastic they may seem to others.

The early 19th century was a time of feverish speculation about the question of life elsewhere in the solar system. The astronomer Sir William Herschel, discoverer of Uranus, went to his grave convinced the Sun was inhabited. Philosopher and science writer Thomas Dick wrote extensively about "Moon men", suggesting telescopes would soon become so powerful that Earth-bound astronomers would view lunar dwellings and communicate with the occupants.

The subject was ripe for spoofing and Richard Adams Locke, newly appointed editor of a small New York-based daily newspaper, **The Sun**, was the man to do it. In 1834 Sir William's astronomer son Sir John sailed to South Africa to chart the southern sky. His reputation was on a par with his father's and great discoveries were expected.

A year later, Sir John reached the Cape of Good Hope and set up his giant telescope. In this pre-radio age, communication between Africa and America was painfully slow, so when would Sir John be able to send back his first report? Readers of the **New York Sun** would soon find out.

This was the moment Locke had been waiting for. He began to publish a series of dispatches that Sir John had purportedly sent to the **Edinburgh Journal of Science**. In the first report, headlined "Great Astronomical Discoveries Lately Made by Sir John Herschel" it was announced that the astronomer had solved all the optical problems that had previously limited telescopes to no more than a few hundred times magnification.

His new telescope had "a magnifying power of 6,000" and could see objects on the moon 18 in/45 cm across. In the dispatches that followed, "Sir John" described each spectacular observation in turn. The glories to be viewed on the Moon included forests, hills, seas, and brightly colored pyramids.

He saw a "goat-like animal" with a single horn, a spherical creature that "rolled with great alacrity across the pebbly beach", and other exotic creatures including a "biped-beaver", which resembled its Earth cousin in all respects except "its invariable habit of walking upon only two feet". Their huts were "constructed better and higher than those of many tribes . . . and from the appearance of smoke in nearly all of them, there is no doubt of its being acquainted with the use of fire."

Lunar animals and other objects allegedly discovered by Sir John Herschel.

The *Sun* never admitted the hoax, but its editor told friends the prank did go further than he had planned, making him the world's best "self-hoaxed man".

Meanwhile, Sir John continued his stargazing, oblivious of the extravagant claims being made in his name thousands of miles away. "Sir John's" dispatches were keeping **Sun** readers spellbound and sales of the newspaper steadily increased. Even the finest minds at Yale University were fooled by the phoney stories. According to one contemporary writer, professors and students waited for the arrival of the next instalment with increasing eagerness. Each report was regarded as "the absorbing topic of the day".

Two Yale professors called at the newspaper's offices to see the original articles. They were told the **Journal of Science** was at the printers and spent all day being sent from pillar to post in a fruitless hunt for a copy before abandoning the quest and going home.

Sir John finally heard about the hoax in a letter and took it in good humor, at first, saying, "It is too bad my true discoveries here won't be that exciting." But as the story spread he was soon being hounded by foreign journalists and scientists eager to know more. "I have been pestered from all quarters with the ridiculous hoax about the Moon," Sir John complained. He had now achieved international fame – but for a scientific spoof.

THE PERPETUAL MOTION MACHINE

Over-ambitious inventors who claimed to have created a machine that would run forever without requiring any source of energy.

John W. Keely, photographed around 1873, sitting proudly next to his Perpetual Motion Machine.

Charles Redheffer was a 19th-century inventor who lived in Philadelphia in the early 1800s. Redheffer was working at a time when scientific and technological advances were being revealed almost daily – and was determined to cash in on the trend.

In 1812, Redheffer told the world that he had designed a machine that would run forever without needing any energy input at all. This would solve all potential supply problems and would revolutionize industry. It was a miracle!

In the late 1800s, John W. Keely, a carpenter and mechanic also from Philadelphia, presented the world with a Perpetual Motion Machine. The "Keely Motor", claimed its inventor, worked using "free energy". Keely called this "etheric energy".

All of Philadelphia wanted to see Redheffer's working model for the

Wondrous Perpetual Motion Machine. It was such a breakthrough, claimed Redheffer, that he would be writing to the city's councillors to apply for further funding to build a bigger, better model that might just power the whole of Philadelphia. A date for a special viewing was arranged; an excited public waited with bated breath.

The public began to spread the word that the machine really did work. Within a year, Redheffer was ready to receive his official inspection from the government officials. They marched around, taking notes, while the inventor himself became edgy. He dissuaded the commissioners from getting too close to his machine, stating that it was a highly delicate piece of machinery and that any undue pressure might disturb its equilibrium and cause it to break down. One inspector in particular thought this was a little peculiar and decided to keep a careful eye out. He soon realized that the machine did not seem to function in quite the way the inventor had described.

Redheffer explained to the inspectors that the machine used a system of cogs to supply the energy for a quite separate machine alongside it, and that this was the key to its success. The beady-eyed inspector, meanwhile, soon noticed that, were this so, the cogs would be turning in the opposite direction. The side machine must have been supplying the energy source for the Perpetual Motion Machine rather than the other way around.

Away from the workshop, the inspectors thought up a cunning plan to expose Redheffer, should their colleague be correct. They commissioned a local

Seemingly undaunted by his unmasking in Philadelphia, Redheffer tried out his machine on the unsuspecting New Yorkers.

engineer called Isaiah Lukens to build a machine that was similar to Redheffer's, except that its mechanism was to be even more carefully disguised. They then invited the inventor to inspect it. Redheffer took one look, realized that his plan had been scuppered, and fled to New York.

No one in New York had yet heard about the Philadelphia scandal so Redheffer was able to start all over again, presenting his model machine in 1813. Again, the crowds flocked to see it. One of these was a mechanical engineer called Robert Fulton who noticed that the machine, rather than being supplied by no source of energy at all, must have been supplied by a hand crank hidden behind the machinery, which was causing the entire contraption to wobble. He was convinced that he had spotted a fraudster at work.

Fulton challenged Redheffer to prove his worth. If Fulton failed to expose the machine as a hoax, he promised to pay for any ensuing damage. Rashly, Redheffer agreed. Almost immediately, Fulton removed some loose boards from a wall beside the machine to reveal a long cord made of catgut, connecting the machine to some unspecified source of power.

Tracking the cord carefully up the stairs, Fulton discovered an elderly man who was peacefully sitting in an upstairs room, gently turning a hand crank while eating his supper. The baying crowds turned upon Redheffer and, in the ensuing chaos, destroyed his machine while he turned on his heels and fled.

As for Keely, when his laboratory was investigated after his death in 1898, false ceilings and floors were ripped up to reveal links to a silent water motor in the basement, while pneumatic switches under the floorboards were used to turn machinery on and off. A three-ton sphere was found in the basement, apparently a reservoir for compressed air. Hidden pipework was everywhere. It was clearly a case of fraud on a grand scale.

WILLIAM T. SUMMERLIN – WHITE MICE FRAUD

Research dermatologist who claimed to have transplanted skin tissue from unrelated animal species when he had merely painted it with dye.

In 1973, a dermatologist called William T. Summerlin was working as a clinical researcher at Stanford University and began to make startling claims that he had found a way to get the human body to accept foreign tissue during transplants. Rejection of foreign tissue had been the most common cause of failure of such operations and such a find would have represented a huge medical breakthrough. Scientists were skeptical since no one else could immediately replicate Summerlin's results. Nevertheless, an eminent immunologist called Robert A. Good took Summerlin on as a researcher at the Memorial Sloan-Kettering Cancer Center in New York City.

Over the next few months, one important breakthrough after another took place, most notably when white mice received successful tissue transplants from black ones. Good was quite happy to be associated with these results and, indeed, co-authored a few of Summerlin's research papers. Laboratory colleagues who worked with Summerlin day in day out were, however, deeply suspicious. By November 1973, even Dr. Good was beginning to have reservations.

Summerlin made new declarations: he had grafted skin from one human being to another, had implanted corneas on rabbits, and had transplanted glands between animal species. Colleagues declared that there was no way these results could be real. It simply wasn't possible. In 1974, Summerlin was asked to make a presentation to Dr. Good to justify his research. During this, other laboratory assistants noticed that the black patches on the white mice were not merely suspicious – they could actually be rubbed off using alcohol.

Summerlin was suspended while a committee looked into his claims. Initial results suggested that a mouse on which Summerlin claimed to have carried out successful grafting was, in fact, a hybrid breed. This meant that its genetic make-up would already have included some of the material that Summerlin claimed to have transplanted. It was also genetically compatible with the animal whose skin it had received and, therefore, much less likely to reject a transplant. Colleagues, meanwhile, said that they believed the black skin patches on white mice, which he claimed to have created using tissue transfer, had in fact been created with permanent marker pen. With regard to the experiments on humans, it seemed that Summerlin had again exaggerated his results. The transplant had failed on three of the five patients and the best that could be said about the other two was that they had not yet failed.

The committee eventually requested that Summerlin appear before them to answer questions in person. Under heavy pressure, he admitted that he had used a colored pen to touch up the mice and that he had never, actually, transplanted a cornea. The committee concluded that Summerlin had probably suffered from some kind of delusion that his experiments had genuinely succeeded. Dr. Good sent Summerlin to undergo a course of tests with a psychiatrist and issued a statement that his researcher was suffering a "serious emotional disturbance". Shortly afterwards, the committee concluded that Summerlin had, for whatever reason, falsified the results. The hospital gave him a year's pay and sent him away on medical leave, with instructions never to return.

The committee also concluded that while Dr. Good had played no active part in the deception, he should have exercized greater control over research that was partly carried out in his own name. Summerlin blamed professional pressure for his behavior and declared that his research work was over.

Good's suspicions did not mean closer supervision of his researcher; he merely stopped co-authoring the results of William Summerlin's work.

Summerlin with a lab rat at the the Memorial Sloan-Kettering Cancer Center.

TOAD'S REVENGE

Some scientists will go to any lengths to prove their theories correct. Biologist Paul Kammerer's research brought him both international fame and public shame – and all because of a toad.

A midwife toad.

Naturalist Charles Darwin caused huge controversy when he published **On the Origin of Species** in 1859, in which he proposed the theory of "evolution by natural selection". But Darwin wasn't the first to claim to know how new species of animals came about.

Before Darwin, many believed that evolution occurred through "inheritance of acquired characteristics", an idea put forward by the naturalist Jean-Baptiste Lamarck and called "Lamarckism". Until Darwin, many 19th-century thinkers subscribed to Lamarckism, including Darwin's own grandfather, Erasmus.

Lamarck said that changes occurring to an animal during its lifetime were passed on to the next generation. For example, a giraffe's attempts to reach up to feed on leaves just out of reach stretched its neck. This characteristic was inherited, so the next generation had slightly longer necks. In the 1920s, Austrian biologist Paul Kammerer (1880–1926) said he had proved Lamarck was right and Darwin, wrong.

Kammerer carried out experiments with amphibians – especially on salamanders and toads – in his laboratory at Vienna University. His approach was to keep the animals in non-natural environments and examine the effect on their offspring.

He began with salamanders. One species, the black **Salamandra atra**, lived in mountains and gave birth to fully formed offspring. The other, the spotted **Salamandra maculosa**, lived in valleys and gave birth to tadpoles. By raising them in the other species' environment he produced black salamanders that bore tadpoles and spotted salamanders that produced fully formed offspring – or so Kammerer claimed.

He then kept spotted salamanders on either black soil or yellow sand. These creatures normally had yellow spots on a black background. He hoped to show that the offspring of those raised on black soil would be totally black and those raised on yellow sand would be all yellow. Again he claimed success.

Finally, he experimented with a species of midwife toad (**Alytes obstetricians**). Unlike other amphibians, midwife toads mate on land, so they do not have black scaly lumps on their back legs that would otherwise allow them to cling on when mating in water. Kammerer wanted to prove that by forcing the toad to mate in water these lumps would appear in later generations of midwife toads.

Kammerer's research seemed to bear his theory out. By keeping toads in a filled fish tank with no opportunity to get onto a dry surface they were forced to mate in water. Generations of toads were born before Kammerer announced success – one litter of toadlings had the black scaly lumps he was waiting for.

If true, it meant scientists must re-write the biology books. For one thing, it made the creation of superhumans possible. For example, children of keep-fit fanatics would be born already fit and muscular. Over generations this line of humans would achieve incredible levels of strength and stamina.

Most biologists still believed Darwin, however. According to "natural selection", each generation was slightly different from its parents and only the most successful would survive and pass on their genes to their offspring. An individual's genes were fixed and couldn't be changed by events occurring during their lifetime.

Kammerer's evidence seemed to prove the contrary. He was invited on lecture tours and gained international recognition. But it did not last long. The biologist was exposed when the curator of reptiles at the American Museum of Natural History examined one of Kammerer's midwife toads and found that the scaly marks weren't scaly at all. They had been made by injecting black ink under the animal's skin.

The author Arthur Koestler claimed in his book *The Case of the Midwife Toad* (1971) that pro-Darwin sympathizers had sabotaged Kammerer's work to discredit him.

Kammerer denied he was the culprit and claimed a laboratory assistant was responsible. Facing ridicule, he committed suicide shortly afterwards.

Paul Kammerer and his amphibian friend.

THE FAKE DNA MAN

The ambitious South Korean scientist who claimed to have cloned a human embryo and produced stem cells from it.

Hwang Woo-suk explains his groundbreaking research – before his unmasking.

Hwang Woo-suk had a remarkably accomplished scientific career, indeed. In 1999 he claimed to have cloned a cow, in 2002 a pig, and then in 2004 the big one: a human embryo. In 2005, Snuppy was produced: an Afghan hound puppy who, his team claimed, was the first cloned dog.

Dr Hwang had an impressive CV prior to that, too. He had trained as a vet at Seoul National University and then gone on to study theriogenology – the science of animal reproduction – at MSc and PhD levels. When he was making his important, pioneering discoveries, he had an army of 15,000 fans who belonged to an online community calling itself "I love HWS".

To announce his human cloning accomplishments to the scientific community, Hwang chose to publish papers in the journal **Science**. The paper was greeted with surprise because it hac thought that creating a human stem cell in this way was more or less impossible, due to the complexity of primates. Hwang said that he used 242 eggs to create one cell line. The following year he said he had managed 11 stem cells with 185 eggs. Great advances in human medicine were expected to follow.

Instead, as a result of the comments of one of his team who had resigned, he was investigated for the way in which he had obtained eggs – from researchers who, it was said, were coerced. But there was worse to come. Hwang's second experiment was scrutinized by the university and declared a fake. For the astute, alarm bells had actually been ringing much earlier – Hwang produced no scientifically viable data for his cow cloning research.

At first Hwang claimed the projects had been sabotaged, but he was fired from his post at Seoul National University and – having received millions of dollars in funding from the state and through private donations – charged with embezzlement.

FAKE PHARMACEUTICALS

Fake pharmaceuticals are flooding the world market and their trade is described as "manslaughter" by medical researchers.

Some years ago, the World Health Organization identified a serious problem, particularly in developing countries: the creation of fake pharmaceuticals.

In China's Guangdong province, for instance, there is a thriving trade in counterfeit "antibiotics" made out of talcum powder, and "birth control pills" containing only rice flour. There is nothing useful about these pills and all are indistinguishable from the real thing.

In 2002, one estimate put the number of Chinese people dying the previous year as a result of fake drugs at 192,000. Some die from swallowing toxins, some from the infection that the drugs are meant to cure. Perhaps half of all counterfeit drugs contain no active ingredients or the wrong kind, and around 10 per cent are harmful.

Fake Viagra has been produced in factories in China, too, and then sold to U.S. customers via Internet retailers based in Nevada and Colorado. Another popular route for counterfeit drugs is into the U.S. from Mexico, where they are produced from active ingredients imported from India and China. Truly, this is a global industry.

The counterfeit drugs that have received the most widespread condemnation are fake anti-malaria drugs. In 2006, international researchers acknowledged that the lives of hundreds of thousands of malaria patients, most of them children, were at risk as a result. The problem was particularly bad in Asia and Africa.

Every year, around 1.5 million of the 300 to 500 million people infected with malaria die. Even so, drugs are reasonably effective – particularly artesunate tablets. But in southeast Asia, between 1999 and 2004 the number of fake artesunate tablets containing no artesunate at all increased from 38 per cent to 53 per cent according to studies by Paul Newton and Professor Nicholas White at the University of Oxford. In some countries, the majority of artesunate tablets are fake.

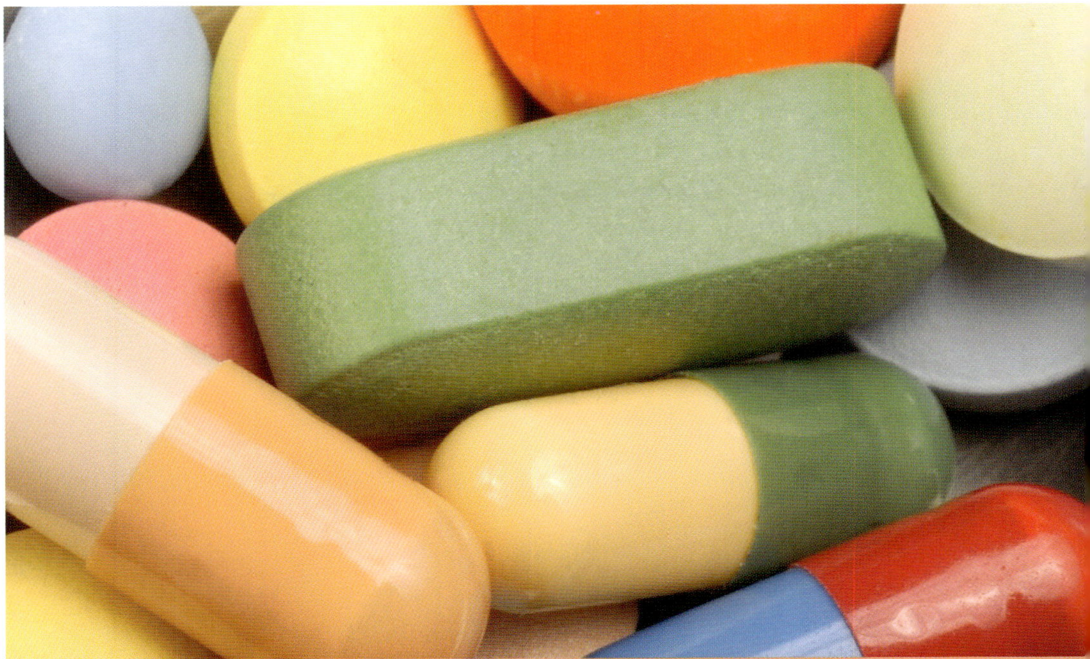

They look genuine enough – but do we really know what's inside?

HOAX WEBSITES

Some hoax websites are harmless pranks. Others are the dangerous brainchild of enterprising fraudsters and designed to strip the unwary of their money.

The number of websites that are forgeries has boomed in the past five years as page-making software has become cheaper and easier to use. The problem with distinguishing a hoax website from the real thing is that it is virtually impossible to check out the credentials of the site. Dedicated websites, such as www.whois.co.uk will reveal the name and address of the person to whom the website is registered, but that often leaves the viewer little better off, as the registered owner of a site is very often an agency or other third party. In most cases it is necessary to take the website at face value, though more diligent research is needed if a person is thinking of parting with a substantial sum of money for what purport to be airline tickets, investments, or other products.

Dehydrated water for sale?

The use of hoax websites is essential to the successful completion of many fraudulent dealings that seek to steal money from the uninitiated. Some of these sites go so far as to have "urls" that are almost identical to the real thing. Cleverly, they put the hapless recipient through to the genuine website once the personal details have been obtained. One entirely spoof site is www.buydehydratedwater.com, which purports to offer for sale dehydrated water. This nonsensical product – water with the water taken out – appears on the website to be a genuine product, the virtues of which are extoled in glowing terms. There is, of course, no such thing. Meanwhile, the website home.inreach.com/kumbach/velcro.html seeks to convince the reader that Velcro is a natural crop produced largely in California and that it is currently suffering a serious drop in production due to the effects of climate change and insect pests.

Equally humorous is the website www.funphone.com, which claims to use the newly discovered technique of "acoustiphotoelectromagnetic resonance" to turn any Internet-enabled computer into a telephone able to make calls to any other computer. If the site's instructions are followed to the letter, the hapless reader will end up shouting at the computer screen to no real effect. Meanwhile, the site www.bandersnatch.com/guide.htm claims to be the General Delivery University, which offers a wide range of educational diplomas by post. The School of Hard Knocks is, it says, an affiliated body. All utter nonsense, of course. Such sites are, by and large, easy to spot as fakes since the content is so patently absurd and most of the links do not work.

Rather more impressive and, at first glance, credible are websites where the designer has taken more care to include apparently genuine photos and links. A typical example is the website www.thedogisland.com, which claims to offer pet dogs a better home when their owner gets bored with them. There is supposed to be an island at some unspecified location where pet dogs are set free to lead a natural and enjoyable life. The website has an extensive FAQ page, where you find out what the dogs eat on the island. Similarly, we discover that "there were 10,000 rabbits

Life's a beach on www.thedogisland.com

Nobody really knows how many hoax websites exist, but they certainly number in the thousands. If a site seems too crazy to be true, then chances are it is.

released on to the island two years ago. We are not sure how many rabbits there are in total now, but they far outnumber the dogs, and continue to reproduce rapidly."

In rather more dubious taste is www.afterlifetelegrams.com, which seeks to convince readers that it is possible to send messages to one's recently deceased relatives by getting a terminally ill volunteer to memorize the "telegram". "Let someone know about an important event that they might have missed such as a wedding," urges the site. It is all done with complete seriousness.

There is plenty of scope for more hoax websites of course. All you need is a few basic web design skills and a bit of money.

MARGARET MEAD – THE ACCIDENTAL FAKER

The young, ambitious US anthropologist who built her entire reputation on believing the tall stories of some naughty Samoan girls.

In 1926, anthropologist Margaret Mead undertook research in Samoa, and this research became her book **Coming of Age in Samoa**. For the greater part of the 20th century, this was considered to be a defining work in the study of female adolescent sexuality and a very important book to science as a whole. And it turned Mead into one of the most famous and celebrated scientists in America. Certainly as recently as the 1990s students worldwide were being taught about the ground-breaking work of Margaret Mead.

But it began to emerge that her research was unreliable to say the least. Central to her whole thesis was the new and daring idea that adolescent girls in Samoa were sexually promiscuous before marriage. It is easy to see why the book attracted the attention it did and stirred up such excitement.

Margaret Mead's Samoan fieldwork between 1925 and 1926 was extensively documented by her, and submitted to the Library of Congress in Washington, D.C. The fact that she, presumably in an open-handed spirit of scholarship, did so would seem to support the idea that she was not the faker. Not intentionally, anyway.

Still, there were problems with the manner of her research, and the part about female adolescent sexuality rested on some fairly flimsy testimony. Essentially it boiled down to interviews Mead conducted with two young women: Fofoa Poumele and Fa'apua'a Fa'amu. In 1926, Mead was only 24, and so – it emerged – was Fa'apua'a.

What appears to be the truth of the matter only came to light 60 years later. Fofoa had died long before, in 1936, but her son, Galea'i Poumele, interviewed Fa'apua'a for a documentary in 1987. To the documentary-maker's surprise, it appeared that Fa'apua'a – by now a very old lady – wanted to get something off her chest. Galea'i asked her in Samoan whether Mead had ever questioned the two of them about what they did at nights, and whether they had joked about this. "Yes we did", she said, going on to say, "we said we were out at nights with boys; she failed to realize that we were just joking . . . " She reiterated this, before adding, "As you know, Samoan girls are terrific liars when it comes to joking." Galea'i then asked about the many subsequent times that they were questioned by Mead. "We just fibbed and fibbed to her," she said.

Mead died in 1978, so never knew the ending to the Samoa story.

So according to Fa'apua'a's new version of events, this was just two girls messing about. But should such a conclusion ever be drawn from such scanty evidence? Mead's supervisor, Franz Boas, must take his share of the blame here. Her destination was his idea, and it was he who put the idea of premarital promiscuity into her head. In a sense, she felt her job was to find evidence for this premise in Samoa.

Also, Mead was constantly worrying about her method. Five days after that first fateful interview with Fofoa and Fa'apua'a she wrote to Boas, asking, "If I simply write conclusions and use my cases as illustrative material will it be acceptable?" His view

Margaret Mead photographed at her home in California in the 1950s.

was as follows: "I am very decidedly of the opinion that a statistical treatment . . . will not have very much meaning, and that the characterization of a selected number of cases must necessarily be the material with which you have to operate."

So given that "Samoan girls are terrific liars when it comes to joking," why should we believe Fa'apua'a's revised account? Relying on the testimony of one person is always risky. What we do know, however, is that with her revised version, she swore on the Bible.

For devout Christian Samoans, apparently, lying under such an oath resulted in immediate sickness or death, followed by eternal damnation.

OTHER SCAMS AND FAKES

The Ponzi Scheme

Named after the famous fraudster, Charles Ponzi , this ficticious investment scheme relies on new clients investing money in an often non-existent product or business. The return from the new investments is used to pay dividends to existing clients. The scheme will inevitably fail as the earnings will always be less than payments made to initial investors.

The Romans

Fakes and forgeries were common practice, even in Roman times. Greek sculptures and works of art were often copied by Roman artists, who then sold them on to unsuspecting buyers as the original articles.

Balloon Boy Hoax

In October 2009, a homemade helium balloon floated above the sky over Denver, Colorado. Anxious parents, Richard and Mayumi Heene, attracted the media's attention claiming their son, Falcon was inside. Police tracked the balloon, but found it to be empty and a large-scale manhunt ensued. Eventually, however, the boy was discovered hiding at home. The Heene's nearly got away with their scam to direct media attention and goodwill donations their way until one reporter asked the boy why he hid. Falcon's response: "Because you guys said that, um, we did this for the show."

William Henry Ireland

William Henry Ireland was a forger of Shakespeare memorabilia. He got the idea from his father who was an avid collector himself. His father was overjoyed with his sons 'finds', which included scripts, letters and legal documents. His father died in 1800, still believing they were the genuine articles.

Joseph van der Veken

Joseph Van der Veken was regarded as one of the best art restorers in his field. However, he will be best remembered for his forgery of the 'Mary Magdalen' painting, originally by Hans Memling. He later went on to sell his work to Herman Goering during World War 2 and was even given a posthumous exhibition entitled Fake / Not Fake in Bruges, in 2004.

Mary Peck Butterworth

The original counterfeiter, Mary used cloth and a hot iron to transfer ink from American bank notes onto blank paper and then added missing detail by hand. She was arrested in 1723, but acquitted due to lack of evidence.

Foreign Lottery scams

Almost 8 million people in the UK receive junk mail through their letterbox promising them millions in overseas lottery wins. The way they make their money is through registration, or administration fees. Unsuspecting victims seduced by promises of riches are enticed to called premium numbers, or pay an administration fee in order to claim a prize that doesn't exist.

Robert 'Forger' Spring

Robert Spring was famous for his autograph forgeries, his most successful being those of George Washington, Benjamin Franklin and Horatio Nelson. He even invented a fake identity, that of Miss Fanny Jackson, in order to sell his wares. Spring went on to fake letters, documents and bank cheques and eventually fled to Canada to escape the law.

Shill Bidding

Shill Bidding is a very common scam used on auction websites such as eBay. It is when sellers, or their friends, bid on their own items to drive up the price. This is an illegal activity and auction sites refer offenders to local law enforcement.

Phishing

Phishing is a modern scam, where mass emails, or instant messages are sent out in an attempt to find secure information, such as user names, passwords and bank details. Often the email will look like they are from a genuine source, such as a bank or a famous website, in order to dupe the unsuspecting victim. Often emails direct you to sites that are very similar to the real ones they are pretending to be: watch out for typos and misspelled domain names, as these are a dead giveaway!

Family Fun Run Fraudster

In 2008, a benefit cheat was caught out in a lie that had cost the UK government more than £12,000 in disability allowance over 3 years. Brian Rawsthorne, from Manchester, claimed he could only walk 20 yards, but was later caught on camera, completing a 10K charity fun run. He continued to claim benefits for another year until he was prosecuted.

Fake Cancer Woman

One woman in America faked having cancer for 2 years to scam people out of thousands of dollars. After discovering a benign lump in 2008, Ashley Kirilow went on to tell the world she was suffering from cancer, she even starved herself and shaved her head to perpetuate the lie. She then created a bogus cancer charity, conning people, including family members, into donating to the cause. Her father became wise of the scam and convinced donators to press charges 2 years later.

The Cardiff Giant

The Cardiff Giant was an American hoax from the 1800s. A tall petrified man measuring 10 foot (3 metres) in height was uncovered by workers behind a barn in Cardiff, New York. The 'giant' was commissioned by Methodist, George Hull after an argument about a bible passage claiming that giants once lived on the earth; the sculptor was sworn to secrecy. The giant was displayed as an exhibition and people were charged fifty cents to view it. Later, famous fraudster, P.T. Barnum, offered $50,000 dollars for the giant. Barnum was turned down and so went on to create his own giant from wax, calling the original giant a fake. Luckily Barnum escaped prosecution for calling the original a fake, as they both turned out to be fake!

Gap Year Scams

These scams prey on the humanitarian nature of students wishing to travel to a 3rd world country and help a local community. Made famous by Prince William's gap year trip, many spurious companies have sprung up offering package tours where gap year students can teach English or help build wells. Often most of the money paid goes into the pockets of the travel company and students are left in a strange country with no support and making no difference whatsoever to a local community.

Priory of Sion

The Priory of Sion is a ficticious secret society founded and dissolved by Pierre Plantard in 1956. Plantard who also made false claims to the French throne is said to have created this fake society to establish a bloodline from the famous Merovingian Dynasty, who themselves claimed to be descended from Christ. The Priory of Sion, although continually debunked as fictious, enjoyed a brief revival in 2003 when it was referred to as factual by Dan Brown, author of The Da Vinci Code. Famous members of this made-up society include Debussy and Isaac Newton.

The Turk

The Turk was a fake chess-playing machine 'invented' by Wolfgang von Kempelen in 1770. The machine was in actual fact a large box with a chess master hidden inside. The chess master would operate the machine through a series of cogs and magnets.

Catherine Murphy

Catherine Murphy was the original faker of counterfeit coins. Unlike Mary Peck Butterworth, the British courts found Catherine Murphy guilty of high treason. She was the last woman to be burnt at the stake, in 1789.

Front cover © Getty Images
Back cover © Thinkstock
Page 2 © Claro Cortes IV/Reuters/Corbis
Page 9 © Lindsey Parnaby/epa/Corbis
Page 10 © Alen MacWeeney/Corbis
Page 12 © Underwood & Underwood/ Corbis
Page 13 Time & Life pictures/Getty Images
Page 14 © Doug Byrnes/Corbis
Page 15 © Paul Almasy/Corbis
Page 16 © Hulton-Deutsch Collection/Corbis
Page 19 © Nicolas Asfouri/epa/Corbis
Page 20 © Bettmann/Corbis
Page 22 © moodboard/Corbis
Page 23 © Azzara Steve/Corbis Sygma
Page 25 © Michael Nicholson/Corbis
Page 26 © Austrian Archives/Corbis
Page 29 © Bettmann/Corbis
Page 30 © Bettmann/Corbis
Page 31 © Corbis
Page 32 © Photonews/TopFoto
Page 33 © Photonews/TopFoto
Page 34 © The Art Archive/Tate Gallery London/Eileen Tweedy
Page 35 © Bettmann/Corbis
Page 36 © WireImage
Page 38 © The Art Archive/Corbis
Page 40 © Bettmann/Corbis
Page 41 © Le Segretain Pascal/Corbis Sygma
Page 43 © Reuters/Corbis
Page 45 © Alen MacWeeney/Corbis
Page 48 © Bettmann/Corbis
Page 49 © Bettmann/Corbis
Page 50 © Bettmann/Corbis
Page 51 © Sol Neelman/Corbis
Page 53 © Bettmann/Corbis
Page 56 © Frank Miller/Corbis
Page 59 © Bettmann/Corbis
Page 60 © Corbis/Sygma
Page 63 © Bettmann/Corbis
Page 64 © Bettmann/Corbis
Page 65 © Reuters/Corbis
Page 68 © Popperfoto/Getty Images
Page 70 © Cleveland Police/Handout/ epa/ Corbis
Page 74 © Jason Reed/Reuters/Corbis
Page 76 © Bettmann/Corbis
Page 81 © Bettmann/Corbis
Page 83 © Corbis/Sygma
Page 85 © Peter Harholdt/Corbis
Page 86 © Shawn Thew/epa/Corbis
Page 88 © Bettmann/Corbis
Page 91 Popperfoto/Getty Images
Page 92 © Hulton-Deutsch Collection/ Corbis
Page 93 © 2004 Fortean/TopFoto
Page 96 © Getty Images
Page 98 © Bettmann/Corbis
Page 99 © Reuters/Corbis
Page 101 © Yann Arthus-Bertrand/Corbis
Page 102 © AFP/Getty Images
Page 105 Courtesy of Brookhaven National Laboratory
Page 110 © Reuters/Corbis
Page 111 © Reuters/Corbis
Page 112 © Amet Jean Pierre/Corbis Sygma
Page 113 © You Sung-Ho/Reuters/Corbis
Page 114 © Sue Ogrocki/Reuters/Corbis
Page 117 © Judy Griesedieck/Corbis
Page 119 © Ed Eckstein/Corbis
Page 122 © Hulton-Deutsch Collection/ Corbis
Page 126 © Bettmann/Corbis
Page 128 © Zahid Hussein/Reuters/ Corbis
Page 129 © Bettmann/Corbis
Page 131 © Bettmann/Corbis
Page 134 © Bettmann/Corbis
Page 136 © Wolfgang_Thieme/ dpa/Corbis
Page 137 © The Natural History Museum, London
Page 139 © Bettmann/Corbis
Page 140 © Stefan Rampfel/epa/Corbis
Page 143 © Bettmann/Corbis
Page 145 © Bettmann/Corbis
Page 146 © Corbis
Page 149 © JP Laffont /Sygma/Corbis
Page 150 © B. Borrell Casals; Frank Lane Picture Agency/Corbis
Page 151 © Bettmann/Corbis
Page 152 © Giorgio Benvenuti/epa/Corbis

Сл... в

...ванскаго

...скій ...ши

...ими Жизн...

...ем Ж...